PERSIAN ART

Text: Vladimir Loukonine and Anatoli Ivanov
Layout and cover: Matthieu Carré
© Confidential Concepts, worldwide, USA, 1996

ISBN 1 904310 13 3
© Sirocco, London, 2003 (English version)
Printed and bound in Slovakia

PERSIAN ART

Vladimir Loukonine & Anatoli Ivanov

CONTENTS

Catalogue descriptions written by:

Adèle Adamova – nos. 156, 161, 197, 198, 208, 209, 225-230, 235, 237, 240-244, 256-260, 263, 264, 285, 286, 289, 290.

Oleg Akimoushkin – nos. 213, 254.

Erkinay Guliamova, Anatoli Ivanov – nos. 98, 100.

Angelina Grigolia – nos. 261, 268, 269, 276, 283, 284.

Anatoly Ivanov – nos. 84, 87, 91-93, 99, 101-130, 132, 134-138, 140, 141-155, 157-160, 162-178, 186-196, 199, 201, 203, 207, 210-212, 214, 215, 218, 221-224, 236, 238, 239, 248-250, 252, 253, 255, 262, 266, 267, 270-274, 277-281.

Anna Yerussalimskaya – nos. 83, 97.

Vladimir Loukonine – nos. 1-93, 131, 282.

Boris Marchak – nos. 85, 86, 88-90, 94-96.

Olga Mironova – no. 217.

Elena Morchakova – no. 219.

Nathalia Pirverdian – nos. 181, 182, 184, 204, 205, 233-234, 245-247, 275, 287-288.

Nathalia Sazonova – nos. 133, 139, 141, 183.

Emma Chernoukha – nos. 185, 202, 232.

Elena Tikhomirova – nos. 179, 180, 216, 220, 251.

Inna Vishnevskaya – nos. 206, 231.

Elena Yablonskaya – no. 200.

که مرم تکسکش سروتزک وال	عمودی بزذرسرترپورر زال	بی کرد رستم ز پرمرفسوس	سدی سدناخن ردری طوس
بزرکونه بلی پکلینه بوش	لفتندکای مردبازرزروروش	بزرکاز نبو ددپذد از خرد	بنزاد ردز زلمی حمله برد
لی داند خواندش سکارسله	دربفست رنج اندرژرشارساله	لکن افلنی پاسبهرنبرد	ریام توجون نزادی جبرد
رسند وزجوونژرشروزت	بکی پاره افلنده ازرژکوبت	زهر لونه داند کار راخواند	نوفرید وزاز ارزبراند
		ورزرنج ربهی کردکم	رزبنساز نافسونزونج
		لون پاره دزمرارندلرد	زرج بردندمرداز مرد
		بزرنج بردندلداری بهما	کسرمزنزارن بزرباد شاد
		بزراندروزراه آورد بی	جنف وابدبرسی خورد بی
		باشد بدسندی مزدآوری	ساباز رزمرونج اوری
		زافسوز سلم ودم جالبقن	زذبروز بارره بوسجنین

سباه اندراورد ردرجارسو	بکی دزمرودزشننه برارزوی	دار زرجوبش جویل مشه شد	سشنک رستم براندسندشند
زره داریاخنجرکابلن	پدروی برلشکرزاولی	برش اوبلما بوفرکوس	بکو ردزربکروری وکوس
زمانه سرزرابی دروزدب	هرانکسرکه ازباره سرزدزد	همه دربد وماننده شلفت	زرستم کمان برد کرفت
جوب اندراشبرالنله شد	بی باره زان سرللمدزکوفت	بدساز کاری می کش جفت	مغربکان انج رازلغت
کماتها وتررخف نله اورد	جونجی زدروار درزلله شنه	پالودنفط سباه ازبرش	ولهانهاد نندزبراندرش
کرای هرانکوراذراندرنداز	بفرهو دررستم لمجلک بده	زهرسو سباه اندرامنده کرد	وآمد ان باره نورکرد
پبشراندروزبزرولسنم	همه سرمداز لدککساد	ممان ازبی بوم وسوبندخوش	زانی کنج ورندخوش
دلربهبرکردنل کودراناهبر	بی باشی بانبرده دا	سبرهاکرفند وبروزکمات	بان پاد بشت نلدازربان
سش جهان افزون شد	ازاشان زکشنی زنی	هرجت بودزران بسناکزبر	آتش زبارزان ننس
نهادنل بک رو	نهش پاله مرونن نشت	سنور وغلام وبرسنلکبنن	زروسبم وکرلمابه بیز
مردن به آبد زبام وزلب	زبراکان ش جهان افرن	مران نلوی پبهسناتکرت	وزلنش سانش رکوفت
بکی خلعنی باشاب ازدکر	حوزنوباشد جنک	بران لو مداراف رانتخشد	وزاد یزدان زهره زان ناخبنه
سه دار ورکلسنوار ورسوار	بعهس لفنی بیتهرورسل	زبانی بانی زبهسته سد	وان زهرو جنل

PERSIAN ART: Stages of development from the 10th century BC to the 19th century AD.

Vladimir Loukonine. Photograph. 1970s.

This book consists of two sections. The wide-ranging introduction attempts to outline the basic stages in the development of Persian Art, from the first appearance of Persian peoples on the Iranian plateau during the tenth to eighth centuries BC up to the nineteenth century AD. Detailed commentaries on the works of art reproduced here provide not only factual information (dates, iconography, provenance, techniques, etc.), but are also in many instances followed by brief scholarly studies of the examples of Persian art housed in various museums of the former Soviet Union that are, in the authors' opinion, of the greatest interest and significance. Some of these objects are reproduced and discussed here for the first time.

As far as possible, we have tried to select only such works as are typical of Persia itself, and not those produced beyond the present-day borders of Iran (Transcaucasia, Central Asia, etc.), however strongly influenced by Persian culture these may have been. At the same time, we have tried to present material to illustrate our basic thesis, namely that Persian art, though it had periods of ascendancy and of decline, remained coherent, individual and profoundly traditional throughout its development, from its formation in the tenth to seventh centuries BC right up to the nineteenth century AD. This is despite the violent, often tragic political upheavals, fundamental ideological changes, foreign invasions and their concomitant devastating effect upon the country's economy.

In attempting to sketch a general outline of the development of Persian art over this vast period we have been obliged to set aside artistic descriptions or analyses. The specific "morphology" and "syntax" of Near-Eastern art differs fundamentally from Western art. There is a lack of source material, insufficient analysis of the work of some periods and art history suffers from terminological inflexibility – how many more arguments could be put forward in support of the indisputable fact that at the present time, so far as Near-Eastern art is concerned, no serious artistic analysis is possible. At the moment, the task of fundamental importance is to interpret the objects in a historical light, to attempt to analyse them as one of the sources for a history of the culture of one period or another and investigate these objects in such a way as to enable them to fill the considerable gaps in our reconstruction of the ideological, political and economic history of Iran.

Our present state of knowledge inevitably means that we can plot the course of the development of art only approximately; nevertheless the points along this course tally with all the sources, written and otherwise, on the history of the period. Research into Persian art is impeded by a number of obstacles that are extremely difficult to overcome. From the foundation of Persian art to the end of Sassanid rule there are very few antiquities extant and the chief danger in suggesting an outline for art of this period is that one is forced to draw excessively straight lines between the rare incontrovertibly established facts. The result is an incomplete and problematic description. Yet even the drawing up of such outlines is made extremely difficult by the need to take into account a whole network of facts – from iconographical analyses of cultural artefacts to linguistic studies. Confidence in the accuracy of the resulting outline is inspired only in those cases where there is no contradiction between any of its component elements. In other words, recourse to a very wide range of sources of the most varied nature is required.

On the other hand, a vast number of objects survive from the Middle Ages, yet here the construction of outlines is far too complex. At every point along the way, the researcher is confused by the attempt to take into account all the twists and turns of development inherent in the material itself and in a comparison of written sources with information contained in any inscription there might be on the object. There is thus a real danger of drowning in a sea of facts, albeit incontrovertibly established facts, without having clarified the general trends.

There is yet another danger – that of the "academic" illusion which links the cardinal ideological or political changes (for example, the change from the Zoroastrian religion to Islam or, say, the conquest of Iran by the Seljuk Turks) far too closely to developments in the art produced by that culture. There are a number of further difficulties – the unreliable dating of individual objects, lack of data as to origin, etc.

As far as possible, we have attempted to draw a clear distinction between two levels, the prestigious works of art reflecting concepts of an ideological, official, dynastic or other such nature, and handicrafts or, more accurately, traded objects in which one can see more clearly changes in the aesthetic taste of a wide range of buyers, the influence of local traditions and developments and innovations in particular techniques. Clearly, both categories of objects are closely linked and to study them together significantly enriches the overall picture of the art of the time, but it is also clear that prestigious objects more obviously reflect changes in the art of the period, whereas the study of handicrafts offers important assistance in dating and identifying the origin of articles. Apart from this, these objects provide evidence of changes occurring in the economy, but only partially reflect social change.

In Antiquity, beginning at any rate in the Median era, prestigious objects were those directly connected to the ruling dynasty, commissioned by the Iranian sovereigns and members of the court and reflecting their tastes and ideological views. They all relate to a specific period in the history of the Ancient East – that of the Ancient World Empires[1] – and they reflect the level of art in the region as a whole and not just the art of a dynasty. At this particular stage, the only possible scientific means of dating is by dynasty.

In the Middle Ages, owing to fundamental changes in the nature of the state and the structure and outlook of society, the objects which had been used to reflect status and ideology in ancient times changed, and new forms of art took over. One cannot say that dynastic dating and dynastic chronology lose their meaning altogether in the Middle Ages, but dynasties degenerate, become local and inward-looking, and their range of subject-matter and technical skills naturally diminishes.

The concept of "prestige" also changes. It is no longer purely an expression of dynastic ideas, but an assertion of high social status based on wealth and influence rather than nobility and ancient lineage.

It is much more difficult to draw up a general outline for the development of art during this period because of the increasing decentralization, and because the range of prestigious works expands and their interpretation becomes more complex, whilst handicrafts and prestigious art objects become more closely allied. For the time being, only what one might term "technical" dating by period is possible, founded largely on mass-produced objects, above all on handicrafts. While observing specific stages in the development of Persian art during the Middle Ages, it is still impossible to say what determined significant changes in various types of art. It is not even possible to say whether we are merely observing changes in various technical skills and devices or a change in fashion.

By no means have all of the suggestions in this essay been proved with a satisfactory degree of certainty. There are a number of questionable hypotheses and the result may well be similar to that in a story told by Jalal al-Din Rumi. The son of a padishah was studying magic and had learned to identify objects without seeing them. The padishah, clasping a jewelled ring in his hand, asked him, "What is this?" The prince decided that the object in the hand was round, was connected with minerals and that it had a hole in the middle. "But what exactly is it?" asked the padishah. After long meditation the prince answered: "A millstone...".

For over a hundred years, specialist studies have looked at the question of when and by what routes the Iranian peoples, above all the Medes and Persians, first emerged onto the plateau.

The first references to these peoples are found in Assyrian texts of the ninth century BC (the earliest is an inscription by the Assyrian king Shalmaneser III, c.843 BC): despite this, specialists have discovered Iranian names for a number of places and rulers in earlier cuneiform texts.

According to one of the most widely held theories[2], the settlement of Iranian tribes on the present territory of Iran dates back to about the eleventh century BC, and their migration route (at any rate, the migration route of a significant proportion of them) passed through the Caucasus. Another theory traces the Iranian tribes back to Central Asia and has them subsequently (about the ninth century BC) advancing towards the western borders of the Iranian plateau[3]. Whatever the case, a new ethnic group gradually penetrated into an immensely varied linguistic environment – into regions where dozens of principalities and small city-states existed side-by-side with lands subjugated to the great empires of antiquity – Assyria and Elam[4]. The Iranian tribes, who were cattle-breeders and farmers, had settled on lands belonging to Assyria, Elam, Manna and Urartu and subsequently became dependent on the rulers of these states[5].

It would seem that these questions of the routes by which the Iranians entered the plateau and of how they settled among the heterogeneous native population of what is now Iran during the twelfth and eleventh centuries BC[6] have only an indirect bearing on the history of the culture and art of Iran. However, it was these very questions which inspired archaeological excavations and research, covering a large area into the pre-Iranian and proto-Iranian period, or, in archaeological terminology, Iran's Iron Age. As a result of intensive work undertaken in Iran by archaeologists from many countries from the early 1950s almost to the present day, the majority of specialists have come to the conclusion that new tribes appeared in the western provinces of Iran (in the Zagros Mountains) during "Iron Age I" (c.1300–1000 BC), bringing about sudden changes within the material culture of this region. Some archaeologists suggest that this invasion was "completely clearcut and dramatic". Pottery shows drastic changes. Red or grey earthenware vessels appear in place of painted ones and they adopt new shapes – so-called "teapots", long-stemmed goblets, "tripods", etc. Burial customs change. Spacious cemeteries appear beyond the city walls and bodies are buried in "stone boxes" or cists[7]. Later, during the Iron Age II (1000–800 BC) and the Iron Age III (800–550 BC), gradual changes occur within the confines of this culture, which was in essence introduced wholesale from outside. Its spread throughout the Zagros region was at first limited and appears, in theory, not to contradict the resettlement of Iranian tribes known from written records.

Later (during the Iron Age III) it took over practically the whole of Western Iran, and this may be linked to the formation and expansion of the Median and Persian states. However, a detailed study of all the hitherto published material destroys this neat picture.

Firstly, there is no hard evidence of any incontrovertible link between new forms of pottery or decoration that would be necessarily and exclusively attributable to ethnic changes rather than to other types of change (technical developments, fashion, cultural influences, etc.).

Secondly, as far as burial rites are concerned (a factor apparently more closely bound to a specific ethnic group), the picture also turns out to be unclear throughout Iran. Burial rites are not consistent and vary considerably.

Finally, a closer examination of the facts relating to the "archaeological revolution of the Iron Age" leads to the conclusion that the beginning of this period in no way demonstrates either a general unity of culture or any sudden changes.

It would be far more consistent with the process established by written sources to postulate a gradual accumulation of new characteristics within the material culture, taking place over several centuries[8].

Disputes about archaeological aspects of the early history of Iran or changes in its pottery and rituals appear to be only indirectly linked to the history of Iranian culture and art. Yet it was due to archaeological work during the 1950s to the 1970s that an unexpected and remarkably vivid page of ancient Iranian culture was revealed.

There were splendid works of art, above all metalwork, that had hitherto remained completely unknown. Archaeologists date these works with varying degrees of success, but the search for the sources of Iranian culture depends on finding an answer to the questions of who produced these works – the local population or the Iranians – and what do they depict, local, ancient oriental designs or new Iranian ones?

In the summer of 1958, whilst clearing away the remains of a collapsed ceiling from one of the rooms in the fortress of Hasanlu (in the Lake Urmia region), the archaeologist Robert Dyson came upon a man's hand, the finger-bones covered with verdigris from the plates of a warrior's bronze gauntlet. When Dyson took over the excavation of the find and began to brush off the bones, a sliver of gold was suddenly revealed. At first the excavator thought he had a bracelet, but the gold went deeper and deeper until a solid gold bowl, eight inches in height and eight in diameter, was revealed. Careful observation of the two skeletons found with that of the man who had carried the bowl resulted in the following reconstruction: the bowl "was being carried out of the flaming building by one of three men who were on the second floor at the moment it gave way. The leader of the group fell sprawled forward on his face, his arms spread out before him to break the fall, his iron sword with its handle of gold foil caught beneath his chest. The second man, carrying the gold bowl, fell forward on his right shoulder, his left arm with its gauntlet of bronze buttons flung

Gold cup, Hasanlu. 9th–10th century BC. Museum of Archaeology, Tehran.

F ca. 63 and 64 – Designs on the sides of the gold bowl of Hasanlu.
12th-11th century B.C. Archaeological Museum, Teheran.

Gold cup, Hasanlu. Decorative détails. Drawing.

against the wall; his right arm and the bowl dropped in front of him, his skull crushed in its cap of copper. As he fell his companion following on his left also fell, tripping across the bowl-carrier's feet and plunging into the debris[9]."

The fortress of Hasanlu, the headquarters of one of the local rulers, was besieged and sacked, apparently at the end of the ninth century BC or the very beginning of the eighth century. The gold vessel which the warriors of the palace or temple guard were trying to save was a sacred object. Its dimensions are 20.6 x 28cm, its weight 950g; around the top are scenes of three deities on chariots, with mules harnessed to two of the chariots and a bull to the other, whilst a priest stands in front of the bull with a vessel in his hand. These probably portray the god of thunder, rain or the sky (water streams from the bull's jaws), the national god wearing a horned crown, and a sun god with a solar disc and wings. In all there are more than twenty different figures on the vessel-gods, heroes, beasts and monsters, scenes of sheep being sacrificed, a hero battling with a dragon-man, the ritual slaughter of a child, the flight of a girl on an eagle.

In all probability, they illustrate local Hurrian myths (which survive in Hittite versions: "The Divine Kingdom", "The Songs of Ullikummi") in which the son of the Hurrian deity Anu, the dragon-slayer Kummarbi, features as the main hero. Iconographic and compositional parallels to the scenes on the vessel are also known in the Hittite reliefs of Malatya and Arslan Tepe and on ancient Assyrian and Babylonian seals[10]. This vessel from Hasanlu is the first of a number of metalwork objects whose technique and style are evidence that a new local school and a large artistic centre had developed in North-Western Iran at the end of the second or beginning of the first millennium BC.

Illegal excavations have always taken place in Iran – peasants have dug up ancient monuments and sometimes remarkable works of art have appeared on the market, though unfortunately lacking any scientific documentation. This continues to be the case. Gold and silver goblets, found somewhere in Gilan, near the town of Amlash (the centre of the region in which the Marlik burial site is situated), appeared in the mid-1950s, both in antique shops and in private collections. Marvellous zoomorphic ceramic vessels, depicting either zebu-like bulls or antelopes, have also come up for sale.

In 1962, the Archaeological Service of Iran sent a scientific expedition to Gilan, 14km (about nine miles) west of the settlement of Rudbar. The archaeologists discovered 53 graves on the hill of Marlik in the form of four different types of "stone box". Golden goblets were found, several of them very large, up to 20cm in height and weighing more than 300g (at one time, one of them was even depicted on modern Iranian banknotes), plus gold and bronze vessels, bronze weapons, parts of horse harnesses, pottery (including a great number of zoomorphic vessels in the shape of zebu-like bulls) and ornaments, etc. So far, however, only preliminary reports of these finds and a spate of popular works have been published.

There are, however, some remarkable metalwork objects among the Marlik finds, although these have not been precisely dated[11]. Judging by their technique and a number of stylistic features, they are attributable to the same school as the Hasanlu bowl, but evidently a considerable time elapsed between the production of these objects. None of the Marlik vessels bear narrative designs; in general they depict real or fantastic birds and beasts. Unlike the decoration of the Hasanlu bowl, the illustrations are clearly divided into registers.

One of the vessels – a large gold goblet (height 20cm, weight 229g) – bears "the story of a goat"[12]. The supervisor of the Marlik excavations, Ezzat Negahban, describes its design as follows:

Gold cup, Hasanlu. Details.

Gold vase "The story of a goat" Marlik.
9th–8th century BC.
Drawing of decoration.

In the lowest row, A, the young kid is suckling from its mother. In the second row, B, the young mountain goat, just beginning to sprout horns, is eating leaves from the Tree of Life. In the third row, C, is a wild boar (apparently the killer of the goat). In the fourth row, D, the body of the goat, now grown old - as indicated by the long elaborately curved horns - lies on its back with two enormous vultures ripping out its entrails. On the fifth row, E, a small creature, an embryo or a monkey, is sitting in front of a small stand. If this is an embryo, it indicates rebirth; if a monkey, it is telling the story. It is common in the ancient fables of Iran for an animal, particularly a monkey, to tell the story [13].

In our opinion register A (the mother goat) is not a goat at all but a deer. This design, a deer with a suckling fawn, is copied almost exactly from ivory plaques in the provincial Assyrian style of the eighth century BC. One finds exactly the same design on plaques from the famous treasure of Ziwiye (see below) [14].

Register B is an ordinary goat. The design is typically Assyrian and known from numerous objects, especially cylindrical seals, and it has a particular symbolical significance in a local (Assyrian) religious context. Finally, register D is an ibex, but the composition - birds pecking a goat - is known from Kassite glyptics (fourteenth - thirteenth centuries BC), Elamite cylinders and Hittite stone reliefs. In the above cultures this motif symbolizes victory in war [15].

Only the boar (register C) and the strange "embryo" have no direct iconographic parallel, although the latter is depicted in front of a typically Assyrian Tree of Life. They alone betray the artistic individuality of the craftsman.

Thus we have before us four different references to the symbolism of different religions (Assyrian, Elamite, Kassite and Hittite), but they have been removed from their context and brought together on one vessel by a local craftsman in a simple, guileless tale of life and death, lacking any of that complex symbolism and meaning which the separate components possessed in their own context. Who was this craftsman? An Iranian or a Mede? At any rate he was not an Assyrian, a Hurrian or an Elamite - he did not understand their pictorial language. To produce his tale he used representations on carved ivories, seals and signet-rings and possibly images from other vessels rather than those on works of official court art such as reliefs. However, the essential difference between what is depicted on the Hasanlu vessel and this goblet is that on the former all the images are used to create a single story which can be clearly deciphered on the basis of a single religious or epic tradition (Hurrian myths). The Marlik goblet, however, tells a new story with the help of old but very varied images. Taking the analogy of language, one could say that the craftsman of the Marlik goblet is employing foreign ideograms in order to create his own coherent text. Perhaps for the first time we are encountering an example of the formation of Persian art as a whole. We will return to this in far more detail, for a great deal of evidence will be required, but

on the basis of this example it is already possible to suggest that Persian art was created from heterogeneous quotations taken out of context, from elements of religious imagery from various ancient eastern civilizations reinterpreted and adapted by local artists to illustrate their myths or (subsequently?) to depict their deities. This theory suggests the possibility of an Iranian interpretation of works that still consisted entirely of foreign ideograms, but only of those works where these ideograms are taken from various artistic languages. In the case of the Hasanlu vessel it is unnecessary to seek an Iranian interpretation of the Hurrian myths depicted. The Marlik goblet is an example of quotations from several languages and periods where the search for another, Iranian, content appears to be feasible.

In 1946, an enormous hoard was discovered by chance near a high hill 40km east of the town of Saqqiz, not far from Hasanlu. The story of its discovery was rapidly transformed into confused legends. For example, the story was told of two shepherds who accidentally stumbled

Gold vase, Marlik. 9th–8th century BC.

Fawn with its mother. Relief.

on the rim of a bronze vessel while searching for a young goat. Trying to dig it out, they are said to have noticed a large bronze sarcophagus packed full of gold, silver, bronze, iron and ivory objects. All of this was distributed among the peasants of the nearby settlement of Ziwiye and in the course of the distribution many valuable objects were broken into several parts, shattered or trampled. At the same time, some of the objects appeared in Tehran in the hands of a few antique dealers. One of them, having first arranged to receive a share of the proceeds of scientific excavations, informed André Godard, then inspector-general of Iran's Archaeological Service, of the find's whereabouts.

In 1950, Godard published part of the gold, silver and ivoryware, gave a confused account of the circumstances of the hoard's discovery and suggested a date for the bulk of the items – the ninth century BC. He defined these objects as "art in the animal style" of the Zagros region with elements from the art of Assyria and nearby regions – an art which was subsequently adopted by the Scythians and the Persians of the Achaemenid period. Godard noted that many objects in the same style had previously been found in this region, some of them at the site of the ancient town which he identified as Izirtu, the capital of Manna.

In 1950, the "Ziwiye fashion" began. The activities of antique dealers led to the dispersal of objects from the hoard into private collections, though some ended up in museums in the USA, France, Canada, the United Kingdom and Japan. Until recently a large part of the treasure was kept in the Tehran Archaeological Museum. One of its first researchers, Roman Ghirshman, drew up a list of finds, attributing 341 objects to the hoard, including 43 of gold, 71 of silver and 103 of ivory [16].

Such variety in the contents of the hoard aroused incredulity. Godard had already pointed out that items ascribed to the hoard had been discovered by chance in neighbouring regions or even in Southern Azerbaijan. In recent years, the disputes have grown even more bitter. Some specialists have flatly refused to consider that the majority of the objects on the "Ghirshman list" were really found at Ziwiye, declaring some of them to be modern imitations. It must be said that these suspicions have some basis, for archaeological investigation of the hill at Ziwiye has, in essence, yielded nothing (archaeologists only gained access more than ten years after the discovery of the hoard). The entire hill had been riddled with holes dug by treasure seekers. Remains of the walls of a small fort which once stood on the hill have been found. Judging by the pottery found there, it was built between the end of the eighth century BC and the middle of the seventh. But the hoard might well be unconnected with the fort. One of those who studied the hoard remarked, "Unfortunately, what is left in an empty stable after a horse has been stolen merely tells us that a horse was once there, but it does not identify the horse" [17]. This ironic remark is, in fact, extremely significant, for the answer to the question of what this collection of objects was hinges upon whether there was a real, not a metaphorical, horse at Ziwiye. Was it a hoard or the remains of the rich burial of an

Iranian – or perhaps a Scythian – chief with his steed, weapons and personal belongings, like the Scythian barrow at Kelermes? Ghirshman considers that the hill of Ziwiye is quite definitely the grave of the Scythian ruler Madias, son of Partatua, who was king of the Scythians and a powerful ally of Assyria (died c.624 BC). But what then of the remains of walls discovered by archaeologists? As has already been stated, together with the other objects from Ziwiye housed in the Tehran Archaeological Museum and the Metropolitan Museum of Art in New York there are fragments of the sides and edge of a large bronze "bath". Similar artefacts, undoubtedly Assyrian and dating from about the second half of the eighth century BC, have been found at other sites. Sometimes they were used as bath-tubs – for example at Zincirli, sometimes as coffins, as at Ur. But whatever the case, whether it was a burial or a hoard hidden in a large bronze vessel, it is clear that all these items were plundered from various places. Among the objects from Ziwiye are many ivory plaques with various designs. Some of them, fashioned with unusual artistry, are undoubtedly Assyrian, similar to those discovered in the Assyrian palaces of Arslan Tash, Nimrud or Kuyunjik. Another group, fashioned under the influence of Assyrian art, bears the stamp of the provincial style of the mid to late eighth century BC, with signs of the influence of Phoenician art, the art of Northern Syria and possibly that of Urartu. The bronze bath already mentioned is also Assyrian. Some of the jewellery has neither been precisely dated nor precisely localized as such earrings, necklaces and bracelets are characteristic of many areas of the Near East. Among the bronzeware – parts of furniture, bells, bronze pins and animal figurines are items that are undoubtedly from Urartu. Several ceramic vessels, supposedly found in the same hoard, are also Urartian or Assyrian (eighth to seventh centuries BC). Most interesting of all are the gold and silver items in the hoard. Some of them, mostly silver objects, are also Urartian, but the majority of the gold objects belong to the so-called mixed style, in which stylistic features that are definitely Urartian and some that are definitely Assyrian, along with others that are apparently from Asia Minor and some almost certainly Syrian, all blend together with new, more vivid representations of a style, technique and, above all, choice of imagery which may be cautiously termed "local".

These are all prestigious items. Richly decorated weapons, insignias of a king's or courtier's power, such as a pectoral, a diadem, a gold belt and so on [18]. On nearly all these objects the composition is based on heraldic principles, symmetrical scenes depicting mythical creatures are displayed on either side of the Tree of Life. There are no less than ten versions of the Tree of Life from Ziwiye, consisting of standard S-shaped curves woven into a complex pattern. The representations of the Tree of Life on Urartian bronze belts of the thirteenth to seventh centuries BC form the closest parallel. The fabulous creatures depicted at the sides of the Tree of Life on objects from Ziwiye are not very numerous – a dozen in all.

There are also purely Assyrian compositions on gold, as on ivory, objects. These include a king with a sword defeating a rampant lion. Apart from this, zoomorphic figures are represented on gold objects and even on fragments of pottery. There is a stag with legs drawn in and branching antlers executed in a typically Scythian style, very close to those on famous objects from Scythian barrows, such as the Kelermes or Melgunov swords or the Kelermes pole-axe; a panther with its paws entwined into a ring, almost the same as the famous Kelermes panther or the panther on the gold facing of the Kelermes mirror; the head of a griffin, identical to that on the Kelermes sword; a mountain ram with legs drawn under it, its pose and the treatment of its body identical to those of the Kelermes stag; and, finally, a hare.

Among the objects from Ziwiye are some which show only mythical beasts (the gold breast-plate, the gold quiver-facing, and others) or only real animals (the gold belt with stags and rams, parts of the gold diadem with panthers and griffins' heads, and others); only one object a gold pectoral, the symbol of power of a king or a courtier shows both types of animal.

Gold belt, Ziwiyeh. 7th century BC Detail. Museum of Archaeology, Tehran.

At this point, an important detail must be emphasized. Without exception, all the images on both gold and silver items as well as some articles of carved ivory are fashioned using the same stylistic devices (for example, idiosyncratic "underwings" appear on the bodies of the fabulous creatures and the panther).

Thus the craftsmen of Ziwiye created prestigious objects such as symbols of power (ceremonial weapons, a pectoral, a diadem, a belt, etc.), employing the pictorial language of Urartu, Assyria, Elam, Syria, Phoenicia and, lastly, the "animal style" of the Scythians, so that their own pictorial language was again created from elements extracted from various alien contexts to produce a new text. They also employed many older metalwork techniques (as seen, for example, in the Marlik objects).

Three facts are of importance here. Many of the objects at Ziwiye were produced for rulers or for the aristocracy, they clearly display the Scythian animal style which was new to this area, and the majority of similar designs (such as the Tree of Life and the monsters) link these objects to the art of Urartu.

All these parallels inevitably pose fresh questions. Above all, for whom were the Ziwiye objects produced? And then, how are these works to be dated? If they were made earlier than the Scythian items at Kelermes, or were even contemporaneous with them, what then is their significance in the formation of the Scythian animal style and of those other aspects of Near-Eastern art to which we have already referred? How are these objects to be interpreted? Lastly, how did these images subsequently develop?

First of all, one has to answer, however cursorily, the question of how the animal style developed. The origin of the nomadic tribes known to the Ancients by the generic name of Scythians or Saka – their first homeland, their migration routes and their ethnic origin – is as controversial as the question of the Iranians' original homeland and of their migration. However, the important thing for the history of Iranian culture is that detachments of nomadic warriors are first mentioned in writings in the Near East during the eighth century BC (the oldest known references are the reports of Assyrian spies from Urartu in the 720s BC). They are known by various names: *umman-manda* (the Manda tribe), *gimirrai* (Cimmerians?), *ashkuzai*, *ishkuzai* (Scythians), *saka* (Saka). In the 670s BC these tribes were already playing an active part in the foreign policy of the Near-East and subsequently they even set up a short-lived "Scythian kingdom" in Southern Azerbaijan, somewhere in the vicinity of Manna. No less controversial is the origin of the Scythian animal style itself. Images of beasts stylized in a Scythian manner connect a number of archaeological cultures covering a vast territory from the Mongolian steppes to the Crimea.

In recent years, the term "Scythian-Siberian animal style" has become current in Russian archaeological literature. It has been suggested that this style emerged in the eastern steppes, perhaps as early as the late ninth century BC, and then migrated westwards along with its bearers[19]. Two

Gold breastplate, Ziwiyeh.
7th century BC.
Museum of Archeology, Tehran.

features of "Scythian stylization" are also characteristic of Ziwiye imagery. One is the generally closed construction of the animal figures (for example, beasts twisted into a circle), resulting in a distortion and simplification of form, and the other is the consequent construction of designs consisting of several entirely distinct planes of geometrical regularity[20].

Thus the question of dating is highly important, but at present it remains unresolved. It is not impossible, of course, that it was the Scythians themselves who brought with them to the Near-East the motif of the stag with legs drawn in and branching antlers, the motif of the panther and the stylised image of the griffin's head[21]. One cannot, however, point to a single similar object of incontrovertible Scythian provenance which is reliably dated and known to be older than the pieces from Ziwiye[22]. At the same time – and leaving aside the stag's or ram's pose, which was already extremely widespread in the art of the Near-East by the end of the second millennium BC – objects have been found on Iranian territory depicting these same beasts but stylised in a different manner.

A griffin's head adorns the butt of a number of Luristan axes as early as the tenth or ninth centuries BC, the stag with legs drawn in is found on Luristan psalia of the late eighth century BC, and there is a panther on a bronze pin from Baba Jan Tepe, also from the eighth century BC.

Let us assume that Ziwiye and the Kelermes burial mounds date from the same period[23]. Despite an abundance of Urartian and Assyrian motifs, the buyer for whom these articles were intended could have been neither an Assyrian nor an Urartian ruler because the pictorial categories of fabulous beasts are grossly confused, which would have been unacceptable in the unified systems of religious imagery of Assyria and Urartu. Thus we must seek another candidate, and he must be an Iranian. Only in this case would the "Scythian animals" have to feature on his belongings, insofar as they were a totem or emblem of his tribe (in Vladimir Abayev's opinion, for example, the term saka – the name by which some Scythian tribes were known in the Near East – signifies "stag")[24].

It should be borne in mind that the craftsmen who incorporated them into insignias of power were employing the very same technical and stylistic devices they used for the ancient eastern motifs with which they were familiar. For example, the stag's antlers are depicted with the same S-shaped curves as the branches of the Tree of Life.

The intended recipient of these articles would have to be a king to account for the royal symbols of investiture. In other words, the most likely candidates are kings of a Scythian power settled in the Sacasene province of Transcaucasia and conducting raids from there on Urartu and Assyria, the rulers of a "Scythian kingdom" (one of these, Madias, has already been mentioned) who may have adopted the customs of eastern potentates, or the kings of Media, the first Iranian empire established on this territory in the 670s BC. Two facts give grounds for considering these objects to have been produced for Median rulers.

Firstly, the political situation in the area in question during the late eighth and early seventh centuries BC[25]; secondly, the subsequent history of objects made in this style.

How rapidly early Scythian articles lose that fabulous imagery which is characteristic of Near-Eastern art! This imagery has already vanished completely from early Scythian objects in burial mounds of the northern Black Sea area dating from the sixth to fifth centuries BC. Here Scythian art comes into contact with the art of Greece. On the other hand, this imagery survives in Persian art of the Achaemenid period. One finds it on Achaemenid seals, on silver and gold vessels (especially on rhytons), in the decoration of Achaemenid swords, and even in monumental art – on the capitals of columns and on reliefs[26].

The most natural explanation for this is that the imagery of the Near East was not interpreted by the Scythians in any way.

On the very earliest Scythian objects it simply constituted a form of exotic decoration. Yet images of actual Scythian "totems", although originally produced by Near-Eastern metalworkers using Near-Eastern models and styles, were to be developed further in Scythian art.

In Persian art, on the contrary, Scythian images rapidly degenerate[27], while it is the fabulous imagery of the Near-East which continues to develop. This indicates that their selection, both at the beginning (at Ziwiye) and subsequently (under the Achaemenids), was not accidental and that they were interpreted in some way.

Thus some of the objects from Ziwiye were produced for Iranian, and in all likelihood Median, rulers. The metalworkers, successors to the Hasanlu and Marlik "school", produced works of art on the same principle as did the Marlik craftsmen, depicting in a single object images of "evil demons" and "good genii" extracted from the context of various religious pictorial systems. The field of selection for such "quotations" is a great deal more extensive than at Marlik, but the choice itself is more limited. Some dozen or so images are repeated on all the objects. In making the selection, no great importance has been attached to the symbolism these images possessed in their own pictorial systems. The quotations sometimes alternate with a "narration in one's own words".

Lastly, even though the Near-Eastern "text" is ideographic, images that are already indisputably Iranian are introduced into it as "phonetic indices". If such a system were to be found in written records, we would conclude that the text, despite the fact that all, or nearly all, of it was composed of foreign words, would have to be read in Iranian owing to the presence of phonetic indices. Here is the situation in the written Iranian language: in the Achaemenid period standard correspondences were beginning to be developed between Aramaic words and expressions and their Iranian equivalents (all the business of the chancellery in Achaemenid Iran was conducted in Aramaic, a Semitic language).

Senior civil servants had the (Aramaic) text read to them in Iranian. Gradually, scribes developed the habit of reading the entire text, even

Ring with seal.
4th – 3rd century BC.
Hermitage Museum, St Petersburg.

to themselves, in their native (Iranian) language. Aramaic spellings turned into a type of conditional sign system for the Iranian words - ideograms or, more precisely, heterograms.

The actual use of heterograms was subject to specific rules: thus, for example, one or two of the numerous Aramaic verb forms were arbitrarily selected all the time to serve any purpose... An Iranian verb ending was often joined to the Aramaic form which had been selected once and for all, as a phonetic complement in order to reveal the real Iranian verb form concealed beneath the heterogram[28]. When they arrived on the Iranian plateau, the Iranians did not have their own written language.

They used the cuneiform script of the Near East in order to set down the official manifestoes of the Achaemenid rulers, and Aramaic writing and language in order to conduct their state and business affairs. Neither did these Iranians have their own representational art. Therefore an analogous process can be traced in art - quotations and a limited choice of images can be explained by the fact that the resulting works were also to be understood in Iranian.

It is only in late Zoroastrian works that we find faint hints of anthropomorphic representation. In fact only a single Iranian goddess - the goddess Anahita - is depicted anthropomorphically. All the other deities of the ancient Iranian religion are represented abstractly, only through their "hypostases" or incarnations (chiefly as certain birds or beasts). The Yasna Haptanhaiti - one of the oldest parts of the Avesta, the ancient Iranian sacred text - mentions the worship of mythical creatures such as, for example, the sacred three-legged ass Khara and a few others, but the deities of the ancient Iranians were not pictorially represented.

This probably explains why, when the need arose to depict the Iranian gods, artists had to seek a suitable iconography among examples of ancient eastern art. These were foreign to them both as regards religious content and, of course, ethnic origin, but they were at the same time widely known and revered and the Iranians interpreted them in their own manner. It was entirely natural for the Median kings to use the very rich figurative art of Assyria, Urartu and Elam as their basis, and especially the art of that region in which their state developed historically and culturally; nevertheless, the selection had to be purposeful and relatively strict. At Marlik and Ziwiye a native Iranian representational language was created on the basis of foreign representational languages; this was, in effect, a native Persian art which, by the Ziwiye stage, one can justifiably term Median.

An inscription of the Achaemenid ruler Darius I concerning the construction of his palace at Susa more than a century after the creation of the Ziwiye complex, states (lines 49-50): "The Medes and the Egyptians were skilled in the use of gold, they crafted works of gold". As we find out in the following lines when he comes to list other craftsmen - stonemasons, specialists in glazed tiles, sculptors and builders (Ionians, Lydians, Babylonians and Egyptians) - Darius's

information is accurate. In all probability he was equally correct in speaking of the Medians as noted metalworkers.

We have already pointed out the characteristics that link the pieces described and the art of Luristan - one of the most distinctive regions of Iran. Interest in the culture of Luristan began in the late 1920s. The story has it that in 1928, in the small town of Harsin, a Lur nomad offered a local merchant a strange bronze object - an idol with a human body ringed with fabulous beasts - in exchange for a few cakes. The Lur had found the idol in an ancient grave. The story may be without foundation but it is well known that when similar objects appeared in the antique shops of Tehran and subsequently those of London, New York and Paris, the interest in them was so great that thousands of Luristan bronzes were soon scattered among private collections and museums and virtually nothing remained for the expert archaeologist arriving in Luristan, except for ancient graves pitted with holes and entirely robbed of their treasures. It required no little time and effort for systematic excavations finally to reveal the ancient civilisation of Luristan.

Nowadays the so-called "typical Luristan bronzes", characterised by their original form and iconography, have been singled out from the wide range of objects from this ancient centre. These bronzes consist of ritual bronze axes, often decorated with cast figures of men or beasts (some of them bearing inscriptions with the names of Elamite kings of the twelfth and eleventh centuries BC), bronze daggers (also frequently bearing inscriptions, for example of the Babylonian king Marduk-nadin-ahhe, 1100–1033 BC), and bronze handles of whetstones, terminating in protomes of a goat with splendid horns or birds.

Of later date (eighth to seventh centuries BC) are the bronze psalia - parts of horse harnesses fashioned entirely in the Assyrian style (similar to those depicted on the relief of the Assyrian king Sennacherib, for example) or showing Elamnite or local Luristan deities, and psalia with depictions of beasts - moufflons, horses, unicorns (similar to those on Marlik metalwork), stags and even elks. Representations of some local deities, fabulous creatures, "demons" and anthropomorphic figures combined with complicated zoomorphic images which appear not only on psalia but on heavy bronze pins, on the finials of standards and on weapons, etc., have no iconographic parallels beyond the bounds of Luristan itself. The most characteristic standard finial takes the form of a hybrid image - an anthropomorphic deity ringed with fabulous animals and birds of prey (these are what were termed "idols") - or a female deity with the heads of birds growing from her shoulders. No less typical are the large, disc-shaped or openwork heads of pins ornamented with floral motifs or representing a female deity surrounded by beasts, birds, fish and plants. Sometimes these are in the form of plaques with a polymorphic deity combining feminine and masculine characteristics or the features of a youth and an old man.

Evidently, it will be a long time before we succeed in understanding this imagery, for in Luristan only one local temple where such items might have survived has been excavated to date. This is the temple of Surkh-i Dumb where exploratory excavations were carried out in the 1930s, but the material from these excavations has still not been published. However, those articles fashioned in the Assyrian or Elamite style were evidently made to order. The craftsmen of Luristan who, as excavations show, had thousands of years of tradition and extensive experience in the field of metallurgy, manufactured weapons and parts of horse harnesses for various customers, among whom were kings, princes and chiefs of tribes of different ethnic origin.

These were the craftsmen who manufactured psalia in the form of Iranian beasts - a stag with legs drawn in, an ibex, an elk; it was they who made bronze quivers with the same pictorial quotations seen in the Marlik age. But no unified representational language was created here out of such images; the articles were simply made in accordance with the customer's taste. A native, and very complex, art coexisted here alongside the foreign articles. But the important fact about them is that they can be dated much more precisely than, say, objects from Marlik and Ziwiye[29], and here it turns out that the "Iranian animals" portrayed on them have a date - the eighth century BC - demonstrably earlier than any item hitherto discovered in the Scythian animal style.

There are no prestigious objects from Luristan exhibiting Iranian characteristics. This is understandable, for in the ninth to seventh centuries BC the Iranian tribes, which had by then already settled in the vicinity of Luristan, had not yet evolved any sort of strong or stable unified state.

On turning to an analysis of the art forms developed in the Achaemenid empire, one of the world empires of antiquity, we should describe at least one architectural complex, such as Persepolis.

Persepolis, Parsa in Old Persian, is situated 50km from Shiraz in the south of Iran. Its construction began c.520 BC and continued until c. 450 BC. The city was erected on a high artificial platform reached by a wide stairway with 111 steps made of limestone blocks.

On the platform there is a unified architectural complex made up of two types of palace - the Tachara (an inhabited palace) and the Apadana (an audience hall).The best known of them is the Apadana of Darius and Xerxes - a square audience hall, its ceiling supported by 72 stone columns. The Apadana was raised 4 m above the terrace and was reached by a wide stairway decorated with reliefs. On the left side are three tiers of identical soldiers of Elamite regiments with spears, bows and quivers, Persian guards with spears and shields, and Medes with swords, bows and spears. There are also warriors carrying the king's throne, leading the royal horses and driving the royal chariots. On the right side the reliefs depict a procession of the nations which formed part of the Achaemenid empire. At the head of each group is a courtier, possibly a satrap - the governor of a province who was always chosen from one of the leading aristocratic families - in ceremonial Persian dress with a high tiara. The different nations are depicted in approximately the same order as that of the kingdoms

composing the empire on official inscriptions of the Achaemenid kings.

Here are the Medes with their famous horses of Nisa, bearing gold vases, goblets and torques, Elamites with tame lionesses and gold daggers, negroes with okapi, Babylonians with bulls, Armenians with horses, vases and rhytons, Arabs with camels, and other peoples.

The stairway leading to another palace, the Tripylon, is decorated along the outside with a solemn procession of the royal guard, and along the inner side with a procession of servants carrying rams, vessels and wineskins. By the east door of the Apadana of Darius-Xerxes is a representation of Darius I, the king of kings of the Achaemenid state, seated on his throne, and behind him stands the heir to the throne, Xerxes. The hands of both of them are raised and stretched out in a gesture of worship towards the symbol of the royal deity - Khwarnah (see below for further details of this deity). At the north entrance to the throne room, the king of kings is depicted fighting a monster with the head, body and forelegs of a lion, the neck, wings and hindlegs of a bird and the tail of a scorpion. Identical monsters appear on several pieces from Ziwiye.

The Persepolis reliefs form a slow procession, a rhythmic, solemn and magnificent parade of hundreds of soldiers, courtiers, civil servants, priests and hundreds of representatives of subject nations, occasionally interrupted at specific points by the figure of the king of kings himself on a throne supported by these same representatives of subject nations, or by the struggle of the king of kings with a monster, or, lastly, by the scene of a lion attacking a bull - an ancient eastern religious symbol. The separate figures and scenes do not themselves form a sequence, rather the sequence is of groups or complexes of scenes ("the Apadana complex", "the Tripylon complex", etc.). Close examination of them gives rise to the impression that the king's army was innumerable, that the whole world was subject to the king, that he himself was like a god and fought with the monsters of evil, as the god of light and goodness himself fought against them.

The laws governing the imagery are meticulously elaborated and carefully observed in such details as weapons, dress, headdress, masterful depiction of valuable vessels, ornaments and details of horse harness. Such articles of Achaemenid applied art as have survived are reproduced with absolute accuracy in the sculpted reliefs at Persepolis. We may restrict ourselves to a single example - the relief on the western doorpost of the Apadana shows Darius wearing a garment, the hem of which is decorated with an engraved procession of lions. A wool hem with the same figures of lions - identical down to the minutest detail! - was found in one of the Pazyryk burial mounds in the Altai.

The "portraits" at Persepolis are extremely stylized but the subjects are distinguished by details of attire - crowns, weapons or bracelets, by their position in the scene depicted or by clearly delineated "ethnographic" features.

In the first Achaemenid capital, Pasargadae, which was built twenty-five years before Persepolis, only remains of reliefs decorating walls and entrances to the palaces have been found. Comparing these to the Persepolis reliefs, one can trace the rise of the "Achaemenid style" of sculpture and its evolution. Above all, at Pasargadae the prototype for these reliefs can be more clearly discerned, going back to the stone orthostats of Assyrian palaces.

Their style and imagery also derive from the Mesopotamian traditions of Assyria and Elam. Several of them have exact counterparts in Assyrian art, especially among the orthostats of Sennacherib's palace at Nineveh, where portrayals of fish-people and "demons" recur with great frequency. These images were probably seen by the Persians as guardians of the Assyrian rulers.

Perhaps some political purpose lay behind the repetition of these motifs at Pasargadae. Perhaps they express an attempt to proclaim the concept of a succession of power from the Assyrian kings. But the pictorial quotations are as chaotic as those at Ziwiye and the total sacrifice of the meaning of the Assyrian composition indicates that the

original religious message was of no consideration. At any rate, we are faced here with the earliest example of imagery intended to convey a message adopted from kingdoms destroyed by the Achaemenids and used by them in order to glorify their own majesty and power.

It is significant that at Pasargadae too a limited repertoire of themes has been selected from the enormous variety of sculpted designs of Assyria and Elam – there are only depictions of "monsters", "demons" and fabulous creatures, a king and courtiers, or processions of warriors and people offering gifts. Achaemenid reliefs have none of the scenes so characteristic of Assyrian art such as hunts, battles, the storming of cities, feasts, depictions of landscapes or various types of religious ceremony.

When analysing Achaemenid monuments we should recall an Egyptian hypostyle hall, the image of the Egyptian winged sun-disc, the Egyptian crown of one of the fabulous creatures on a relief at Pasargadae, the obvious Ionic influence in the form of the columns, and especially the Lydian features in the layout of the palaces and the Urartian techniques of erecting buildings on enormous artificial platforms, as well as the already mentioned Assyrian and Elamite reliefs.

We have already referred to the inscription of King Darius to mark the building of his palace at Susa (written in the three officially accepted languages of Achaemenid Iran: Akkadian, Elamite and Old Persian). It lists a wide variety of materials delivered to Susa from many of the kingdoms subject to the Achaemenids (from the Mediterranean coast as far as India) and a host of craftsmen of all nationalities (Ionians, Carians, Egyptians, Medes, Babylonians, etc.).

Carl Nylander[30], an expert on Achaemenid art, describes something like the following situation. Having subjugated Media and Asia Minor and destroyed Babylon, the Achaemenid king of kings, Cyrus II, became the ruler of an enormous powerful state. He ordered building to begin at Pasargadae, in view of the new political and religious tasks which confronted him. The buildings of his official residence were to be constructed of stone and decorated with reliefs. Median concepts and techniques were employed[31], or those used in Assyria and Elam which Cyrus had subjugated. In other instances ready-made traditional forms were lacking, so there was a certain synthesis of other elements. But as all the palaces were to be constructed of stone and at that time such buildings only existed in Asia Minor it was essential to attract stonemasons from Sardis and Ephesus, in addition to those craftsmen schooled in the Mesopotamian and Median traditions who were employed above all as sculptors.

A school of craftsmen developed at Pasargadae which later flourished at Persepolis; this united various formal languages in a single style which reflected state requirements. In other words, we are faced, in theory, with a pattern similar to that which characterized the formation of early Median art, which was itself a determining factor in this new school.

The Achaemenid age was the first period of a native Persian art from which many objects have survived, as well as written records. Such of its

Bronze pin, Luristan.
8th - 7th century BC.

Persepolis. c. 520-450 BC. Grand staircase.

features as are formulated below may well help reconstruct the history of Median art from a few surviving objects and at present a comparison is possible only of general patterns and theories rather than of actual objects.

Thus, first of all, Achaemenid art cannot be characterized any longer as one of direct visual references, despite the colossal number of borrowings – in this instance from prestigious branches of the art of subjugated lands. Such borrowings quickly lose their original meaning. The paradox of Achaemenid art lies in the fact that all, or nearly all, the details of any particular image or any particular architectural construction can be traced back to prototypes of previous ages and various lands, but the image itself, nevertheless, remains distinct from anything known and is specifically Achaemenid.

Secondly, the entire pictorial repertoire of art of this era, established with the participation of craftsmen of various nationalities, fairly rapidly spread down to the minutest details to all the monuments – from reliefs on palaces and kings' tombs to metalwork, textiles, ornaments, etc. A single imperial Achaemenid style was created and this unified culture can, moreover, be traced from the Indus to the shores of Asia Minor.

The plan of the Apadana at Persepolis, for example, was repeated by Darius at Susa, and in Armenia (at Erebuni) an Urartian temple was rebuilt according to the same plan; the same sort of palace was erected for the Achaemenid satrap at Khwarazm (Kalaly-gyr). In many instances, however, local traditional materials were used instead of stone.

Thirdly, the art of the Achaemenids as we now see it, primarily in the monuments of Pasargadae, Persepolis, Susa, the Behistun rock reliefs and the rock tombs of the Achaemenid kings at Naqsh-i Rustam, as well as in numerous articles of metalwork and glyptics, is in essence intended to proclaim the majesty of royal power and the majesty of the empire. This characteristic in particular also explains the paradoxical selection of themes in Achaemenid art. Only such proclamatory themes interested the Achaemenid monarchs and not tense, dynamic hunting or battle scenes.

There is conscious selection, or a strict pictorial system dictated by

specific aims. One might say that the reliefs of Persepolis, for example, are thematically monotonous because Persepolis itself was a ritual city. Apparently the solemn celebrations of the sacred Iranian New Year (Nawruz) were performed here, when the coronation of the king of kings took place. We can thus conclude that it is this ritual that is depicted on the Persepolis reliefs, the sculptural reflection of the myths and images of the ancient Iranians.

These include the struggle of good and evil symbolized in the battle of the king with the monster, festive processions and subjugated nations presenting New Year gifts and tributes to the king of kings[32]. It could be said that the reliefs of Pasargadae constitute the specific political programme of the Achaemenid empire's founder, Cyrus.

Yet these very images took over the whole of Achaemenid art. It seems that the programme was a great deal more extensive, reflecting more than the specific aims that arose during the construction of Pasargadae and Persepolis. Canons stipulating certain "principal" scenes were laid down at this time: the scene of the king's triumphal reception, the scene reflecting his religious faith (the king at a sacrificial altar with a burning flame – see below for more about this) and certain symbolical compositions. These canons were to endure in Iran for several centuries.

Like all Near-Eastern art, that of Achaemenid Iran is distinguished by its realism in the portrayal of everyday objects which are faithfully reproduced down to the tiniest detail, combined with stereotyped, idealized portraits lacking any individual features. Unlike the art of the Near-East, however, there is nothing that might be termed personal or private in Achaemenid art, for nearly all compositions have a specific symbolic meaning. Thus, for example, the symbol of the supreme god of the Assyrians, Ashur, was chosen as the symbol of the deity of fate, success and "royal predestination", Khwarnah. There was not even any need for any serious iconographic changes in doing so – in late Assyrian cylindrical seals Ashur is depicted in a sun-disc in the form of the figure of the king between two outspread wings.

Persepolis. Reception hall (throne room).

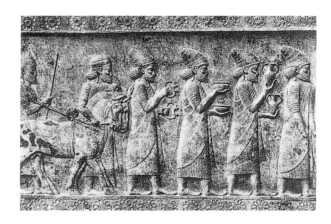

Relief decoration, grand staircase

The symbol of Khwarnah probably appeared at the time of Darius and evolved during his reign: the rock at Behistun bears an image in which a sphere with a star crowns the deity's tiara and in his hand he holds a torque - the insignia of power. At Persepolis, Khwarnah is depicted exactly like the king, Darius. The Assyrian "gatekeepers", *shedu*, repeated on a gigantic scale in the "Gateway of All the Nations" at Persepolis, perpetuate many details of the prototype used and transformed by the Iranian sculptors, but here they symbolize an Iranian deity - Gopatshah. This image was also very popular in the applied arts. Above the door of the rock tomb of Darius at Naqsh-i Rustam is a sculptural composition that in effect repeats the throne compositions at Persepolis in which representatives of subjugated nations support the ceremonial dais. Darius himself is shown on a stepped pedestal leaning on a bow with one hand raised towards an altar on which a fire is burning. Above this scene soars the symbol of Khwarnah. This scene soon becomes part of the artistic canon and tombs of later Achaemenid kings repeat it in detail. It also appears on Achaemenid seals.

In the spring of 330 BC, Alexander the Great burnt down the Apadana of Persepolis; this event was to be a turning point in the history of Iran and of its culture. Alexander's campaigns in the East began an age usually referred to as the age of Hellenism[33]. Along with Alexander's phalanxes, the artistic tastes of the Greek world, its craftsmen and its works of art all penetrated Iran.

The efforts of Alexander's successors, the Seleucids - his generals who became the monarchs of the lands he had subjugated - to create unity throughout lands with varied social conditions, beliefs and customs, complicated by the formation throughout the East of cities granted the right of *polis*, were simplified by the fact that in theory a social structure and political norms similar to those in Greece had existed in the East even before the arrival of Alexander's troops. As a result, an ideology of "cosmopolitanism" was to dominate for an extremely long period.

Initially, the Greeks themselves did not attempt to hellenize the conquered lands. Convinced of the superiority of their own political system and way of life, they nevertheless tolerated local cults and even supported them. In the end there was collaboration between the Persians and Greeks. The Persians began to aid the conquerors both in the creation of the machinery of state and in the sphere of religious cults and all of this simplified the process of syncretization. Despite the shift in power, local rulers preserved the ancient traditions in many of the satrapies[34].

There is no need to list here the examples of Hellenistic art found on Iranian soil - the Greek inscriptions, the statues of Greek deities or Greek architectural monuments - since there are a number of specialist studies on this subject. The picture became a great deal more complex in the second century BC when Iran was conquered by a dynasty of Eastern Iranian origin, the Parthians, who brought their own culture to Iran, and a new, Parthian, empire arose which was to last for more than 500 years.

Even today the world of Parthian art remains a colourful mosaic of isolated works, varying styles and concepts which it is difficult to amalgamate into a coherent picture. Consequently, it is necessary to bear in mind that Iranian territory during this period is a 'blind spot'. We know a good deal about many works from Central Asia, Afghanistan, North-Western India and Mesopotamia, but hardly anything about Iran itself, since there has been no archaeological research of this period. One could, of course, gloss over this period, uniting, say, the art of Mesopotamia with that of Central Asia and Eastern Turkestan. One would then find that this art (as opposed to the art of Greece or Achaemenid art) is characterized by refinement of form, a wealth of symbolism and frontal representation. In addition there is greater movement and space, and a more illusionistic approach than is seen in Achaemenid art[35].

The process of artistic syncretism, especially as one era ends and another begins, is, of course, linked to definite social, economic and political changes. The rulers of both empires - the later Seleucids and the Parthians - tried to embody their own divine reflection in the form of single deities and nearly every religious system in the East of that time aspired to the role of world religion. In the early Hellenistic period a common religious language appeared. The cult of a sun deity, under various names - the Semitic gods Bel (in Elam) and Aphlad (in Syria), the Iranian Ahura Mazda and Mithras - spread across the whole Parthian empire. The same happened with the cult of the god of victory (the Iranian Verethragna and the Greek Heracles) and with the cult of the mother-goddess or goddess of fertility, called Anahita by the Iranians, Nanai or Atargatis by the Semites and who was compared to the Greek Artemis or the Cybele of Asia Minor. It is easy to imagine how many new features the religious art of the Parthian period had to absorb. There is much greater thematic variety than in Achaemenid religious art.

Relief decoration, grand staircase.

During this very period some Iranian deities were endowed with an anthropomorphic aspect. It has been established[36] that an enormous role was played at the courts of the Parthian rulers by *gosans* or minstrels who sang the epic ballads celebrating the exploits of the ancient Iranian heroes, the Kayanids (the kings who first embraced the Iranian faith of Zoroastrianism), or of heroic warriors battling with demons such as Thraetaona, the dragon-slayer, or Zarer, the conqueror of nomads.

These traditions were more secular than religious and formed an extremely important part of Parthian dynastic doctrine, for the Parthian kings traced their lineage back to these ancient epic heroes. Dynastic legitimacy was founded on the epic. The epic justified the divine right of the Parthians to the throne of Iran, the epic was Iranian dynastic history. Fragments of it survive in sacred texts often preserved by Zoroastrian priests. But the Iranian epic tradition, which was vitally important for Persian art of all ages up to the nineteenth century, was born in North-Eastern Iran and came to the Iranian plateau by the North-Eastern Iranians led by the Parthians.

This epic tradition gave rise to such essential themes of Iranian court art as the depiction of hunts, battles and feast scenes. The epic cycles may have been illustrated in polychrome wall-paintings in palace. Archaeologists have found such wall-paintings, together with clay sculpted portraits of noble ancestors – on the north-eastern frontiers of Iran, particularly in Parthia, whereas in Iran itself no wall-paintings or other depictions have yet been found clearly representing such scenes, with the exception of some wall-paintings of dubious date at the palace of Kuh-i-Khwaja in Seistan.

We may, however, safely assume that these themes, so decisive for Persian art, appeared during the Parthian period under the influence of the art of the north-eastern provinces (Central Asia and Afghanistan).

Towards the end of the existence of the Parthian state, Christianity arose and spread across its western boundaries. In the state of Kushan, on the eastern borders of Parthia, at approximately the same time, one of the most important Buddhist movements was taking shape – the doctrine of the Mahayana. In Parsa, in the south of Iran, Zoroastrianism was developing into a state religion. Syncretism and the common religious language that had arisen in the Hellenistic period were giving way to the search for a dogmatic religion.

Some knowledge of the Iranian religion, Zoroastrianism, is necessary as it formed the ideological basis of Iran's art for at least two millennia. Its name comes from that of its prophet – Zarathustra (subsequently transmitted to Europe in its Greek form as Zoroaster). Zarathustra was evidently a real figure, as is corroborated in particular by his "peasant" name meaning "owner of an old camel"; he was a member of the Spitama tribe and probably lived in the seventh century BC. He was expelled from his community for having

Relief decoration, grand staircase.

preached doctrines to which its priests objected and went away into the east of Iran, to Bactria or Drangiana, where he was received by a king belonging to the ancient dynasty of the Kayanids, Wishtaspa (Hystaspes), who was the first to be converted to his faith. Zoroastrianism is known primarily in its later, Sassanian version. At its heart lies a dualism: this asserts that there are two principles in the world – Good and Evil – and the essence of existence is the struggle between them. At the same time Zoroastrianism is a monotheistic religion, for Ahura Mazda (later Ormazd) is the one god, a god of goodness and light, while his antithesis, "the lord of darkness" Angra Mainyu (literally "evil intent", later Ahriman) and his forces, are fiends (*daevas*).

According to this doctrine, space and time are infinite. Space is dual – "the kingdom of good" and "the kingdom of evil". Within infinite time (*zrvan akarana*) Ahura Mazda creates a finite, closed period which lasts 12,000 years. The concept of cyclical development is fundamental to Zoroastrian philosophy. Thus, according to sacred texts, the first 3,000 years of this period were devoted to an "ideal creation" of the world, the world of ideas; in the second 3,000 years the material world was created. Here the struggle between Ahura Mazda and Angra Mainyu takes place (everything good is created by Ahura Mazda, everything evil by Angra Mainyu). The following 3,000 years is the history of the struggle between the two forces before the appearance of Zarathustra. Finally, the last 3,000 years is "our time" in which Zarathustra appears and three "saviours" (Saoshyants) are awaited, who will announce the decisive moment in the struggle between the forces of light and darkness. The forces of darkness will suffer a final defeat and the world will be purified by fire.

A distinctive feature of Zoroastrianism is its assertion of man's active role in confessing the good faith of a worshipper of Mazda and thus contributing towards the final victory of good.

Zarathustra's doctrine and his preaching, as well as numerous pre-Zoroastrian religious hymns and liturgies and a plethora of ancient Iranian myths, were brought together in the Avesta, the sacred texts, which were, however, written no earlier than the fifth century AD, in a very complicated alphabet created especially for that purpose by the Zoroastrian priesthood. For more than 1,000 years before this the priests had learned the texts by heart.

Apparently no more than a quarter of what once made up the Avesta has survived. Its foundation is the *Gathas*, the preaching of Zarathustra himself, and the *Yasna*, hymns to the gods. After its codification in the fifth century, parts of the Avesta were translated into Middle Persian and the Zend, an extensive commentary on it, was written. The liturgical texts (*Yasna*) have, of course, survived longer

Persian warrior. 5th century BC. Hermitage Museum, St Petersburg.

than anything else, and although they as well as their supplement (*Vispered*) and the priestly codex (*Videvdat*) are in the main monotonous incantations to the gods, they contain a number of myths and legends of great antiquity. The gods of the *Avesta* are not as a rule given human form in the sacred texts.

The single exception is the goddess Anahita, who, in one of the *Yashts*, is described as a beautiful woman dressed in a silver beaverskin cloak and wearing various ornaments. But many of the Zoroastrian deities are personified mainly as various animals or birds which serve as complete representations of these deities (see below for further details). The evil *daevas* have a single personification.

These are such evil deities as Azhi Dahaka, a three-headed snake, or the daeva of plague and death, Nasu, represented as a fly coming from the North, or the demon of laziness, the long-armed Bushyasta.

During the Achaemenid period there also existed the Mazdaism of the Magi (an ethical and religious doctrine) and the religion of the Achaemenid kings, which in many ways differed both from the doctrine of the Magi and from ancient Iranian beliefs (thus, for example, in the official texts of the Achaemenid kings the name of Zarathustra does not occur and Ahura Mazda is not the only god but simply the supreme one).

Consequently one can say that in the late sixth and early fifth centuries BC, Zoroastrianism was only just beginning to assert itself in Iran and the Achaemenid kings, while valuing the superiority of Zarathustra's doctrine as their new official religion, nevertheless did not cast aside the cults of the ancient tribal gods. At the same time Zoroastrianism had not yet become a dogmatic religion with firmly established norms and there were slight modifications as the doctrine developed. Zoroastrianism was widespread in the Parthian empire: for example, shards from the wine store of Mithradatkirt (discovered during excavations at Nisa in Turkmenistan) bear more than 400 proper names of various people, of which a third, the so-called theophoric ones, are given in honour of Zoroastrian deities. However, symbols and religious formulae are lacking on Parthian coins, while at Mithradatkirt works of art used in the funerary cult of kings display an abundance of typical Hellenistic imagery.

Only in one province of Iran, in Parsa, are the old Achaemenid traditions preserved. Here a local dynasty was in power, and although very few works from this province have survived (its capital, Istakhr, situated not far from Persepolis, has still not been excavated), from about the second century BC its rulers issued coins bearing their Zoroastrian (even Achaemenid) names, the symbol of the royal Khwarnah and the symbols of Zoroastrianism – an altar with a blazing fire and a Zoroastrian temple (possibly a temple of the goddess Anahita).

The Sassanian state, formed in the third century AD, began with the creation of a strong centralised power which fairly soon united the whole of Iran under the control of the Sassanid monarchs.

The province of Parsa was the centre of the development of this state and its historical and cultural nucleus for the entire duration of its 400-year existence, and the Sassanids themselves were hereditary priests of the Temple of Anahita, one of the Zoroastrian holy places of Parsa.

Consequently, the keyword in the unification of the country was the "renaissance" of Iran's ancient grandeur and the ancient grandeur of the Iranian religion. Before long, the Sassanid monarchs were starting to trace their lineage back to the Achaemenids. It is natural, therefore, to regard the history and culture of this period as a nationalist Iranian reaction to Hellenism. The first works of the Sassanian period seem in fact to be totally unlike works from the age of Hellenism or the few that have reached us from the Parthian age.

Above all, the thematic restrictiveness of Sassanian works of art is striking. Monumental reliefs depict nothing but scenes of the king's investiture by a deity, military triumphs, single combat or the king of kings and his courtiers. In the main, carved gem-seals reproduce official portraits of civil servants and priests, while metalwork items show scenes of kings and courtiers hunting or again display official portraits. Such was the art of Iran during the course of the third century AD, and although new themes can be distinguished here in comparison with Achaemenid art – military triumph, tournaments, hunting scenes – it seems as if we are, in fact, faced with a rebirth of ancient Persian art, evident in the symbolism of the scenes, in a particular sort of extended narrative quality, in the emphasis on the divine essence of royal power, even in the choice of location for the largest reliefs which were carved into the same rocks out of which the tombs of the Achaemenids were hewn.

Once again, we are confronted with an artform that aims to reflect the specific ideological principles of a new state. Once again we are confronted with an "imperial style", with a strict canon and a comparatively narrow choice of themes reflected in all branches of art, from reliefs to carved gem-seals.

This period must be regarded as the closing stage in the development of ancient Persian art. The art is characterized in particular by naturalism in the portrayal of iconographic details such as the insignia of power of the shahanshah (king of kings) – a crown and ornaments, a particular type of dress, the exact rendering of weapons, or horse harness. Such iconographic details vary only slightly as a result of variations in the material.

For example, all the basic elements of the individual crowns of the shahanshahs are portrayed absolutely identically whether on colossal rock reliefs and on miniature gem-seals, in soft stucco and in silk textiles. Until the end of the Sassanian period each shahanshah was portrayed on such works wearing an individual crown of a pattern that was unique to him and with the symbols of his own guardian deities.

A few palace ruins have survived from the Sassanian period (Firuzabad, third century AD; Sarvistan and Ctesiphon, fifth to sixth centuries AD, and others), a few Zoroastrian temples, the so-called *chahar taqs* – domed constructions with a windowless central space, which became widespread throughout Iran probably in late Sassanian times – and a few towns, in general still unexcavated. The outstanding works of art of this period are the numerous works of applied art, above all metalwork but also carved gem-seals, textiles, ceramics and glass, which are to be found in various of the world's museums. The Hermitage in St Petersburg justifiably prides itself on possessing the largest collection of such pieces in the world. These works recreate the image of a state which was one of the great powers of the East from the third to the seventh centuries AD and a centre of learning and culture; a state which not only left as its heritage one of the first medical academies and one of the first universities of the Near East, but also the first authentic chivalrous romance and the first authentic record of the codification of the ancient Iranian encyclopaedia – the *Avesta*.

In almost all fields of culture of the Sassanian era one can discern clear links with the culture of previous periods – not only with that of the Achaemenids but also the Hellenistic period. The artistic imagery and ideas of Sassanian works exerted a perceptible influence over a vast territory from the Atlantic to the Pacific, and in turn one can distinguish features from the art of the Caucasus, Central Asia, Eastern Turkestan, even China, in works of art from Iran.

The dominant theme of early Sassanian art (third to fourth centuries AD) was the proclamation of the state's power. From the very beginning of the Sassanian era official portraits of the Sassanid shahanshah and his courtiers as well as his military triumphs were the images most often seen. In essence, Sassanian art begins with the creation of the iconography of the official portrait and the triumphal composition.

Religious art also follows the same line as official art. From the very beginning its basic subjects were anthropomorphic portrayals (also, in their way, official portraits) of the major Zoroastrian deities – Ahura Mazda, Mithras and Anahita, depictions of the interior of the monarch's coronation temple and portrayals of the shahanshah's investiture by these main deities. Such works of art reflected the fundamental, divine nature of power cherished by Iran's rulers in a language of clearly understood symbols. The scene of the divine investiture, the handing over of the insignia of power to the shahanshah by Ahura Mazda, Mithras or Anahita, was mainly sculpted in reliefs, but also featured on the reverse of early Sassanian coins and on early Sassanian gems. The canonic form of the interior of the king's coronation temple shows an altar on which a fire blazes, sometimes flanked by the figures of the king and a deity, the design being almost the same as in Achaemenid reliefs; the altar is occasionally on the dais of a throne constructed just like those of the Achaemenid rulers. This altar appears on reliefs and coins as well as on gems.

These official works reflected the initial period of development of the Sassanid monarchy's state ideology; they emphasized the real political successes of the first shahanshahs and proclaimed their faith, Zoroastrianism. The religious theme becomes more complex at the end of the third century AD, as if it had become obscured by the introduction into the official-portrait iconography of incarnations of Zoroastrian deities of a lower order (in the beginning, it is true only of one deity the companion of Mithras, the god of victory Verethragna). The main incarnations of Verethragna are a wild boar, a horse, a bird, a lion and the fabulous Senmurv (half-beast and half-bird), and they appear in depictions of the shahanshahs' crowns and the headdresses of princes and the queen of queens. Strictly speaking, the emergence of such imagery marks the beginning of a new theme, that of Zoroastrian symbolism. The earliest pieces only present these incarnations themselves or their protomes, but very soon they give way to a different type of composition, above all to scenes of the royal hunt which are also widespread at the end of the third century AD.

Subsequently all three themes that followed developed along different lines. At the end of the fourth century AD the state political theme gradually loses its significance. Rock reliefs, the chief monuments exhibiting this theme, are no longer produced: thirty reliefs are attributed to the period from about the 230s AD to the beginning of the fourth century, but only two to the period from the first decade of the fourth century to the beginning of the sixth century. The official portrait of the shahanshah appears primarily on coins, the official portraits of courtiers mainly on gems.

Triumph of Shahpur I. 3rd century. Relief. Naqsh-1 Rustam.

Zoroastrian symbolism, with various symbols of the guardian deities, occupies an ever greater place on the crowns of the shahanshahs. The scene of the altar flanked by the figures of the king and a deity on the reverse of Sassanian coins gradually becomes a canonical image, but one which has already lost its meaning. Zoroastrian symbolism, on the other hand, seems to overwhelm various branches of art. Incarnations of many Zoroastrian deities and symbolical compositions become the main subject of gems and are often depicted on stucco decoration and on textiles.

However, the initial meaning of this theme is also lost. The symbols of the Zoroastrian deities – various birds, beasts and plants – become benevolent. Imagery that is foreign to the Sassanians makes its appearance, borrowed from the West and in the main connected with Dionysian beliefs. Having been subjected to a Zoroastrian interpretation, not always of any great profundity, it is included in Zoroastrian benedictory or celebratory compositions. Such a subject as the royal hunt loses its initial, strictly symbolical, meaning and a new, narrative, theme arises in Sassanian art on its foundation; the symbolical composition simply turns into a literary subject.

All these processes had already begun in the fourth century AD and were, of course, linked to definite changes both in dynastic doctrine and in the Zoroastrian canon, although there was no such hard and fast correspondence between the two as there was between official ideology and official art during the first stage.

In the sixth and seventh centuries AD, art as a whole was characterized by a flowering of the narrative theme and benedictory subjects, although in some works political and religious themes did reappear. There was even an emergence of what might be termed narrative-Zoroastrian themes – various Avestan myths were illustrated in works of art.

The link with ancient Persian art is particularly significant for Sassanian religious iconography. The portrayal of Zoroastrian deities in the form of their hypostases or personifications is a device with which we are already familiar and which was encountered in the art of both the Medes and the Achaemenids. Several such hypostatic images were passed on to Sassanian art. Among them one finds the already familiar Gopatshah who has the Assyrian *shedu* as his prototype, winged and horned lions, winged griffins, the scene of a lion attacking a bull and even such ancient images as a stag, a panther and a vulture. The changes are truly of great significance.

We have already referred to the creation of anthropomorphic images of the main Zoroastrian deities. It is true that they repeat the real iconography of royal portraiture. Ahura Mazda, in the dress and insignia of Iran's shahanshah, is depicted on the same pattern as the Khwarnah of the Achaemenids, except that the dress of the Achaemenid king is exchanged for that of a Sassanid king; Anahita is depicted in the dress and insignia of Iran's queen of queens; Mithras is also in royal dress, but with a radiant crown around his head.

Triumph of Shahpur I.
drawing of relief by Sir Robert Ker Porter.

The link with Achaemenid culture is apparent in many spheres. One could point out, for example, that in official manifestoes of the Sassanid shahanshahs the standard formula of Achaemenid royal inscriptions is employed. Nowadays it has become evident that Sassanian state Zoroastrianism was initially nothing but the Zoroastrianism of Parsa of the Parthian, or even the late Achaemenid, age. In the formation of Sassanian art the Parthian contribution was no less important than that of the Achaemenids and of post-Achaemenid Parsa. A certain number of reliefs and graffiti as well as coins of the Parthian age have the same composition, sometimes the same portrait iconography. The contribution of the late Hellenistic art of Mesopotamia to Sassanian art is also extremely significant[37].

Vessels of precious metal play an important role in Sassanian art. Such vessels were used at royal feasts, but the feasts themselves also had particular significance. Herodotus wrote that the Persians decided all their most important questions of state at feasts. Precious vessels were offered to the kings of neighbouring states as valuable gifts; they served as rewards to courtiers for outstanding exploits.

They were valued for their marvellous craftsmanship and for their imagery, but the metal of which they were made was itself of no small value in Sassanian times. According to the Sassanian Code of Law, for example, "worthy" provision for a free citizen of the empire consisted of 18 silver drachmae a month (about 75g of silver); the silver bowls in the Hermitage weigh at least ten times that amount. The earliest of the silver ceremonial bowls which have come down to us date from the 270s–290s AD.

Late Roman art and especially late Roman silver "portrait" vessels heavily influenced Sassanian metalwork during its early stage. Apparently under their influence this traditionally Persian art form was reborn. The vessels were of prestigious or propagandistic significance and their simple ceremonial role was merely secondary. At first, such vessels featured official portraits of the Iranian kings, employing the same iconography as on reliefs and coins. Fairly soon, within fifty years or so, the portraits depicted on the vessels were no longer of shahanshahs, but of great courtiers and priests. Towards the middle of the fourth century such vessels disappear completely. The first known plate bearing a depiction of kings and incarnations of Zoroastrian deities also dates from the 270s–290s.

The first known plate depicting a hunting scene was produced at about that time. This form of art was new to the Sassanians and exhibits some innovations. First of all, there is a wealth of Zoroastrian symbolism (other objects of this period presented only what might be termed basic symbols).

At this point, it is necessary to summarize briefly what little we know about the hypostases or incarnations of Zoroastrian deities, from the Yashts of the *Avesta*. The first of the *yazads*, Mithras, according to the *Mihr Yasht* a sun deity of victory, royal majesty and justice, does not have

an earthly incarnation, but even in the Achaemenid age a lion was the symbol of the sun and royal majesty. In the *Mihr Yasht*, the deity of victory Verethragna, in the form of a boar with sharp tusks and iron claws, flies in front of Mithras as he defeats his enemies. In other *Yashts* Verethragna appears before the hero-kings in different guises: in the form of a bull, a camel, the bird of prey Varaghna, a white steed, Senmurv, a ram, an ibex, a bear and a beautiful youth. The deity of fate, success and "royal predestination", Khwarnah, appears in the *Yashts* in the form of the bird Varaghna, a fish, a gazelle (?), Senmurv and a large ram. In the *Avesta* Mithras is extremely closely linked to Verethragna and Khwarnah. The bull was also revered (the deity of the "soul of the bull" and Gopatshah, the man-bull) as was the star Sirius (Tishtrya) which appeared in the image of a steed, a golden-horned bull and a youth. This covers almost the entire animal repertory of early Sassanian art.

Fragments of Eastern Iranian epic cycles are preserved in the Avestan texts, where they narrate the struggle of the hero-kings to acquire the qualities of these deities – strength, invincibility and success. The visible incarnation of the deity had to be literally captured or seized. Not only the hero-kings of the Iranian epics but also the founder of the Sassanian state, Ardashir, had to first obtain possession of the "good fortune of Khwarnah of the Kayanids" in the form of a large ram, according to the account in the romance devoted to him (*The Book of the Deeds of Ardashir, Son of Papak*).

This solves the mystery of the symbolism of the hunting scenes on Sassanian silver plates. The three divine qualities of a true, legitimate ruler of Iran, granted to him by the god Mithras, by Verethragna and by the deity of royal predestination, constitute the sole symbolism found on ceremonial royal metalware of the early Sassanian era, presented in strict, exact compositions repeated without alteration from one object to another.

These pieces were fashioned in a central royal workshop up to c. 480. Divine essence and the legitimacy of royal power are symbolically represented by the "capture" of Khwarnah in the form of the most popular hypostasis, a mountain ram, the strength of this power by the struggle with the lion, and its triumph by the struggle with the wild boar. Silver plates bearing such compositions were essentially for propaganda purposes.

By the end of the fourth century, however, scenes of royal hunts on silver plates were gradually giving way to depictions of the heroic or epic victory of the king of kings. Of course, one cannot say that the Zoroastrian symbolical composition in its pure sense was no longer recognized – it still occurs on fifth-century objects – but the range of buyers for metalwork had widened and this, it seemed, had somewhat altered the repertory of subjects. This development of iconography is characteristic of the evolution of all Sassanian art; it is a movement from orthodoxy to the everyday subject requiring no religious interpretation.

Boar hunt. 6th–7th century AD. Relief. Taq-i Bustan.

The theme of the heroic hunt flourished especially in the fifth century. Later, this subject, too, was reduced to a simple genre scene, or even to the level of literary illustration of some particular hunting story. Royal horsemen were already being depicted wearing, as a rule, standard "impersonal" crowns.

Three silver plates – two in the Hermitage, one in a private collection in the USA – provide examples of such a hunting story, representing one of the exploits of Prince Varahran.

These depictions are the first and possibly the only clear examples of genuine illustrations of oral or written tales of the skill and valour of an Iranian knight. But in the sparse Sassanian literature of the sixth to seventh centuries that has reached us we find tales of skill and prowess in chivalrous sports (hunting, polo, the mastery of various weapons and especially skill at archery) and also of proficiency in games (at chess - *shatrang* - and backgammon - *nevartashir*). One of those works, *Khusrau, Son of Kavadh, and His Page*, tells the story of the beautiful women who played the *chang* and who accompanied kings on their hunts; they are often depicted, for example in hunting scenes of the Shahanshah Khusrau II (reliefs at Taq-i Bustan). Judging by the story of Firdawsi, a woman playing *chang* also took part in the marvellous gazelle hunt of Bahram Gur, though on silver vessels showing this scene she has no instrument in her hands. A host of such beauties with harps, flutes and changs are depicted on silver vessels - ewers, flasks, deep hemispherical bowls and shallow dishes.

These vessels also show various birds and beasts, including fabulous ones, genre scenes, depictions of architectural monuments (which have not survived), illustrations of myths that are not fully comprehensible, plant motifs, flowers, trees, etc.

This group of Sassanian metalwork, unlike silver plates portraying Sassanid shahanshahs, can only be dated with difficulty (apparently most of these festive utensils relate to the fifth to seventh centuries). It is even more difficult to interpret their subject-matter. The very fact that we are dealing with festive dishes may, in many respects, call into question any interpretation of them as religious and symbolical images. The Dionysian background of the main characters and most of their attributes are indisputable. The origin and prototypes of the iconographic details can, in the main, be traced back to the West and in this sense the entire group is comparable to those few Sassanian dishes on which a western subject is reproduced in full by Iranian craftsmen - the dish with the Triumph of Dionysus from Badakhshan (now in the British Museum, London), later replicas in the History Museum in Moscow and the Freer Gallery in Washington, the Bellerophon dish in the Metropolitan Museum of Art in New York, and several other vessels. In all probability such vessels were used at banquets during Zoroastrian festivities, the most sacred of which were Nawruz, the celebration of the New Year (meant to coincide with the vernal equinox), Mihragan, the autumn harvest festival dedicated to Mithras, and Sadeh, the winter festival dedicated to the divine fire.

Judging from accounts in written sources, the climax of all these festivals was a ceremonial banquet, which took place after a special service in the fire temple, and various rites (the offering of water, wine, etc.) in which silver vessels were used. The *Nawruz-nama*, a work on ancient Iranian customs ascribed to Omar Khayyam, contains the following passage:

"The king said: this [water] has been stolen from two who are blessed and highborn. [This refers to two amashaspands, Haurvatat and Ameretat.] And they adorned the neck of the jug with a necklace of olivines and chrysolites strung on a golden thread. [The necks of some silver flasks are decorated with convex "pearls" in imitation of such beads.] And girls alone stole water for the New Year ritual from beneath water-mills and out of canal cisterns".

The depictions on ceremonial vessels may be linked to rituals whose details remain unknown to us. It can, however, be gathered from written sources that various contests and exchanges of gifts took place during these festivities, and that musicians, dancers and girls who served wine and water in special vessels took part in them. These festivities and the carnival processions did, of course, have a definite religious symbolism and ritual significance, but evidently they were taken over by ancient folk customs and their symbolism. The longer this continued the farther religion receded into the background. Thus, the Muslims of ninth-century Baghdad wholeheartedly celebrated several Zoroastrian festivities, and as late as the tenth century the Muslim rulers of Iran delighted in celebrating the Zoroastrian feast of Sadeh which, moreover, coincided with Christmas. On that night they would light bonfires and drive wild beasts into them, release birds into the flames and sing around the fires.

We can clearly see how the themes of Sassanian metalwork gradually change. The theme of state propaganda is very short-lived and soon changes into the religious propaganda of Zoroastrian symbolism in its "pure" phase, but both themes have a comparatively brief existence and eventually heroic and narrative themes predominate. All this can be demonstrated from stage to stage in the development of the royal hunt motif, which may well be the only motif in metalwork that relates directly to the art of official propaganda.

Of course there are vessels which employ only Zoroastrian symbolism or illustrations of Zoroastrian myths; there are also vessels portraying the "wonders of the world" or "marvels" like the complicated clockwork mechanism that once decorated the throne of one of the Sassanid shahanshahs, and depictions of subjects that were exotic or foreign to Sassanian society.

All this variety, initially clearly differentiated in terms of iconography and subject-matter, becomes confused towards the end of the Sassanian period, its previous exactness and rigour of selection seeming to break down. Judging by those Sassanian items known to us today, it is possible to state that all art of this period, and not just metalwork, follows this line of development, a process by which themes of a propagandist nature die out, and heroic and epic, benedictory and everyday themes come to dominate.

This is one of the fundamental reasons why a wide range of similar compositions subsequently pass into Islamic, Umayyad and early Abbasid art. For it is Sassanian jugs of wine, and bowls served by Zoroastrian girls, that are mentioned in these verses of the famous Arab poet Abu Nuwas (died in the ninth century)[38]:

She is a Zoroastrian, her blouse complains it has no room because of the twin pomegranates of her breasts.

Her chief business is to bow down to the first ray of the rising sun when it appears.

"She gives wine in marriage to water [mixes wine with water] in golden bowls whose interiors are filled, Girdled with images that do not heed the caller and do not speak. Before the figures of Papak's sons [the Sassanid shahanshahs between whom a moat is trenched.] When the wine is above them they are as batallions of an army drowning in the depths".

The bowl described here is apparently a boat-shaped vessel with deep fluting at the bottom and images on the internal surface, so that there really does appear to be a moat trenched "between Papak's sons". In recent times such vessels have been found in North-Western Iran during unsupervised excavations of Sassanian sites of the sixth and seventh centuries.

The Zoroastrian girl mentioned by many Persian and Arab poets of the Middle Ages is of particular interest. She would usually be serving them wine, which was forbidden by Islam, in taverns or among the ruins of a temple. Are these not fragmentary survivals of rituals connected with wine from Zoroastrian feasts, and is this not the reason why there are so many girls with wine and vines and other

attributes of the "Dionysian background" both on these Sassanian silver vessels and on early Islamic ceramics?

Thus, looking at Sassanian art as a whole, one reaches the conclusion that it began with a fairly limited range of themes strictly stratified according to genre, as an art that was, so to speak, "conceptual", or at any rate subject to an absolutely specific interpretation, and "imperial", an instrument for political and religious propaganda. In late Sassanian art, however, genres blend; complex religious symbolism changes into benedictory symbolism; the symbolic banquet, battles and hunting scenes become ordinary tales of hunting exploits, many feasts and chivalry.

The further art develops, the more all these initial, symbolic scenes and compositions become either illustrations or mere ornamentation. One could go so far as to say that towards the end of the Sassanian period the illustrative and ornamental themes played the main role in art, although, of course, the propagandist themes of the "imperial style" also survived until the very end of the period, especially in official works of art (rock reliefs, palace decorations, coins and gems). In discussing the illustrative aspect of late Sassanian art one cannot avoid mentioning Sassanian literature.

About a hundred titles of various religious, literary and scientific works of this time are known from different sources. A few dozen books of various kinds have reached us, mostly via translations into Arabic and later also into Persian, a hundred or more years after the fall of the Sassanian state, or even in revised versions of a comparatively late date. It is difficult to distinguish between their various accretions from different periods, to make any sense of the blending of various styles and genres. In the course of translation from Middle Persian a sort of compendium was usually produced.

Boar hunt. Relief. Detail.

In official manifestoes of the shahanshahs and rock inscriptions (third century) mention is made of official state records, statutes and codices produced under each king. This is also reported by much later foreign sources relating the history of the Sassanids. Probably it was these official state-records that were reported by the Arab historian al-Mas'udi, who in 915 AD saw a manuscript in Istakhr which contained the history of the Sassanids – all twenty-seven shahanshahs who had ruled, as the manuscript stated, for 433 years, one month and seventeen days.

All these kings were portrayed in the manuscript. Another medieval historian, Hamza Isfahani, saw just such a manuscript (or perhaps the very same one). He left a description of the portraits of "kings and courtiers, famous guardians of the fire, all priests and others noted among the Persians". These illustrations were typical official portraits.

Pitcher, 9th century. Hermitage Museum, St Petersburg.

The crown was precisely depicted, the kings stood or sat on their throne. The manuscript was translated from the original into Arabic for the Caliph Hisham. It was completed in 731 AD and this is probably the earliest record of the translation of Middle Persian works.

A few compendiums of the tenth to twelfth centuries preserve fragments of similar translations and they confirm that in terms of their content such books were records of state affairs, arranged not by year but by separate reigns. Around the fourth century comes the first reliable report of literary works being among such records, and of their being collected into specific anthologies, their abundant subject-matter relating as a rule to distant antiquity. We know in particular of one such story, *Rast-sukhan* (*The Truthful Word*).

The story has not survived, but apparently it contained the legendary history of the founder of the Sassanian state – Ardashir, the son of Papak – and was similar to the *Book of the Deeds of Ardashir*, known in a late Sassanian version (fourth century). It is possible that both these works were combined into one text in the sixth century. Despite the fact that it recounts various stories in terms of feats of chivalry – the struggle with a fabulous "serpent", the freeing of beautiful women, tournaments, miraculous portents, military stratagems and so on – this story was indisputably semi-official insofar as it defends the legitimacy of the Sassanid rulers' power, asserting that they are descended from the ancient Iranian kings. It is curious that at the same time an "anti-romance" also existed and was widely known in certain circles opposed to the dynasty. In it, Ardashir turns out to be the son of a soldier called Sasan and of the wife of a cobbler called Papak (Papak, it is true, was a sorcerer).

Fragments of Eastern-Iranian myths about the hero-kings, the Kayanids and Peshdadians, survive in isolated *Yashts* of the *Avesta*, written in the alphabet specially created for it in the fifth century, and subsequently glossed and partly translated into Middle Persian (the language of the *Avesta* is very archaic). Names of heroes and various of their feats are mentioned (for example, their battles or their victory over the forces of evil), but not a single more-or-less complete myth has reached us.

These legends became especially popular in the fifth century, perhaps as a result of the Sassanids' capture of the city of Balkh in Eastern Iran – according to legend the very city once ruled by the Kayanids. This was the period when the Sassanids began tracing their lineage back to these epic hero-kings. At the same time, epic poems dating from the Parthian era were being recorded.

Only one of them has survived, *The Chronicle of Zarer*, relating the Iranians' struggle for the Zoroastrian faith against their famous enemies, the "Turanians" (in the Sassanian version they are called Chionites, but that is a prose retelling). Even later, in the sixth and early seventh centuries, there were cycles written about individual Sassanid shahanshahs, such as the conqueror of the Turks and the usurper of the throne, Varahran Chobin. Apparently there were also books in existence at that time concerning the "wonders of the world", similar to the stories of Sindbad the Sailor, and there was a geographical literature and stories of the exploits of holy men. It is well known that in the sixth century a collection of edifying novella-type tales, *Kalila and Dimna* (or *Pañchatantra*), was translated from Sanskrit into Middle Persian. This book was by no means mere light reading – it was valued as "a book full of wise thoughts".

Thus, towards the end of the Sassanian period several literary genres already existed as well as official history and religious works. Tradition relates that the last of Iran's shahanshahs, Yazdegerd III, commissioned a scholar called Daneshvar to compile a dynastic history.

This book, the *Khwataw-namak* (*Book of Rulers*), grouped together myths, historical romance and royal records in a single cycle. This marked the beginning of a written tradition, although one must bear in mind that such works would hardly have found a wide readership. Written Middle Persian was extremely complicated and hard to understand. It involved a vast quantity of heterograms and in addition the lack of vowel points and the enormous polysemy of individual signs made the writing so difficult that contemporaries had good reason to name it "the devil's script". When reading these books, *dabirs* (scribes) and priests often had to "translate" them into spoken Persian.

To make this clearer (for the problems of literature and language will play an important role later on in this account), we will cite the literal translation of one section from the Sassanian romance, *Book of the Deeds of Ardashir*:

"(1) In the book of the deeds of Ardashir, son of Papak, it is thus written that after the death of Alexander Rumi in the kingdom of Iran there were 240 rulers of principalities. (2) Isfahan, Parsa and the adjacent provinces were under the hand of the governor Ardawan. (3) Papak was marzban and governor of Parsa and was among those designated by Ardawan. (4) Ardawan sat at Istakhr (5) and Papak did not have any son to bear [his] name. (6) And Sasan was shepherd to Papak and always to be found among the sheep, but [he] was of the line of Darius."

Everything underlined in this text was written in heterograms. And this is one of the easiest texts! Consequently, as previously under the Parthians, the basic literary works – epics, folk tales and true histories – were recited by poets and *gosans*, versifiers of epics, at courts and the castles of "knights". Their names have survived and in later works there are a number of stories about their talent and their outstanding role in court life, for example the story of Barbad, the *gosan* of the shahanshah Khusrau II. We know only four lines from one of his poems, but these are the oldest verses at present known in the Dari language – the spoken language of late Sassanian Iran, which was to become the Iranian literary language two centuries later. They were preserved by the Arabic-speaking historian, Ibn Khurdadhbih: "Caesar [here the Byzantine emperor] is like the moon, but Khakan [king of the Turks] is like the sun. But my lord [Khusrau II] is a mighty cloud [Khusrau II was called

Parwiz, "cloud"]. When he wishes he will cover the moon; when he wishes, the sun".

These unsophisticated verses are one of the first examples of the ruba'i, the quatrain, a literary form that was to become extremely widespread in the Iran of the age of Islam.

It is beyond the scope of this study even to draw up a brief list of the problems connected with the new Islamic religion, which has been the dominant ideology in Iran from the seventh century to the present day.

However, one of its aspects is of great importance. From the very beginning Islam rejected figurative representation, or more exactly the depiction of living creatures, as a means of propagating its ideas[39]. In this respect Islam differed from Buddhism, Christianity and Zoroastrianism, which made widespread use of figurative representation and had for a long time anthropomorphized their deities. This hostile attitude towards the depiction of living creatures – though in essence only towards anthropomorphic representation as an object of worship – had a number of consequences that were decisive for the development of art in Iran.

Firstly, it caused a gradual decline of monumental art forms such as rock reliefs, stucco panels and wall-painting (although we know that the latter existed in Eastern Iran up to the thirteenth century, and in central and Western Iran up to the seventeenth century).

Secondly, it diminished the status of the artist, at any rate during the first centuries of Islam when it expelled him from the ranks of those creating works pleasing to God, and transformed his occupation into something not entirely commendable from the point of view of religious morality.

Thirdly, it narrowed the range of new themes that could emerge, above all the religious ones which were central to all Christian and Buddhist art – the depiction of God and his deeds, the stories of prophets and saints – everything on which an artistic impression of the world was founded in non-Muslim cultures during the Middle Ages. The reasons why anthropomorphic representation was unnecessary in the propagation of Islam are complex and have not been satisfactorily elucidated. We will examine a few of them here.

Theology, in the true sense of the word, took shape very late in Islam. Early Islam was interested only in external ritual observance and it elaborated questions of religious law, but despite this, in the eighth century, as Vasily Bartold writes, in Islam "the same disputes about God and his relationship to man were arising as in Christianity; apart from the direct influence of Christian dogma on that of Islam, this can be explained by the identical conditions in which both religions found themselves"[40].

Especially important is the school of theology of the Mutazilites (from the Arabic for "separatists"). This school, which created Islam's first carefully elaborated theological system, made widespread use of Greek devices and achievements in logic and philosophy, particularly those of Aristotle. Its fundamental thesis was "the cognition of the divine unity".

Stucco panel.
7th–8th century.
Chal-Tarkhan.

The Mutazilites resolutely opposed the concept of God in human form and of his attributes or qualities which were invented by man, even those such as "omnipotent" or "all-seeing", for these are "conceivable" categories. According to the doctrine of the Mutazilites, God is a unity that is pure, undefinable in human terms and unknowable.

It was during the flourishing of the Mutazilites that the following *hadiths* (traditions of the words and deeds of the prophet Muhammad) first gained popularity: "artists will be tormented on the Day of Judgement", "and they will be told: bring your own creations to life".

But one must bear in mind that from the point of view of its structure Islamic theology was in no way comparable to, say, that of Christianity. Firstly, though it became a state religion, even the dogmatic theology of the Mutazilites remained such for only a few decades. Secondly, Islamic law pervaded all aspects of social life (even contracts for buying and selling had to be agreed upon in the presence of a religious judge, a *qadi*), yet it was not founded on any absolute and clearly formulated law, but had four bases: the Koran, the *hadiths*, *ijma* – consensus of opinion between the *faqihs* (the authoritative theologians), and *qiyas* – the method of analogy with the Koran or the *hadiths*.

In consequence, one can fully understand why the faqihs held various opinions on the subject of the "*hadiths* of the artists", but views such as the following, expressed by Abu al-Farisi in the mid-tenth century, were more or less general:

But if someone should say: "surely it is said in the hadith, "the artists will be tormented on the Day of Judgement", and in other hadiths, "and they will be told: bring your own creations to life", then the words "the artists will be tormented" relate to those who depict Allah in the flesh. And as far as any addition to that is concerned, these are communications of isolated individuals who are unworthy of trust. And as we have noted, the *ijma* does not dispute this opinion[41].

Oleg Bolshakov, who has studied the known sources on this question, formulates his conclusions as follows: "Defining the permissibility of this or that depiction, the jurists proceeded first of all from the consideration of the extent to which they are dangerous as potential objects of worship. Disagreement between the various scholars arose over the attempt to define this very matter"[42].

But the existence of persistent disagreements even between the *faqihs* did not, and never could, give rise to any official and general prohibition. Of course, in the history of Muslim theologians' attitudes towards figurative art there have been periods when a more rigorous attitude prevailed, and even periods of persecution and extreme reaction (not until the seventeenth and eighteenth centuries, it is true, and then only in individual Islamic countries), but one thing is clear: the question was always one of religious anthropomorphism – and of that alone.

Therefore there is absolutely no reason to see figurative art in Islamic culture as the perpetual overcoming of a prohibition existing within the religion.

On the other hand, the arrival of Islam in Iran brought about the abolition of other restrictions which had an important bearing on the development of art.

By the eighth century the Islamic state, the Caliphate, included not only the whole territory of Iran but also part of Byzantium, North Africa, the Iberian Peninsula, Central Asia and Afghanistan, and it subsequently extended even further; yet this state was by no means a world empire like the empires of the Achaemenids or the Sassanids. Its ruler, the *caliph* (from the Arabic "successor" or deputy of the prophet Muhammad), inherited from the prophet the Imamate, the spiritual leadership of the Muslim community, and the Emirate political power. According to Islamic law, he either had to be elected by the whole community (this was, of course, only in theory), or appoint a successor during his lifetime, with the approval of the *faqihs* (this latter requirement was also not followed in practice).

And although it was considered that the power of the *caliphs* had been established by God, the Islamic state was theocratic but far from despotic.

In theory, the Islamic state was considered to be a state of equals and the basic confrontation within it was not in terms of estates or between the nobility and the oppressed, but in terms of Muslims and infidels[43]. In Sassanian Iran, and this was especially noticeable towards the end of the Sassanian period, divisions in society were strictly upheld – they were specifically sanctioned by Zoroastrianism. Priests, warriors, scribes and the common people each formed separate "estates" and movement from one estate to another was impossible or at least extraordinarily difficult. In artistic terms, this social system fostered the creation not only of a hierarchy of forms and themes but also of a hierarchy of individual types of art ("prestigious" and "non-prestigious"). The Islamic conquest swept away the social system of castes and estates and in so doing significantly changed the hierarchy in subject-mater and the branches of the fine arts. The Sassanian royal and "chivalric" culture was destroyed.

Lastly, it is necessary to say something about the conception of a world culture which also suffered notable changes after the arrival of Islam in Iran. Mention has already been made here of this conception as understood by the Achaemenid and Hellenistic eras. Its character during the Sassanian period is described thus by Vasily Bartold:

"The world situation of the Sassanian state in the sixth and seventh centuries clearly had an even greater effect on the success of imperialism (Bartold uses this term only in the narrow political sense of the "creation of empires") in individual countries than did the formation of Alexander's empire in its time. This was the period of the unification of China under the rule of the Suis dynasty (589-618), followed by the T'ang dynasty (618-907), with their extensive claims in Central Asia; of the might of the kings of Kannauj on the Ganges, considered to be the imperial city of India during the first centuries of Islam; of the unification under the power of a Turkish dynasty of nomads from China to India, Persia and Byzantium.

These events formed the basis of the Buddhist concept of four world monarchies at the four corners of the world: the empire of the king of elephants in the south, the king of treasures in the west, the king of horses in the north and the king of people [because of the vast population of the Chinese empire] in the east. With a few alterations, this same concept was transmitted to Muslim authors: the king of elephants was also called the king of wisdom because of a fascination for Indian philosophy and science; the king of people was the king of state government and industry because of a fascination for Chinese material culture; the king of horses was the king of beasts of prey; in the west two kings were differentiated – the king of kings, that is the king of the Persians and then of the Arabs, and the king of men, because of a fascination for the racial beauty of the [Byzantine] empire's population[44]."

The Islamic modifications are of interest here. In Sassanian Iran the conception of the "four kingdoms" manifested itself as a concept of Greater Iran as a centre of civilisation surpassing, or at least equal to, other nations in terms of its culture. Islamic "democracy", on the other hand, stresses the differences and the specific contributions of individual civilizations towards the single world of culture created by them, for the theory was that the Islamic state should in the end become worldwide and integrate all these achievements, since, after all, the "infidels" had been conquered by the Muslims.

Thus the Islamic conquest swept away a number of restrictions within Iranian culture, and not only religious ones but also those relating to estates. The Zoroastrian or state propagandist interpretations were eliminated from all artistic forms, themes and compositions which had been developed in Sassanian Iran; kings finally became simply kings; heroes, warriors and hunters simply themselves; beasts, birds, flowers and plants simply beasts, birds, flowers and plants. And this repertory, which included a great number of images and compositions imported from other cultures, passed into the art of medieval Iran, developing along the same general lines which characterized medieval art, such as an intensification of decoration and a striving towards abstract compositions.

And yet the art and culture of Iran did not fuse into a general Islamic culture. On the contrary, after the Iranian renaissance (tenth to eleventh centuries) the Modern Persian language became the language of Islam together with Arabic and under the influence of the Iranians Islam itself became a multilingual, multinational culture and religion. In the words of one contemporary historian, "Iranian civilisation played the same role in the development of Islamic culture as Greek civilisation did in the formation of Christianity and its culture"[45].

From the seventh to the ninth centuries the eastern province of Iran, Khurasan, was of special significance in the founding of the new culture (in the Middle Ages it encompassed the north-east of present-day Iran, the south of present-day Turkmenistan and the north-west of present-day Afghanistan).

In the sixth to seventh centuries the situation there resembled that of Syria, for example, in the second century, in terms of the intensity of its conflict of ideas. In the Marv region, archaeologists have discovered a Christian monastery and cemetery; there was a large Jewish community which buried its dead in day ossuaries bearing Hebrew inscriptions; a Buddhist monastery was situated there, as was one of the most ancient and revered Zoroastrian temples. In 651 AD the last Sassanid shahanshah, Yazdegerd III, met his death here while fleeing from the Arabs. Medieval historians relate that his death was shameful: he was robbed and murdered in his sleep, his body was thrown into a river, and afterwards he was buried by the Christian bishop of Marv, Elijah.

One immediate consequence of the Arab conquest of Iran was an influx of Arabs settling in many cities or setting up military camps which soon became cities. This Arab immigration was on a mass scale; in the tenth century, for example, the Arab population already constituted a majority in the city of Qum.

The second consequence was the spread of Islam and of Arabic. During the first two centuries of Islam in the territory of Khurasan, the religion of the Arabs underwent an intensive process of transformation into the religion of the entire Caliphate, while the language of the Koran and various Arab tribes developed into an Arab literary language; in all of this the Persians, who had converted to Islam, played no small part. It was here that Shi'ism, one of Islam's most important movements, developed, and in particular its extreme faction, Ismailism, and other doctrines that were to serve as rallying points for many national uprisings.

Thus during the early Islamic period (under the Umayyad Caliphate) Khurasan was a stronghold of Islamic science and Arab literature. It was here too, in Khurasan, that the anti-Umayyad rising began, instigated by Abu Muslim, leader of a political and religious party supporting the Abbasid family.

The common people were widely involved in the rising: peasants, craftsmen, and also the Khurasan *dihqans*, descendants of the Sassanian nobility. There were also Muslims and Zoroastrians among the rebels. Having established themselves on the caliph's throne, the Abbasids were naturally quick to settle with all the dissatisfied. One of the consequences of the Abbasid victory was a complete "Iranization" of the Caliphate. The Abbasids offered a number of high positions in the state to the Iranian nobility that had helped them to seize the Caliphate. The state system of their Caliphate followed the Sassanian pattern.

There was yet another important consequence of the change of power. Before the Abbasid age the Islamic community of Iran had consisted primarily of Arabs and only afterwards of Persians converted to Islam, who were considered as clients (*mawali*) of the Arab families and tribes and did not possess equal rights with true Arabs. The Abbasids ended this division and in the same period many *dihqans*, who had preserved or even raised their social status, adopted Islam. This Iranian elite did a great deal for Islam.

The supporters of the Iranophile cultural movement, the so-called Shuubiyya, wrote their works in Arabic. This movement flourished especially in Khurasan under the Abbasids, and despite the fact that it inculcated into an Islamic culture the pre-Islamic ideas, traditions and customs of Sassanian Iran, in objective terms it led to the enrichment and widening of Islam itself and to a rejection of the provincial narrowness of Muslim culture. In the court of the Abbasid caliph al-Mamun (813–833) translation in particular blossomed: works of many types were translated into Arabic – ethical and didactic (*andarz*), historical (numerous "Histories of the Kings of Fars" linked to the *Khwataw-namak* cycle), literary (such as *Kalila and Dimna*) and many others. At the same time scientific tracts and parts of religious and philosophical books were translated. It is interesting to note that at approximately the same period a Zoroastrian orthodoxy, that was not in any way prohibited by Islam, held power in Fars; basic Zoroastrian works such as the *Denkart* were written here. In honour of the arrival of al-Mamun in Marv (809 AD), a certain Abbas-i Marwazi delivered the first verses in the Modern Persian language.

These were all the first steps of the "Persian Renaissance" leading to a flowering of Modern Persian literature by the tenth century and, in the final analysis, to that of the Iranian cultures of Firdawsi, Nizami, Sa'di and Hafiz.

The creation of Modern Persian literature was also a factor of the utmost importance for medieval Persian art, for it was this which was to serve as the basis of figurative art. The essential preconditions already existed.

The illustrative quality and the variety of forms within late Sassanian art, the rich artistic traditions of wall-painting in Eastern Iran and Central Asia and the no less rich traditions of Christian art in the eastern provinces of Byzantium, etc. But before discussing what happened to Persian art in the early Middle Ages, it is necessary to know something of the "Persian Renaissance" which flourished in Eastern Iran, mainly during the rule of its Samanid dynasty – a line of Iranian nobles who claimed descent from the Sassanian general and usurper Varahran Chobin.

Modern Persian literature began as courtly literature. At that period the demotic language in the whole of Iran, Khurasan and Central Asia had for a long time been Dari, or what was to be Modern Persian. The Arabs themselves promoted the spread of Dari over a vast territory and its transformation into a language of communication between different ethnic groups; they used it to communicate with the local population in Iran, Khurasan and Central Asia[46]. The adoption of Arabic script (more convenient than Middle Persian or Sogdian) for the Dari language was a natural process. In 967 AD the *Pharmacology* of al-Harawi was written in Dari and in 982 a geographical treatise *The Limits of the World* was published. But the first prose work in Modern Persian was a compilation of "universal history" (from various Arabic translations of the Sassanian *Khwataw-namak*), produced in 959 on the order of the ruler of the city of Tus, Abu Mansur ibn Abd al-Razzaq, by four Zoroastrians (to judge by their names), "scholars of the past of the Persian kings".

In lyrical poetry the famous poets of the "Persian Renaissance", Rudaki, Daqiqi and others, comprehensively exploited all the achievements of Arabic literature, but also utilized non-Arabic verse forms which were evidently still Sassanian or were re-created on the basis of Sassanian verse.

Their work was founded on oral tradition, the poetry of those same *gosans* who, in the courts of local rulers during the early Islamic era, continued to be "…entertainers of king and commoner, privileged at court and popular with the people; present at the council and at the feast; eulogists, satirists, story-tellers, musicians; recorders of past achievements, and commentators in their own times"[47].

The greatest literary achievement of this period was the Iranian national epic, the *Shah-nama* of Firdawsi, who wrote this long poem on the glorious past of his country. Although he undoubtedly considered his subject matter as history, he wrote it in the form of a narrative poem, creating characters and combining various events from different periods or episodes from various legends around them so that the acts of his heroes and their ethical and moral, or even political consequences should stand out in sharp relief. Firdawsi's poem, like Iranian poetry of that period in general, could be said to "discover" the individual as an independent, creative being, as a personality and as the creator of his own fate and history. Man as an individual, and not as a typical representative of an estate, caste or class – it could be said that this is the leitmotif of Persian literature and social life at the time of the "Persian Renaissance".

It is clearly unnecessary to discuss the social and economic basis of this process at any length – it is completely comprehensible and has frequently been described. This, incidentally, was the golden age in the development of cities, but they differed from those of Western Europe, above all, in that their citizens had no special class privileges. The city was simply a conglomerate of manufacturing, territorial, religious and other self-governing corporations under the aegis of a civil service[48]. Like the poets at court, the cities' craftsmen were bound together by close ties. All of these highly important circumstances bear witness to the enormous changes taking place in society, its social structure and its psychology.

Mention must be made of the fundamental difference between the medieval art of Europe and that of Iran. In western medieval art prior to the Renaissance, the acts of God, the saints and ascetics formed the subject of man's "visual" impression of the world and of its morality and history; in the medieval art of the East, however, during the course of this entire period man himself and his acts became the main focus.

During the Middle Ages the range of subjects in western art was universal, that of Persian art was national. This was a consequence of the fact that Iranian fine art was extremely closely linked to written and oral literature whose basic protagonists were ancient Iranian epic heroes and rulers, lovers, warriors, famous poets, and only very occasionally prophets and holy men.

At the time of the formation of the Caliphate and the emergence of Islam as its religion, it was natural that works of art from the preceding historical phase, such as metalwork, carved seals, stucco decoration, coins and silk textiles, should not change their range of subjects and motifs. The first Arab rulers minted coins on the Sassanian pattern, simply using the stamp for a Sassanian drachma with the addition of the Muslim religious formula "in the name of Allah" on the coin's face and, moreover, depicting themselves in the regalia of a Sassanid king of kings.

Some Sassanian metalwork may perhaps already be attributable to particular periods, although as far as its themes are concerned (hunts, royal or courtly banquets, genre scenes, dancers, etc.) no essential changes took place. Purely Sassanian themes and motifs survived longer in such regions as Tabaristan and Gilan. In Eastern Iran a canonic scene, "the king on an ottoman throne", was reproduced on articles of metalwork and possibly on silver medals.

During the tenth to thirteenth centuries this spread from the Indian frontier to the Mediterranean. In this scene, the king sits cross-legged on an ottoman-throne, holding a bowl and surrounded by his servants, dancers and musicians; this scene combines features that are above all Sassanian, but also Buddhist and Sogdian.

On the whole, it can be said that Persian art of the eighth to eleventh centuries was first of all unusually varied as regards its range of themes and subjects and its influences. One of the major historians of Islamic art, Oleg Grabar, wrote: "Every newly discovered monument reveals to us completely unknown aspects of this art[49]." It is true, as we have already mentioned, that there were attempts to create specific styles at the courts of rulers, such as a court style in Khurasan under al-Mamun (early ninth century) and under Mahmud of Ghazni (early eleventh century), but these were merely episodes not leading to any sort of lasting unification.

Such variety is characteristic of all types of art at this time. In the architecture of Iran, for example, the hypostyle plan was introduced as the basic mosque layout, brought by the Arabs from the West (the mosques in Siraf, Nayin and Damghan), but at the same time the so-called "kiosk-mosques" were being built, based on the Zoroastrian plan of the *chahar taq*, and tower mausoleums were spreading (there are Middle Persian inscriptions on some of the mausoleums, alongside Arabic). Mosques were decorated with stucco panels consisting of plant and geometrical motifs, while in the east of the Islamic world, as in Nishapur, these motifs are extraordinarily close to those used in the west, for example in Iraq. At the same time we know of stucco panels of that period (mid-eighth century, Chal-Tarkhan) which depict not only Sassanian animals but even Sassanian deities (Mithras on a stag) and heroes of Sassanian legends (Bahram Gur and Azadeh)[50].

All in all it could probably be said that during these centuries a process of selection was taking place in Persian art, involving a choice of forms and themes from traditional art together with various innovations. Historians of Persian art are unanimous in mentioning the slowness of this process. The most innovative art was produced in the north-west of the country.

It is especially important that in the same period one sees how the propagandistic and class character of the hunt, feast and battle scenes have entirely disappeared – they have become standard scenes, lacking any significant meaning. Sassanian symbols degenerated into purely visual motifs. The same thing happened to Sassanian depictions of birds, beasts and plants. Although they only had a benedictory significance even in late Sassanian art, during the eighth to tenth centuries they become mere ornamentation.

Strange new motifs appear during the ninth and early tenth centuries on Nishapur ceramics, and there alone. The designs portray birds, beasts (most often a goat), various monsters, horses being attacked by beasts of prey, dancers, figures in rich clothing holding goblets and flowers, and riders on horseback. All these designs do, of course, have their prototypes in Sassanian art, but they are very primitively executed with no regard for proportion and are sometimes mere caricatures, though this style gives the faces a lively character and expressive quality.

Ceramic cup. 9th-10th century. Nishapur.

Ceramic cup. 11th century. Garrus.

This ceramic style, which appeared suddenly and vanished just as suddenly, possibly in the course of a single century, is an example of those completely new aspects of art appearing in connection with the new discoveries which Oleg Grabar mentions.

Ceramics from the Garrus region (North-Western Iran) are also curious, executed in a technique involving the carving out of a layer of slip, which results in a low-relief design. One such bowl portrays a character from an Iranian epic, the tyrant-king Zahhak who killed Jamshid[51]. Some scholars assign these ceramics to the twelfth century.

From the beginning of the eleventh century changes in Persian art are clearly distinguishable and this new phase covers a lengthy period of about 300 years, until the mid-fourteenth century. In future, detailed studies of various aspects of art will probably enable us to specify the date when each of them arose and declined, but in the meantime it should be noted that ceramics and metalwork depicted the most vivid figurative images of this period. The golden age of miniature painting dates from around the end of this phase of Persian art (after the Mongol conquest) and this form was subsequently to occupy a dominant position in figurative art.

The political history of this period involves the rise of the Turkic dynasties of the Ghaznavids in the east and of the Seljuks, and the crushing Mongol conquest. In view of the fact that works of art have as yet been insufficiently researched it is impossible to relate them precisely to historical events, and, on a wider scale, to events in the field of culture (often it is necessary to date objects of this period from the eleventh to twelfth or twelfth to thirteenth centuries; although in the course of these centuries extremely important changes occurred both in politics and ideology).

Nevertheless, the general conclusion is totally clear. In essence, the art of this period should not be termed a "renaissance" in the generally accepted sense of the word, since one can hardly consider its aim to have been the rebirth of old traditions, for they had never died out completely. It should also be said that, to a great extent, this applies to the literary "Persian Renaissance" as well. However, we will not enter into disputes which appear to be largely terminological. One thing is indisputable – the eleventh to the mid-fourteenth centuries represent the golden age of art in Iran. In architecture, for example, mosques on the four-*iwan* plan appear and spread throughout Iran.

Whichever way they are interpreted (they are even regarded as an adaptation of the plan of the Buddhist *vihara*), they are truly Iranian and for many centuries were the glory of Iranian architecture.

We need name only such classical monuments as the minaret of Jam, the mosques of Isfahan, the mausoleum of Sanjar, the mosque of Varamin and others[52]. Significant changes also occurred in metalwork, above all in Eastern Iran[53].

Sassanian traditions still survived at this time and partly on this basis, though to a much greater extent on the basis of Eastern Iranian

traditions, processes came about which led to the formation of a new phase in art. This phase was to reach its zenith in the fifteenth century.

As before, we are faced with a geographical factor, involving separate historical and cultural regions. It is clear, for example, that the most outstanding mosques of this time are the Isfahan mosques built between the 1130s and 1150s; the most outstanding mausoleums are those in Khwasan and Azerbaijan from the twelfth to thirteenth centuries; the most sophisticated ceramics are those of Rayy and Kashan, while the bronze inlay was produced predominantly in Khurasan.

Although outstanding craftsmen, as well as poets and writers, congregated at the courts of Iran's rulers, and this had its effect on the general direction of artistic development, no dynastic art of any sort was created.

The art of Iran at this period was the art of cities, of cultural centres, an art of master craftsmen, calligraphers and painters scattered throughout the country, an art for various customers – for the sultan, of course, but also for the merchants and wealthy citizens. Possibly the most exciting branch of art of the twelfth to mid-fourteenth centuries was the production of ceramic vessels and tiles. At that time, the technique of manufacturing lustreware was becoming widespread. It was complicated, demanding double firing, but produced an object that was brightly coloured, glossy and polished, shot with gold in reflected light and imbued with rich tones in the shade. Ceramic dishes became expensive articles of display.

The lustre technique originated in Egypt as early as the eighth century (the first examples of it come from Fustat, near Cairo). Some scholars suggest that the secret of lustre was actually imported into Iran by Egyptian potters who had moved from Cairo to Rayy after the fall of the Fatirnid dynasty (1171). The first precisely dated piece of Iranian lustreware is a jug from 1179 (British Museum, London). This does not, of course, mean that all other lustreware is later than this jug, but this is the first example on which the inscription includes a date.

A vessel in the Metropolitan Museum of Art is the first in the *haflrang* (or *minai* – painting in coloured enamels) technique which, apart from its date (1187), also mentions the name of the artist (Abu Zayd al-Kashani)[54]. The style of painting on this vessel definitely has a number of connections with the Mosul school of miniatures. But the people depicted on it are generally round-faced ("moon-faced", as the poets wrote) with narrow eyes and a small mouth; their hair, sometimes even that of the men, is braided into plaits and falls to their shoulders; their heads are, as a rule, surrounded by haloes. This is clearly a Turkic facial type; and the clothes are also Turkic. This "ideal type" is used without exception on all lustreware, tiles and *haflrang* ceramics. Its emergence coincides with the arrival in Iran of the Seljuk Turks, and the closest surviving parallel for these portrayals is provided by the Manichaean wall-paintings of Turfan.

Ceramic cup.
Late 12th century, Kashan.
Metropolitan Museum of Art, New York.

The dishes with scenes of court receptions are probably closest of all to the Turfan paintings. We have already spoken of the canonic nature of such scenes, elaborated several centuries earlier (there are even two cheetahs here at the foot of the throne, as on the silver saucer Cat. No.96), but one should note the multitude of courtiers' and women's faces surrounded by haloes, which is highly reminiscent of the Turfan paintings. Throne scenes were frequently depicted, not only on lustre vessels but also on *minai* (*haftrang*). Such vessels also show scenes of feasts and hunting which were similarly standard motifs.

Inscriptions are found on many vessels (both lustre and *minai*) as well as on star-shaped and cruciform lustre tiles in friezes decorating the walls of private buildings (with the same designs as those on vessels) or lining the walls of mosques. Sometimes these are Koranic texts, but very often they are lyric verses or extracts from long poems (*Shah-nama* of Firdawsi, *Khusrau and Shirin*, *Laila and Majnun* of Nizami, and others).

Unfortunately, the content of the verse frequently does not coincide with the image. A number of literary subjects are found on ceramics and tiles. Sometimes they are well known. Again one finds Bahram Gur and Azadeh (on several dishes and tiles), the hero Faridun with his cudgel, riding a zebu, *The Iranians Leaving the Fortress of Furud* (an episode from the *Shah-nama*; on a star-shaped tile), subjects well known from Nizami's poem *Khusrau and Shirin* (on a stamped vessel of the twelfth or thirteenth century, in the Hermitage, St Petersburg), and others.

The entire range of objects allows one to construct a certain, albeit sketchy, picture of Iranian figurative art over this period.

It has its standard themes (the royal banquet, the hunt, throne scenes, battles) founded on a tradition of great antiquity, but generalized and lacking any individual traits. It has many motifs or subjects linked in some way to oral poetry, to ballads and epics and to written literature.

These subjects are entertaining stories of ancient heroes and kings, of love and life's pleasures, etc. By the eighth century they had probably already begun naming ancient ruins after such ancient heroes and kings. One also finds extremely rich ornamentation: flowers, trees, fruit, birds and beasts, often of a standard type and serving as a background or even as an independent subject, although still remaining ornamental.

All these subjects appear on ceramics, in bronze and in stucco decorations (for example, the large stucco panels from Rayy). Pieces with such subjects were sometimes made for a particular person, but more often than not they bear inscriptions invoking success and addressed to an anonymous owner, to anyone who might buy them in the bazaar. These inscriptions are sometimes dedicated to the object itself.

The craftsman praises his work, glorying in his art. Illustration overwhelms the object: even the letters of the inscription are formed with their tips in the shape of human or animal heads (see Cat. No.116) or simply in the form of fighting warriors (for example, on the famous early thirteenth-century bronze goblet in the Cleveland Museum of Art)[55].

The works themselves cease to be anonymous. The craftsmen who made them sometimes added their names to the object and the date when it was completed, as did the scribes of manuscripts and their illustrators. The terminology used by the craftsmen to name themselves or designate their work is interesting. Inscriptions on ceramics (whether vessels or tiles) where name and date are marked, often used the standard formula: "Such and such a craftsman painted this". This signifies that he applied both the inscription and the design to the object. On many objects (bronzes and ceramics) another Arabic word is used: *'amila* (made). But this same verb was also used by the artist in his inscription to a miniature in the manuscript *Varqah and Gulshah*. Miniaturists called themselves *naqqash*, as did the artist of *Varqah and Gulshah*, for example; yet metalworkers gave themselves the same name.

In the miniatures of the manuscript *Varqah and Gulshah* (this is a rare case) the names of the characters are written alongside, just as characters' names are written on lustre ceramics and tiles. In miniatures from the famous Demotte *Shah-nama* (see below) the name of the subject is included in the composition, and the same is also seen on the lustre tile showing the scene from the *Shah-nama* mentioned above. Could an artist in ceramics, an artist drawing designs for a bronze object, a miniaturist and a fresco artist all be defined in the same way, or at least be very close in terms of their training ?

At this point it is necessary to look more closely at the history of Persian manuscript illumination. The first Persian manuscript with real miniatures that is known to us is the above mentioned Persian poem of Ayyuqi, *Varqah and Gulshah*[56], commonly assigned to the early or mid-thirteenth century. It was probably produced in Upper Mesopotamia (Jazira) or Anatolia.

The miniatures were painted by the artist Abd al-Mumin ibn-Muhammad al-naqqash al-Khowi, and some of the miniatures reveal the following characteristics: the frieze-like compositions of several miniatures are analogous to frescoes, with the interrupted action continuing beyond the frame in a linear development; some of them are painted against a vivid, often deep red, background which is characteristic of frescoes and also, for example, of the miniatures of the Kyzyl Manichaean treatise; absolutely every detail of iconography and style in this group of miniatures coincides exactly with those found on contemporary lustreware, and especially on *minai* ceramics; finally, luxuriant plant ornament serves as a background to some of the designs in this group of miniatures, exactly as on ceramics.

It is the influence of the Iranian miniature which is adduced to explain the illustrations on metalwork and even the style of painting of Iranian ceramics. But is there any evidence at all, even circumstantial, bearing witness to the existence of miniature painting in Iran during the period before the end of the thirteenth century? We do have a manuscript treatise on astronomy, Abd al-Rahman al-Sufi's *Book of the Fixed Stars* (completed in 400 AH/1009–10 AD)[57].

It contains fine drawings and scientific illustrations which are of a set type and are treated exactly like all illustrations to scientific works of the time. These are not, of course, miniatures in the true sense of the word; they lack any artistic perception of the world.

Information about illustrations in early manuscripts is also extremely sparse in written sources. In fact, only three references can be mentioned. Nizami Aruzi Samarqandi (twelfth century) relates that when Abu Nasr Arraq, the famous mathematician and nephew of the Khwarazmshah Abu al-Abbas Mamun, visited Mahmud of Ghazni (the action takes place in the early eleventh century), the latter ordered him to paint a portrait of the renowned scientist Abu-All ibn Sina, who not long previously had refused to work at the court of Mahmud and had lied to Iraq [58].

Miniature. *Rustam besieging the fortress of Kafur.* c. 1330.

Mahmud wanted the portrait to be duplicated in order to send it to various provinces to identify the runaway. This reference is probably pure legend, and if it is not, then the story may be of more interest to the history of criminology than to that of the Iranian miniature! More reliably, al-Rawandi relates that in 1184 he copied a collection of various poets' works in which the artist (*naqqash*), Jamal-i Isfahani, had included the portraits of these poets [59]. Finally, one source reports that during the siege of Marv by the Mongols in 1220, at their demand a list of artists (*naqqash*) and craftsmen of the city was compiled [60]. Naturally it would be difficult to maintain that the terra *naqqash* in this text applies to miniaturists.

Even earlier accounts are just as sparse and imprecise. There are the accounts of the already mentioned "official portraits" of the Sassanid rulers in the book of Sassanian history kept at Istakhr (Fars) during the early tenth century [61] and there is the information that the collection of fables, *Kalila and Dimna*, translated in the eighth century from Middle Persian into Arabic, had been illustrated by Chinese artists. Only this last report seems to be direct evidence of miniatures decorating a manuscript, but here it is a question of an Arab manuscript and Chinese artists and this is evidently credible, since it is known that Chinese artists, among other craftsmen, were captured by Arabs at the battle of Talass and taken to the Caliphate. From Chinese sources we even know the names of two of them – in the end they managed to return to their native land [62]. All other reports speak not of early Iranian manuscript illumination but of portrait painting or scientific illustration.

We have already seen that the portrait miniature as a genre had already established itself in the Sassanian period [63], and developed, even flourished, in Iranian painting during the following centuries. This movement undoubtedly had its specific characteristics, which have apparently still not been studied.

Thus the facts available at present attest that fresco painting existed on Iranian territory in the tenth to twelfth centuries, and that it was above all widespread in the north-east and beyond the borders of Iran; that portrait painting has been known in Iran since the Sassanian period; that there are a number of illustrations of literary and epic subjects on works of applied art, and even cycles of such illustrations, and finally, that the very earliest manuscript miniatures in Persian works known to us (*Varqah and Gulshah* and the Shiraz *Shah-namas* – see below) bear witness to the influence of fresco paintings and the decoration of ceramics.

One can suggest that the illustrative, narrative quality, which had already been present for a long time in Persian art - in wall-paintings, metalwork, stucco and textiles - became widespread during the eleventh and twelfth centuries in ceramics as well (on vessels and on lustre tiles, often forming what were, in essence, almost wall-paintings); only afterwards did those same artists – at any rate artists with the same technical training – also create Iranian manuscript illustrations. This is all the more likely, since, as scholars point out, one characteristic of Persian artistic perception is an extremely close connection between word and object, literature and fine art.

As a rule comparisons run both ways: life is breathed into objects, human attributes and feelings are ascribed to them, while human experiences and states of mind easily find a precise symbol among objects in the immediate environment.

Because of this the actual circumstances of reading poetry take on another sense: the participants of the scene are no longer surrounded by everyday objects, but by object-symbols with all their various, and as a rule human, characteristics. The bowl in the hands of those listening to verse is no longer a simple bowl but a metaphor brought to life: the open tulips of wine bowls are hearts filled with blood, the lips of the cup are the lips of a beloved, the bowl itself is the bowl of the heavens tilted above the world, and the turning of a round bowl repeats the whirling of the wheel of fate[64]. It is interesting to cite the viewpoint of scholars studying comparatively early miniatures of the so-called Shiraz school (the miniatures in the *Shah-nama* of 1333).

These miniatures differ fundamentally in their draughtsmanship from what we are generally accustomed to seeing in later Persian miniatures (15th–17th centuries). "[...] What one might call a painterly basis dominates here, [...] in terms of their technique these miniatures are on the one hand connected to fresco painting and on the other – and this is of vital importance – to paintings on ceramics of the so-called Rayy type, in which, as is well known, peculiarities of brushstroke and contour are explained by technical demands, i.e. the need to paint the object rapidly[65].

Of course, it is difficult to imagine a direct link between wall-painting and designs on metal and ceramics that does not take book illustration into account. It is, of course, far easier to consider that early illustrated manuscripts have simply not survived to the present day. But all the facts cited above tell us that we have no right to insist categorically that Iranian illuminated manuscripts existed before the mid-thirteenth century at least. How, in actual fact, could absolutely all the illuminated manuscripts have disappeared? Surely they would have been carefully preserved in court libraries. On the other hand, why have a number of Arabic manuscripts with illustrations remained, produced in the middle of the Abbasid Caliphate?

The total silence of early Persian sources on the subject of manuscript illumination is also strange. How many stories they tell of wall-painting! There are the anecdotes about Attar whose father, a merchant of perfumes (true, a fairly wealthy one), out of loyalty ordered a portrait of Mahmud of Ghazni to be set in the state apartments of his house, or the story told by Baihaqi about the erotic paintings in Mas'ud's pavilion, or the famous verses of Farrukhi (although this poet greatly disliked both antiquity and pictures): "Painted at several noble places in that palace [the palace of Mahmud of Ghazni] are pictures of the King of the East [Mahmud]. At one place in battle with a spear in his hands, at another place – at a banquet with a goblet in his hand." And not a single reliable reference to Persian illuminated manuscripts or Persian miniaturists before the fourteenth century.

In the fourteenth century the feudal system was at its height in Iran. At the same time, from the middle of the century, it was the age of individual rulers each striving to create their own magnificent court, with their own poets, scholars and artists. But the "prestige" of such a ruler, which he could flaunt to his rivals and subjects, was no longer a matter of precious vessels of gold, silver or bronze inlaid with gold and silver, of expensive ceremonial dinner services made in the lustre technique or painted in enamels, or of tilework decorating the halls of palaces, mosques or tombs.

Miniature. *The fall of Bahram Gor into the ditch.* c. 1370-1380.

Manuscript frontispiece. c. 1340.

These rulers were both weaker and poorer than their predecessors and there had long been no vast frescoes in their palaces, no stucco panels depicting the heroic exploits of their noble ancestors and no portraits of themselves.

Miniature painting and calligraphy appear to have become the chief "prestigious" branches of art. Costly manuscripts of ancient narrative poems or verses written by the ruler's court poets or by historians praising his, or his ancestors', grandeur, and decorated with miniatures executed by court painters or simply by skilled miniaturists involved in commercial production were highly prized. As for ceramics and metalwork, they were "democratized".

Craftsmen produced these articles for the middle ranks of society. Thus there were no longer ceramics bearing texts of great poems and decorated with pictures that were either themes from these poems or,

much more frequently, pictorial equivalents of the verses; the inscriptions on metal objects, which were more durable and expensive, are popular quotations or specific catchwords – albeit from the works of great poets – and not poetic texts. The social class of customers was changing and Persian miniature painting occupied the position of the most prestigious branch of art.

For many centuries, miniature painting was to be the leading genre in the Iranian fine arts. Oleg Grabar's assertion is perfectly correct: "The Rashidiyya school of painting did have a greater importance in the development of Persian art after the death of its founder in 1318 than the architectural style of Azerbaijan in the thirteenth century." [66]

The previously mentioned Shiraz school of miniature painting is represented by illuminated manuscripts from the first decade of the fourteenth century onwards. Eight examples are known, four of them being Firdawsi's poem, the *Shah-nama*. In the earliest copies the miniatures are executed in a flat style with strong affinities to wall-painting and painting on ceramic.

The large number of miniatures in these early manuscripts is interesting, but it is even more important to note that many of them are simple, standard compositions, such as scenes of a palace reception, a battle or various sorts of garden scenes or hunts. Thus, in the manuscript of the *Shah-nama* dating from 1333, for example, out of 52 miniatures more than 30 are standard scenes of battles, hunts and "conversations", etc. Such neutral, standard compositions have been aptly compared to the so-called *wasf* in literature [67]. The *wasf* is obligatory in almost all genres of Persian literature; it is that part of a work which contains descriptions of nature, royal hunts and feasts, battles or, say, weapons, jewellery and carpets. The descriptions had no independent significance at all. They were vivid literary pictures, like decorations against whose background the action unfolded. The beauty of these decorations in literature was often arrived at through "combinative methods": poets would from time to time interchange the same standard descriptions and motifs, complicating the images more and more and illuminating them in a clever play of words [68].

Early miniatures are extremely exact illustrations of the text. Like those in medieval western manuscripts, they are based on a standard subject into which some significant concrete detail from the story they illustrate has been introduced. Therefore, when depicting Zahhak, the artist reproduced the standard scene of a king on a throne but added the snakes that grow from the king's shoulders.

This manner of illustration develops from one manuscript to another and gradually establishes its own standards with subjects that were, initially, original. The miniaturist proclaims his identity in the character of the painting – in the colour scheme and the attention to intricate detail. Within this framework a great artist could rival a great poet.

But all these features were to emerge somewhat later. To return to the Shiraz school in its first phase, it should be observed that these miniatures are marked by imperfection, coarseness and standardization. In artistic terms they are not very interesting works. They are, so to speak, stereotyped miniatures.

Yet at the same period in Tabriz the masterpiece of Iranian illumination was produced, the Demotte *Shah-nama*, which we have already mentioned. At that time the Mongol dynasty of the Ilkhans, or Hulaguids, ruled in Tabriz. These were the descendants of Hulagu, the grandson of Chingiz Khan. One of them, Ghazan Khan (1295–1304), attempting to rescue the country from the cruel devastation that had been a consequence of Mongol invasion and rule, announced a series of important official reforms which were put into practice by his vizier, Rashid al-Din.

Rashid al-Din was an advocate of strong power and a centralized political system which, as it happened, were stubbornly opposed by the Mongol nomadic military aristocracy. In the consolidation of central-ized power Rashid al-Din was helped by the propagation of his own concept of an "Iranian empire of the Hulaguids". He called the Mongol khan the refuge of the Caliphate, an Iranian Khusrau and successor to the Kayanid kingdom [69].

Rashid al-Din's chief work, *Jami al-tavarikh* (*Collection of Chronicles*), is permeated by these concepts. The work was conceived as a genuinely universal history which would include the history of all the then known peoples, from the Franks to the Chinese. To realise this grandiose plan an entire "academy" was founded, which included scholars, calligraphers and artists – among them were two Chinese scholars, a Buddhist monk from Kashmir, a Catholic monk from France, scholars of Mongol traditions, etc. The manuscript of the Collection of Chronicles was illustrated by artists who strove to portray "ethnographic pictures" of the various peoples. The very strong influence of Chinese painting is noticeable in the illustrations – there were very many Chinese articles and Chinese craftsmen in Iran at that time, brought there by the Mongols [70].

Not long afterwards (perhaps during the third decade of the fourteenth century, at the court of Ilkhan Abu Sa'id) [71] a sumptuous manuscript of the *Shah-nama* was produced, astounding in the quality of its miniatures and the originality of its approach. It has been suggested that the choice of themes for its 120 or more miniatures was governed by a definite programme.

First of all this programme stressed the legitimacy of royal power, the same concept as Firdawsi's "divine Khwarnah (*farrah*)", which alone provides the strength and might of a legitimate lord and his divine predestination to power. However, the important fact is that the miniatures are painted with overwhelming mastery; they are already far from being simply illustrations, although there are plenty of standard motifs in this *Shah-nama* – throne scenes, hunts, banquets and battles. The miniatures of the Demotte *Shah-nama* are the first to represent a new movement in Iranian miniature painting, one that has nothing to do with illustration, for "the elaboration of the narrative through the image of man leads the viewer to a highly moral interpretation of the epic" [72]. But the Demotte *Shah-nama* is a unique manuscript that did not give rise to any imitations. In essence, the style of Iranian miniature painting was laid down in the 1360s and 1370s in the cities of Baghdad and Shiraz, and this was the style which was to determine its development for several centuries.

The first manuscripts with miniatures clearly displaying this style are the *Shiraz Shah-nama* of 1370 and the manuscript of poems by Khwaju Xirmani, copied in 1396 in Baghdad by the calligrapher Mir Ali Tabrizi. Around this time, the initial stage of development of Iranian miniature painting – the stage represented by the miniatures in *Varqah and Gulshah* or the Shiraz Shah-namas of 1330 and 1333, or by the so-called "Small Shah-namas" of the same period – was gradually but inexorably becoming a thing of the past.

It is possible that the first examples in architecture are to be assigned to the early eleventh century (for example, at Rabat-i Malik), although in ceramics "plaited" Kufic script is already well represented in the tenth century. At the same time *naskhi* writing begins to be used as a monumental script[85]. It has also been established that during the eleventh century specific types of mosque, *madrasah* (mosque school) and minaret became prevalent throughout Iran, though these types were not genuinely new but had already been developed during the preceding ages[86]. In the sphere of architectural decor much that is new emerges in the eleventh century, and frequently these innovations occur during the period preceding the creation of the great Seljuk empire[87].

It has been suggested that radical changes took place in art with the consolidation of Seljuk power. But as we have attempted to show, these changes were already perceptible much earlier, before the founding of the Seljuk state in Eastern Iran[88]. The Seljuks' contribution to art appears to have been very small; it is even difficult to speak of the Seljuk sultans' patronage of art as their dynasty never founded a permanent capital city which would have become a centre for the artistic movements of the period.

The changes in Persian art coincide chronologically with the Seljuk conquest, but it is necessary to seek the cause of these changes in the life of the Iranian cities where craftsmen and artists congregated. But by founding an empire from the Amu Darya (Oxus) River to the Mediterranean, the Seljuks furthered the spread of Persian art to the west[89]. A large number of Iranian craftsmen moved to Iraq and Anatolia in the eleventh and twelfth centuries and collaborated in the creation of a new style in these areas (another group of craftsmen went to the western regions a little later, at the time of the Mongol invasion).

Of course, within this long period in the history of art in Iran (from the early eleventh to the mid-fourteenth centuries), one could probably distinguish shorter chronological intervals[90] and, for example, define more precisely the consequences of the Seljuk conquest or of other political events.

Large Pot, by Mahmud al – Qazwini. 12th - early 13th century.

The Mongol invasion did not cause any significant changes in the art of Iran until almost the end of the thirteenth century[91], when one begins to sense the influence of China on miniatures and applied art. During the first three decades of the fourteenth century Iranian craftsmen also took over and reworked elements of Chinese art, but around the mid-fourteenth century a period of changes began in all branches of Persian art.

As we have already stated, the greatest difficulties arise when we attempt to fix a periodic classification for architecture (to the present day many studies adhere to a dynastic chronology). However, Leonid Bretanitsky[92], who has researched the development of architecture in Azerbaijan, has pointed out that several changes can be observed between the fourteenth and fifteenth centuries, and this phase culminates in the sixteenth century.

Apparently some new phenomena occur at the turn of the eighteenth century too. The period of change in architecture at the end of the fourteenth century corresponds to the beginning of the new stage indicated by Grube – around 1350.

Nor have the problems of classifying the periods of late Iranian ceramics been fully solved yet. Arthur Lane considers that the late phase in the development of Iranian ceramics covers the period from the fourteenth to the first half of the eighteenth centuries[93]. This chronology has met with determined opposition from Gerald Reitlinger, who considers that the age of Timur is the watershed between the early and late periods – that is, the last quarter of the fourteenth and the early fifteenth centuries[94]. This is close to Grube's point of view[95].

To explain the changes which occurred in the Iranian applied arts during the fourteenth century apart from metalwork one can study carved gems. It was during this period that Kufic script fell into disuse and inscriptions were as a rule executed in *thuluth* script, covering the entire surface of the seal[96]. These signs of a new style appear around the fourteenth century and end in the mid-sixteenth century. The last rare examples of seals with depictions of animals (see Cat. No.186) and people are found among fourteenth-century seals.

During the course of the fourteenth century an important change also occurs in calligraphy – a new script is developed, *nastaliq*, which becomes extremely widespread throughout Iran during the following century. The majority of surviving manuscripts were copied out in this script. Historical tradition associates the invention of this script with the name of Mir All Tabrizi who worked in the middle to late fourteenth century. True, one can scarcely consider him the creator of *nastaliq* but his work apparently laid down those rules which served as models for other artists.

For a long time the design of manuscripts did not attract the attention of scholars. But studies of manuscripts of the fourteenth to sixteenth centuries have shown that the fourteenth century marked the turning point in the history of this art form. Between the 1340s and the 1390s[97]

Bowl. first half 14th century.

important changes occurred in the decoration and use of colour and this almost coincides with the end of the second inter-regional period.

But the most clear-cut changes of all can be seen in Iran's metal manufacture. Earlier Islamic metalwork had been made from an alloy of copper, bronze or brass, but mostly of brass[98], and decorated with copper and silver inlay, or, after the mid-thirteenth century, silver and gold. In the fourteenth century pure copper begins to be used (see Cat. No.148). Such pieces were tin-plated so that food could be stored in them. The first copper vessels are not distinguished in form or ornament from contemporary bronze (brass) articles inlaid with gold and silver. The inscriptions on the copper vessels are also benedictory and in Arabic. They were presumably made for the middle ranks of the Iranian urban population.

At present, it is still difficult to determine with any great precision when the use of the new metal began in Iran, but if we take into account the fact that copper was used in the Syro–Egyptian region from the 1330s then we may suppose that the articles which concern us in Iran also existed in the second quarter of the fourteenth century[99].

Together with the appearance of the new metal, certain techniques began to be used in decorating objects. Although first used on bronze (brass) objects of the preceding period, these techniques were only developed fully during the course of the new period. For instance, the practice of setting off the inscription and ornament against a cross-hatched background: the first examples of this are observed on articles from the first half of the fourteenth century (see bucket dated 733 AH/1333 AD, Cat. No.146). This treatment of the background apparently only appears on copper items at the end of the fourteenth century (see bowl dated 811 AH/1408-09 AD, Cat. No.150). But as the comparison of precisely dated items demonstrates, this technique of treating backgrounds is a very important aid in dating works, distinguishing an entire phase in the history of Iranian metalwork from about the mid-fourteenth century to the last quarter of the sixteenth century[100]. The hatching is usually large on copper, but on bronze (brass) objects with inlay it is very fine, which may be connected with the much smaller dimensions of the latter.

Contemporary with the appearance of the new metal and the new treatment of background came the development of new types of copper objects. According to approximate preliminary calculations about forty new forms appeared, although very few examples of any one form have been found and bronze (brass) items of the fourteenth century remain almost unresearched. It is possible there will be new finds which will provide us with a more exact impression of how the new forms evolved, but in principle it remains a matter of importance to stress that the beginning of the new phase is characterized by the creation of new forms.

During the course of this new phase, from the mid-fourteenth to the second half of the sixteenth centuries, the art of inlay gradually declines and disappears. This decline seems to be most pronounced during the second half of the fifteenth century and the last pieces with inlay decoration can be assigned to the end of the sixteenth century. The art of inlay naturally serves to link the preceding phase very closely to the new one.

But on bronze (brass) objects of the fourteenth to the first third of the fifteenth centuries, inlay – primarily silver – covered a fairly large surface (broad letters in the inscriptions, elements of floral ornament and human figures), whereas on new bronze (brass) items of the second half of the fifteenth century we see only thin lines of inlay, whether on inscriptions or decoration. This may be a special characteristic of the Khurasan school of coppersmiths, although it is true we do not yet know of any other school of this period.

Another new feature of decoration on copper appeared at the end of the fourteenth century, namely filling a cartouche or medallion with an inscription. At first, the inscription on bronze (brass) articles with gold and silver inlay is stretched out along a line and its background filled with scrolled tendrils. From the end of the fourteenth century, however, the inscriptions on copper objects begin to fill the space completely, the letters of the words arranged one on top of the other with hardly any space left between them; what limited background remains is cross-hatched.

This tendency to fill the cartouche is exactly paralleled in the execution of inscriptions on seals of the late fifteenth and first half of the sixteenth centuries (see Cat. Nos.187, 188).

The rivalry between the Persian and Arabic languages in inscriptions on objects was already noticeable during the tenth to early twelfth centuries, but it developed differently on the various materials. On bronze (brass) this process proceeded fairly slowly. Up to the fourteenth century there are fewer Persian inscriptions than Arabic. It must be stressed that there are few known versions of the latter, but they were very often reproduced on objects. On the other hand, Persian inscriptions occupied a place of honour on the famous ceramics of the late twelfth and thirteenth centuries decorated with lustre and enamels, to which we have already referred.

These consist of quotations from the work both of famous poets of the past (Firdawsi, Omar Khayyam) as well as of contemporaries (Nizami, Kamal al-Din Ismail Isfahani, Jamal al-Din Muhammad Isfahani). Probably this bears witness to the literary taste of the craftsmen themselves, to the links between literary and artistic circles in the cities and to the spread of Sufi poetry. The interest in Firdawsi's *Shahnama* is connected rather with some sort of anti-Mongol sentiment, for the earliest extracts from the poem appear on tiles only after the 1260s[101], *ie* during the Mongol period.

But with the onset of the new phase in the mid-fourteenth century fundamental changes take place. A set of Kashan lustre tiles dating from the 1330s bears an exact reference to the place of manufacture. After this period we know of no large-scale output either of lustre vessels or of size-

Belt. First half of the 17th century.

able sets of lustre tiles (the lustre tiles on tombs of that date and of the fifteenth century are clearly not mass-produced)[102]. In general, the mass-production of lustreware dies out for almost 200 years. As far as one can judge from preliminary observations, the seventeenth-century lustreware which has survived also appears not to be mass-produced and, above all, there is no longer any reason to link it with Kashan (in late historical sources Kashan is not referred to as a centre of ceramic production).

New centres of ceramic production such as Mashhad apparently arose during the course of this new phase, beginning somewhere in the mid-fourteenth century. The most surprising new feature of Iranian ceramics of the later period is the almost total absence of inscriptions on dishes and, probably, tiles, though these latter may not have been produced in any quantities in comparison with the preceding phase. Ceramic mosaics were widely used in the decoration of buildings.

The small number of inscriptions which appear on faience dishes of the fifteenth to seventeenth centuries should be regarded as exceptions, and by no means as a continuation of the tradition of the late twelfth to the first half of the fourteenth centuries. But the role which ceramics played in pre-Mongol and Mongol times in disseminating Persian inscriptions passes to metalwork in the new phase. The period of transition occupies the second half of the fourteenth century to the first half of the fifteenth century, insofar as the number of Persian inscriptions also increases slowly, though often they are only benedictory Persian verses. But from the beginning of the fifteenth century verses of Hafiz are found on copper items (see Cat. No.150), and from the second half of the fifteenth century we see numerous extracts from the works of famous poets – Hafiz[103], Sa'di, Jami[104], Qasim-i Anwar Tabrizi (see Cat. No.162), or such little-known authors as Salihi Khurasani (see Cat. No.163).

The number of Persian verses on copper and bronze (brass) objects increases during the course of the sixteenth century. Arabic inscriptions meanwhile, especially benedictory ones, practically fall into disuse towards the beginning of the sixteenth century, but at the same time two new Arabic inscriptions appear, linked to the rise to power of the Safavid dynasty in Iran (1501–1736) – these are verses in honour of Ali and blessings on the Shi'ite imams, and they become prevalent on all types of object, in architecture and the applied arts. Thus, in the mid-fourteenth century a new phase begins in the history of art in Iran. The transitional period probably lasts a fairly long time, more than fifty years. One feature which characterizes the art of this age is a loss of interest in the depiction of people on objects of applied art. This is indeed a surprising fact and one which has not yet been explained, for in this phase the Persian miniature flourished (although it was perhaps not at the height of its development) and was being rapidly produced at various centres.

In the first half of the sixteenth century depictions of people and living creatures appear only on carpets and textiles. It is difficult to assess whether this is the continuation of an older tradition, as we do not know of any carpets or textiles from the fifteenth century. Nor are there any carpets or textiles with living creatures depicted in fifteenth-century miniatures. Possibly we are here encountering the influence of the Safavid court miniature, which is how this phenomenon is usually explained. Unfortunately, no concrete facts have yet emerged to enable anyone to defend this thesis and the effect of manuscript illumination on textile production still remains unclear. A new phase in the art of Iran begins to establish itself in the mid-sixteenth century. And here the tentative nature of the accepted dynastic periodic classification becomes clearly evident, for the new Safavid dynasty had already been ruling Iran for fifty years. Yet its accession to power did not herald any sharp changes in art[105].

The only new phenomenon in art which we can distinguish at the beginning of Safavid rule is the formation of a Tabriz court school of miniature painting at the end of the 1520s, *ie* the creation of a "prestigious" form of art.

Real changes, which were most clearly expressed in metalwork and seals, began in the mid-sixteenth century.

In metalwork, hatching replaces cross-hatching in the treatment of the background to ornament, and inscriptions. The *thuluth* script gives way to the *nastaliq* script which was to dominate the following phase (only Arabic inscriptions were sometimes to be written in *thuluth*). The inscriptions themselves began to be laid out in a line instead of completely filling an allotted space. Elements of floral ornament were engraved on the free background and in the seventeenth century we see scrolled stalks with flowers and leaves. At the end of the sixteenth century representations of living creatures begin to appear among the ornamentation[106], and in the seventeenth century we again see human figures.

But these subjects did not, it seems, become very prevalent. During this phase, new forms of ware and new Persian inscriptions appear (sixty inscriptions have been noted for the second half of the sixteenth and early seventeenth centuries alone).

A certain watershed in the development of the decoration of seals is clearly visible. It has been possible to isolate the changes because the number of precisely dated examples increases during the course of the sixteenth century, especially towards the end of the century. In the second half of the sixteenth century the *thuluth* script gives way to *nastaliq*, the inscription no longer fills the surface of the seal so compactly and a scrolled tendril appears in the background.

Scholars of the Persian miniature are inclined to believe that the last quarter of the sixteenth century was not only a time when old traditions were followed but when a new style was formed which found its expression in the works of the Isfahan school[107].

Unfortunately, other branches of Persian art of the sixteenth century, above all applied arts such as ceramics, carpets and textiles, although they are represented by hundreds of examples in the world's museums, have not yet been sufficiently researched to enable one to confirm or deny the idea that a new phase in the history of art was formed in the second half of the sixteenth century. Perhaps the lack of thorough research on these materials, and especially on the evolution of their ornamentation, is a factor here.

But it is possible to assume that the changes in art during the second half of the sixteenth century were not as great as during the second half of the fourteenth century and therefore they are not reflected in all art forms (for example, it is entirely unclear whether there were any sort of changes in architecture). In other words, we can now consider the second half of the sixteenth century to be a time of transition to a new phase, although this latter is not as clearly distinguishable as its predecessors. It is therefore difficult to speak of a canon style during this phase.

We now see a renewal of interest in representations of the human form, which is probably most clearly visible in textiles, although one may suppose that such fabrics do not represent a large proportion of the entire range of textile production. In seventeenth-century ceramics the strong influence of Chinese art can again be observed, but now aroused by the interest of Europeans in Chinese porcelain. Other art forms do not seem to experience any new Chinese influences.

During this phase active contacts with European art begin – first of all in painting. Traces of European influence can already be observed in the mid-seventeenth century. First and foremost, this influence involves the court miniature, but it then spreads to other branches of art where it is reflected to varying degrees.

Here it is important to stress the fact that interest in European art initially arose in court circles, although there were various channels through which the influence was transmitted[108].

Apparently, the appearance of this new factor in seventeenth-century Persian art did not yet signify the emergence of a separate phase, nor even the onset of a transitional period – which became noticeable only from the end of the seventeenth century. An analysis of metalwork serves to support this argument.

Although there are few precisely dated pieces from the late seventeenth and early eighteenth centuries, a chronological series can be reconstructed. Changes are noticeable which could be explained by a decline in the quality of pieces, linked to their increased mass-production. For example, on copper and bronze (brass) items the surface of the background to the design is not entirely hatched. Although hatching was obligatory during the seventeenth century; we now see in places only the engraved design against a plain background. The omission of the hatching increases during the first half of the eighteenth century

Curtain. 18th-19th century.

and around the middle of the century a complete break with tradition takes place, for in the second half of the century the background of Iranian copper and bronze (brass) objects is tooled with punches and the hatching disappears completely.

Inscriptions on metalwork continue to be executed in the nastaliq script, but the letters become wider (especially the curves of the letters). By the end of this stage the inscriptions entirely fill their allotted space, leaving very little free background. These indications help us to identify metalwork of the first half of the eighteenth century.

If we compare objects from the seventeenth and early eighteenth centuries with those of the second half of the eighteenth and nineteenth centuries, then the most striking changes are the disappearance of most forms of objects (in the nineteenth century only ten early forms survive) and the sharp reduction in the incidence of inscriptions: in nineteenth-century objects it has so far only been possible to record eleven surviving samples, as opposed to more than eighty known from the seventeenth century.

But are the great changes in the decoration of metalwork also paralleled in the other applied art? During the first half of the eighteenth century the characteristic scrolled tendril in the background of the inscription on seventeenth-century seals either degenerates into a few small spirals or disappears entirely. The character of the writing also changes gradually: Letters become thicker, especially were they curve. This process culminates in the nineteenth century.

As we pointed out earlier, Arthur Lane considers the fall of the Safavid dynasty to mark the end of the development of late Iranian ceramics, around the 1720s–1730s. In actual fact there is a clear boundary, expressed in the decline of technical skill – the objects are overloaded with decoration, the cobalt and lustre painting is of poor quality – which distinguishes even late Safavid faience from late eighteenth- and early nineteenth-century ceramics.

It is more difficult to discuss carpets and textiles, since their relative chronology has not been studied at all and a history of their development remains to be written. Only in the last decades has serious research begun into this area. We must limit ourselves here to the most general considerations, which become apparent on contrasting examples of the seventeenth century with those of the nineteenth. Thus we can see that ornamentation grows smaller during the hundred years that separate these carpets and textiles, but whether this change took place during the first or second half of the eighteenth century remains unclear.

It used to be customary to end the history of the Iranian miniature with the fall of the Safavid dynasty[109]. In recent decades, it is true, this tendency has begun to change and eighteenth-century painting is attracting ever greater attention[110], although no general works on miniature painting and lacquerware of the period have yet been published. As we mentioned above, an abrupt alteration in the style of miniatures occurs in the second half of the seventeenth century, linked to the influence of European painting and, possibly, to that of the Indian miniature. The style of the Isfahan school of miniatures, known to us in the work of Riza-i Abbasi, survives until the beginning of the eighteenth century (see the work of Mu'in Musawvir) but then vanishes completely. Thus one can assume that a new period begins in the history of Iranian painting at the turn of the eighteenth century[111]; a new style immediately becomes prevalent in lacquerware also[112].

As far as the history of architecture is concerned, Leonid Bretanitsky draws a line between the seventeenth and the eighteenth to nineteenth centuries. Some changes also occurred here, possibly throughout the eighteenth century[113].

Thus we can state with some confidence that at the end of the seventeenth century Persian art entered a period of change, heralding the beginning of a new phase. Evidently the first half of the eighteenth century is a sort of transitional period and new elements are finally victorious in the mid-eighteenth century.

Unfortunately, the new phase begins with a "dark age" characterized by a decline in technical skills. This was reflected in all aspects of applied art in Iran, in ceramics, metalwork, carpets and textiles, but was not caused by any great social crisis in society; rather it was a result of the collapse of life in the cities where crafts were concentrated, largely as a result of the extremely unstable political situation in the country. Wars and invasions brought desolation and ruin to the cities, something that is mentioned by all travellers in the second half of the eighteenth century and at the very beginning of the nineteenth century[114].

The unification of part of the country under the power of Karim-Khan Zand did not last very long and was therefore not reflected in any resurgence of crafts. It was probably only miniatures and oil paintings – aspects of court art – which were of a comparatively high standard, although one should point out nevertheless that few specimens of eighteenth-century miniatures and painting have survived: apparently here too the number of artists declined.

Turning to the new phase which began more or less during the middle of the eighteenth century, we are treading on extremely unstable ground, composed of assumptions and hypotheses, for not a single aspect of the art of that time has yet been researched. Generally speaking, interest in nineteenth-century Persian art emerged only about twenty-five years ago and at first was only concerned with painting and lacquerware. Applied art (with the exception of carpets) did not attract the attention of scholars, which, it may be said, is quite comprehensible, for periods of decline do not arouse enthusiasm. More literature has been devoted to carpets than to any other branch of Persian art, but until recently works on carpets have been inclined towards too subjective an approach and evaluation and this makes them of little help in drawing up a chronology.

It would now seem that court art during the rule of Fath-Ali Shah Qajar (1797–1834) experienced something of a resurgence. This affected painting, miniatures, lacquerware – the work of court artists – as well as jewellery and weapons of various sorts. These works were produced for the upper ranks of society and show clear signs of ancient artistic traditions. This was probably dictated by some sort of "imperial" ambition on the part of Fath-Ali Shah, as is suggested by the creation of rock reliefs – a tradition lost since the time of the Sassanids but reborn during his reign.

However, mass-produced objects such as ceramics and metalwork, which were used by a wide cross-section of society, bear witness to a clear decline in technical skill in comparison with the preceding phase in Persian art. The crisis as a whole begins in the 1840s, when Persian art fell into a decline as a result of the factory goods from European countries which poured into Iran at that time. The total rejection of the old techniques of miniature painting and the definitive acceptance of European ones apparently dates from the same period.

A few words should be said about one curious phenomenon in Persian art, or rather in the applied arts of the second half of the nineteenth century. This is the reversion to Achaemenid patterns in art, inspired by the reliefs of Persepolis and Naqsh-i Rustam.

In recent times it has become evident that these patterns were used widely in carpets (see Cat. No.288), in the manufacture of brass- and silverware (see Cat. No.281) and in the extant reliefs in nineteenth-century Shiraz palaces. Apparently these motifs were not reflected in painting (pictures, miniatures, lacquerware), since the new trend in miniature painting which emerged at the end of the nineteenth century took as its model the seventeenth-century Isfahan school. It is not clear what caused this fascination for such a distant historical past, although this type of work continues to be manufactured to the present day.

Nevertheless, it should be noted that Persian art of this final phase, beginning in the second half of the eighteenth century, has still not been studied.

In examining the problems of a periodic chronological classification we have concentrated mainly on highlighting the provisional boundaries between phases and very little has been said about the reasons behind changes in art. This question is even more complex than the chronology itself and very little is known about it. The time has not yet come when all these problems can be solved, nor is a limited introductory essay the place where they can be properly assessed.

Casting one's eye over the history of art in Iran in general after the consolidation of Islam one can say, if only by way of preliminary hypothesis, that its progressive development continued until the first half of the fourteenth century, when the art of medieval Iran reached its height.

This is clearly seen in miniatures, metalwork, textiles and, though possibly to a lesser extent, in ceramics. The following centuries were a period of gradual decline, although at first glance this is contradicted by the flourishing of the miniature in the fifteenth century, when it developed and perfected those principles and devices that had been created during the preceding period. Such a deduction completely corresponds to ideas of the historical development of Iran in the age of feudalism; at any rate, it roughly coincides with the overall chronology accepted by Russian historians.

Within the larger phases one can, of course, distinguish shorter periods during which there was intense developments within one or other art form. For the time being, it is interesting to note that the length of each phase gradually diminishes as one approaches the modern era. This may be explained by the acceleration of historical development, but may also be the result of our as yet extremely limited knowledge of the art of earlier ages.

If a work on the history of eastern culture across several ages demands the drawing of conclusions, then we have probably not achieved that end. But in actual fact "deductions" set forth in one or two pages could only vulgarize and generalize, in effect reducing to banalities – or to excessively speculative categories – all the complexity and colour of the "motion" in the history of a culture; they would eclipse a multitude of unelucidated questions and unproved assumptions. Consequently we shall only allow ourselves one generalization – a statement by Nikolai Konrad ina work with a bold title, *On the Meaning of History*:

"In different lands, humanists have seen different aspects of the human personality as constituting its value. Their views have naturally been contingent upon their historical circumstances. Participants in the Chinese Renaissance saw the value of the personality chiefly in the human ability to attain self-perfection; the humanists of Iran and Central Asia saw it, mainly, in the fact that the highest moral qualities are accessible to man: spiritual nobility, magnanimity, friendship; the representatives of the Italian Renaissance regarded human beings as, above all, the bearers of reason, considering reason to be the highest manifestation of humanity's essence[115]."

Although its underlying meaning is to assert the existence of Iran's own special "renaissance", the description of Iranian humanism given here seems, nevertheless, to be correct, despite the fact that a search for "renaissances" in various historical and cultural areas is not, as we see it, a problem that is particularly relevant to the history of Iranian culture. How many as yet unresolved, and consequently more relevant, problems there are in this field! For the task of precise dating is still incomplete, as is that of precise location for many, if not the majority, of pieces. Nor is there yet any closely argued historical and cultural interpretation of subjects and styles that uses all the available sources – if not for the majority, at least for very many of the pieces.

Such a complex task requires the scholar to refrain, for the time being, from any generalizations or outline sketches. That is why this outline is incomplete: indeed, many of its judgements may appear premature. How could one, then, even consider a "conclusion"?

NOTES

1. For a characterization of this period see IDM 1982, vol.II, pp.15-18.

2. Grantovsky 1970.

3. Dyakonov 1956.

4. In Western Iran, apart from the Assyrians and Babylonians who spoke the Akkadian and Elamite languages, there were numerous tribes and small organized states with dynasties of Hurrian or Qutian-Kassite origins.

5. See König 1934.

6. For further details see Dandamayev and Lukonin 1980.

7. For further details see Cuyler Young 1965, pp.53-87; Dyson 1973, pp.686-715.

8. For further details on the archaeology of Iran of the 13th-7th centuries BC see Dandamayev and Lukonin 1980, pp.39-103, which contains a basic bibliography on this subject.

9. Porada 1965, pp.97-98.

10. Mellink 1966, pp.72-87.

11. There may be material from several burial sites of various periods at Marlik, the dates of these sites differing from each other by up to 1,500 years. See Negahban 1964; Negahban 1972, pp.142-152; Negahban 1977; Hakemi 1973; Moghaddam 1972, pp.133-136, fig.1-3.

12. The vessel is a tall stemless vase or goblet (of the same form as almost all the gold vessels from Marlik, Hasanlu and finds from other sites). The technique of all these vessels is also standard – embossing with subsequent engraving.

13. Negahban 1964, pp.54, 55 (English text), p.57 (Persian text).

14. Wilkinson 1975.

15. Porada 1971, pp.163-182.

16. The most recent summary of data is in Ghirshman 1979.

17. Wilkinson 1975, p.7.

18. For further details on pieces from Ziwiye see Lukonin 1977b; Ghirshman 1962; Porada 1965.

19. For a characterization of the "animal style" see Artamonov 1962, pp.31-46.

20. See Rayevsky 1984.

21. It is true that there is another point of view which holds that the art of the Scythians was non-representational before their arrival in the Near-East (see Rayevsky 1984).

22. The panther twisted into a ring from the Arzhan barrow (8th or early 7th century BC) is a completely different motif: among the objects from Ziwiye there is an attempt to do something similar (on the gold pommel of the spear), but it is clear that the craftsmen of Ziwiye were ill-acquainted with such stylization (for further details see Sorokin 1972).

23. The finds from Ziwiye are assigned to the 7th century BC only in accordance with a historical interpretation, or because some of the motifs are close to those of Kelermes. But the only items in the hoard open to more or less precise dating are the fragments of a bronze sarcophagus (Assyria: late 8th-early 7th centuries BC), carved ivory articles and the Assyrian pottery (8th-early 7th centuries BC). The Kelermes objects are variously dated. In the catalogue *From the Land of the Scythians* (New York, 1978) the date suggested for them is late 7th-early 6th centuries BC.

24. Abayev 1958, pp.607, 608.

25. Dandamayev and Lukonin 1980, pp.71-86.

26. This is not just the case with imagery – for example, on the beautiful 6th-century silver-gilt dish exactly the same stylized palmettes are depicted on the bodies of the goats as are also found on the goats of the Ziwiye pectoral. For further details on the Ziwiye style in Achaemenid art see Lukonin 1977b, pp.33-36.

27. In Achaemenid times – as traditional motifs, no longer meaningful and very deformed – they only survive on the chape of scabbards (see Cullican 1965).

28. Dyakonov 1961, pp.193, 194.

29. On the culture of Luristan see Vanden Berghe 1982.

30. Nylander 1970.

31. On the architecture of the Median temple, ruler's residence and fortifications recently discovered by archaeologists see Stronach 1973.

32. Ghirshman 1962, pp.137–150.

33. Hundreds of works have been devoted to the campaigns of Alexander the Great, to the Seleucid monarchy founded after him, and also to the culture and art of the Hellenistic period. See, for example, W W Tarn, *Hellenistic Civilisation*, London, 1941; Ghirshman 1962; Schlumberger 1970; Frye 1972; Lukonin 1977b.

34. For further details on the social system of Seleucid and Parthian Iran see Lukonin 1977a.

35. See Schlumberger 1970.

36. Boyce 1957, pp.10–45.

37. For a detailed analysis of art of the Sassanian period see Ghirshman 1962 and its bibliography; Lukonin 1977b.

38. Krachkovsky 1930, pp.177–180.

39. Bolshakov 1969, pp.142–156.

40. Bartold 1969–77, vol.VI, p.121.

41. Bolshakov 1969, pp.148, 149.

42. *Ibid.*, p.150.

43. See Petrushevsky 1966, p. 159.

44. Bartold 1969–77, vol.VI, p.216.

45. Frye 1972, p.344.

46. According to one theory (Tavadia 1952, p.384), the term "Tajik" is the Sogdian form of the Persian word *tazi* – "Arab" or "Muslim". Initially the inhabitants of Central Asia called the Arabs and Persians, who converted to Islam, "Tajiks".

47. Boyce 1957, pp.17, 18. For further details on the poetry of the "Persian Renaissance" see Bertels 1960.

48. Belenitsky, Bentovich, Bolshakov 1974.

49. Grabar 1968a, p.359.

50. Thompson 1974.

51. Grube 1966, p.42, fig.19 (the dish is assigned to the 11th century); see Fehérvári 1973 (dated 12th or 13th century). Pottery of the Garrus type was found in layers from the Seljuk period during excavations at Kangavar, see Fehérvári 1973. Despite its indisputable interest both from a technical point of view and because of its designs (usually human figures), this pottery remains insufficiently researched. Almost all the motifs on the published vessels are somehow linked to the epics (the king enthroned and two dragons, a dancer with a mask in her hand and dragons, etc.).

52. There is a good brief outline of Iranian architecture in Pope 1969. See also Hill and Grabar 1964.

53. See Marshak 1976, p.161.

54. Grube 1966, pl.16.

55. Rice 1955.

56. On *Varqah and Gulshah* see Melikian-Chirvani 1970. The manuscript of the *Andarz-nama*, dated 483 AH/1090 AD, has given rise to numerous doubts as to its authenticity.

57. Guest 1943.

58. Nizami Aruzi Samarqandi 1963, pp.112–114.

59. Bahrami 1937, p.31.

60. Thiesenhausen 1884, p.30.

61. In Sassanian times depictions (for example, on reliefs) were called *ptkry*. In Zoroastrian texts there is no reference to the terms "artist" or "graphic artist", but in Manichaean texts (in the Parthian and Middle Persian languages) there are, of course, a number of such references (see, for example, "artist" – *nigargar*, Parthian *zxrwb*, and even "artist-illustrator of manuscripts" – *nibegan-nigar*, see Tafazzoli 1974, p.195). These references are connected to Mani's aim of illustrating the manuscripts of his works, an aim that was seen as heretical from the Zoroastrian priests' and rulers' point of view. The polemics against Manichaeanism – "let him bring his picture to life!" – are referred to in New Persian literature too (before the 12th century?). No illustrated manuscripts from Mani's lifetime have survived, but judging from the Turfan Manichaean manuscripts, in this case too it was probably only a question of portrait painting. Middle Persian terms for the professions of sculptor, metal-

worker, ceramics artist are entirely different from those in Manichaean texts, for example, *asem-paykar* – "one who adorns silver vessels with depictions".

62. Shefer 1982, p.353.

63. Or early Islamic? The book which Mas'udi saw at Istakhr was an early 10th-century copy, made from the Sassanian original. However, the existence of official miniature portraiture – for example, sketches for coin dies – is perfectly feasible during the early Sassanian period too.

64. Vorozheikina 1984, p. 173.

65. Gyuzalyan and Dyakonov 1934, p.XIV.

66. Grabar 1968a, p.628.

67. See Dodkhudoyeva 1982, pp.32–34.

68. Bertels 1962, pp.409–411.

69. The correspondence of Rashid al-Din. See Rashid al-Din, *Collection of Chronicles*, vol.I, Moscow and Leningrad, 1952, p.20 (in Russian).

70. On dishes with underglaze painting of the "Sultanabad group", for example, on a dish from the Leman collection (New York). For a good colour reproduction see Grube 1966, pl.40 – the image was executed by the same miniaturists as those who illustrated the *Collection of Chronicles* by Rashid al-Din.

71. The formation of a new miniature style took place in the middle of the second half of the 14th century, as has become clear since the publication of essential works on the history of the Iranian miniature by I S Stchoukine and B W Robinson (see Stchoukine 1954 and Robinson 1958).

72. Grabar and Blair 1980, pp.23, 24.

73. Quoted from Akimushkin and Ivanov 1968, p.9.

74. Grube 1970.

75. Ivanov 1971a, pp.15–18 and also Ivanov 1961; Ivanov 1969b, pp.32, 33.

76. Grube 1970, pp.13, 14.

77. Marshak 1976, p.166.

78. For further details on these see Ivanov 1985.

79. Four of them bear the signatures of the craftsmen – Bu Nasr al-naqqash, Abu Nasr Muhammad ibn Ahmad al-Sijzi, Muhammad ibn Ahmad and Bu (?) Ja'far al-naqqash. The names of the craftsmen on three of the bowls (in the Metropolitan Museum, New York, in the H Kevorkian collection and in a private collection, Daghestan) are very close and it is tempting to think that we are dealing with one and the same person. However, at the present stage of research this would be difficult to prove, since we hardly know any series of works by a single coppersmith, in order to be able to judge an individual style.

80. Melikian-Chirvani 1976b, p.288;

Melikian-Chirvani 1977a, pp.381, 382.

81. Melikian-Chirvani 1974, pp.145, 146, fig.37.

82. Ivanov 1970a.

83. The ewer in the Herat Museum bears a small silver-inlaid inscription which R Ettinghausen has dated to the late 9th–first half of the 10th centuries, and has assumed that it refers to the ruler of Karaj in Kurdistan who died in 285 AH/898 AD (Ettinghausen 1957, p.333). If this is correct, then this silver inlay was also fashioned in Western Iran and not in the east. Ettinghausen considered that the name on the ewer was that of the owner and that it was added later. Melikian-Chirvani considers that this is the name of the craftsman, although the inscription gives no indication of this; in that case the inscription is contemporaneous with the ewer (see Melikian-Chirvani 1972b, p.139, n.2).

84. At a colloquium in Oxford in 1969, which examined problems of the history of the Islamic world from 950 to 1150 AD, two reports (M Rogers and J Sourdel-Thomine) were devoted to the questions of architecture and the evolution of architectural decoration. See *Islamic Civilisation: 950–1150*, Oxford, 1973.

85. For further details on this see the articles by Rogers 1973 and Sourdel-Thomine 1973.

86. Grabar 1968a, pp.134, 135; Ettinghausen 1969, pp.277–298. On the emergence of four-*iwan* buildings

in earlier, pre-Seljuk times see Fehérvári (s.a.), pp.3-5.

87. See Rogers 1973; Fehérvári (s.a.), p.5; Meinecke 1971, pp.212, 213, 219, 220.

88. In the works of Turkish authors the changes in the art of Iran during the 11th and 12th centuries are ascribed to the appearance of large numbers of Turkic nomads in this area, see Erginsoy 1978, p.552.

89. Melikian-Chirvani (s.a.).

90. See, for example, Grabar 1968b.

91. Of course, the Mongols' annihilation of the cities of Khurasan and Northern Iran led to the extinction of craftwork production in these areas, if only for a certain period, but during that time the manufacture of various types of applied art developed in other centres.

92. Bretanitsky 1964, p.138; Bretanitsky 1966, p.511.

93. Lane 1957, pp.XIV, 71, 74.

94. Reitlinger 1961, p.400.

95. The development of Iranian ceramics is examined by Maslenitsyna, who has also come to the conclusion that "we cannot speak of any fundamental changes taking place earlier than the second half of the 14th century". Maslenitsyna 1976, p.179.

96. In the catalogue of seals and talismans in the Bibliothèque Nationale (Paris), published by L Kalus, the 14th century is also distinguished as the beginning of the "post-classical period" in the history of seals. See Z Kalus, *Catalogue des cachets, bulles et talismans islamiques*, Paris, 1981, pp.32-34.

97. Akimushkin and Ivanov 1968, pp.52, 53.

98. Selective analyses have shown that among early objects one comes across alloys of copper and zinc, *ie* brass. Pending analysis, therefore, the dual description - bronze (brass) - has been preserved.

99. Ivanov 1971a, pp.4, 5.

100. Ivanov 1961; Ivanov 1971a, p.5.

101. See the tiles of 665 AH/1267 AD in the Louvre and the Metropolitan Museum. See Bahrami 1937, p.107.

102. See Watson 1975.

103. See the small jug of 866 AH/1461-62 AD (fragments of two *ghazals*) reproduced in SPA 1938-39, vol.VI, pl.1376b; small jug No.78.12-30.731 in the British Museum, London; candlestick reproduced in SPA 1938-39, vol.VI, pl.1375a.

104. See Ivanov 1971c.

105. See Ivanov 1973, pp.4-6; Ivanov 1976, pp.45-47; Komaroff 1980.

106. From the preceding phase we know only of a copper plate of the late 15th or early 16th century, with a design of peacocks (see Melikian-Chirvani 1976d, fig.64) and a copper *kashkul* (begging bowl) with a design of peacocks and fish of the early 16th century, from a private collection in Geneva.

107. Stchoukine 1964, pp.222-224; Ettinghausen 1964, p.45.

108. See Carswell 1972; Ivanov 1979b; Gyuzalyan 1972.

109. Stchoukine's book on the 17th-century miniature also ends with this period. See Stchoukine 1964.

110. See Robinson 1967, pp.76, 77; Robinson 1979a; Robinson 1980, p.348; Robinson 1982.

111. See Akimushkin and Ivanov 1968, p.43.

112. See Adle 1980.

113. See Bretanitsky 1964, p.133; Bretanitsky 1966, pp.510, 514.

114. See Petrov 1949, pp.328, 329; Hambly 1964, pp.70-72.

115. See N I Konrad, *Selected Works*, Moscow, 1974, p.318 (in Russian).

CATALOGUE OF WORKS OF ART

1. Hilt of a sword.
12th–11th century BC

Bronze, cast. Length 17.5cm.
The Hermitage, St Petersburg.
Inv. No.19536. Acquired 1974 (chance find in North-Western Iran).

Bronze swords – as a rule cast and with a crescent-shaped pomme – were widely produced in North-Western Iran during the 12th and 11th centuries BC.

It is possible that the hilt and pommel were once inlaid with ivory or wood between the tangs.
Bibliography:
Lukonin 1977a, pp.46, 47.

2. Vessel.
10th–8th century BC

Clay, thrown on a potter's wheel, cov-ered with red slip and burnished. Height 31cm; diameter of body 20.3cm.
The Hermitage, St Petersburg.
Inv. No.19502. Donated 1970 by J Gluck, scholar of antique and medieval art.

Similar vessels with very thin walls have been found at burial sites in the Caspian region (Kaluraz and Amlash). It is possible that they had no practical purpose and were manufactured especially for burial rites. On one such vessel (Archæological Museum, Tehran), for example, found at the Kaluraz burial site, the spout is fixed to the body almost at the base and, furthermore, turned backwards. Pottery of this type is usually assigned to the Iron Age II.
Bibliography:
Lukonin 1971, p.9; Lukonin 1977b, p.39.

3. Vessel with a long lip.
10th century BC

Bronze, forged from a thick sheet; pouring lip and handle soldered on. Length 17.2cm.
The Rudaki Museum, Pyanjikent. Acquired 1970 (found in the village of Fatmev, Tajikistan).

This is an extremely rare metal vessel, if not the only surviving one of its kind, from the Iron Age II or the end of the Iron Age I. Its pouring lip and feet mimic the long beak and claws of a bird.
Similar vessels, made of clay, are found in North-Western Iran. The vessel was discovered by chance in the mountains of Tajikistan, in the village of Fatmev, which marks the north-eastern boundary beyond which no vessels with this particular design have been encountered.
Bibliography:
Lukonin 1977b, p. 40.

4. Vessel with a long lip.
10th–8th century BC

Clay, covered with black slip and burnished (body thrown on a potter's wheel, lip modelled separately). Height 20cm; diameter of body 16.5cm.
Museum of Oriental Art, Moscow. Inv. No.1821-II. Acquired 1946 (gift of the Iranian newspaper Iran-e ma [Our Iran]).

This vessel is typical of the Caspian region during the Iron Age II. Its lip is in the form of the head of a bird with a long beak.
Such ceramic vessels, apparently specially produced for burial rites, were copies of metal vessels (see Cat. No.3).

Bibliography:
Maslenitsyna 1975, ill.14; Lukonin 1977a, p.40.

5. Vessel in the form of a falcon.
10th–8th century BC

Hand-worked clay, covered with slip, with traces of colouring. Height 19cm; length 27cm.
Museum of Oriental Art, Moscow. Inv. No.4972-II. Donated 1970 by the Government of Iran to the Government of the USSR.

The purpose of this vessel is unclear, but similar decoratively-shaped vessels, or rather clay sculptures (in the form of various creatures), are found in burials of the Iron Age II in the Amlash area (Caspian region). However, vessels shaped like birds have not been found at any of the sites in this region excavated by specialists.
Bibliography:
Lukonin 1971, p.10; Maslenitsyna 1975, p.178, ill.5.

6. VESSEL.
7TH CENTURY BC

Clay, painted and burnished. Height 21.5cm; diameter of body 19cm. Museum of Oriental Art, Moscow. Inv. No.4414-II. Acquired 1945.

The vessel comes from the excavations at Sialk (near Kashan). It is painted red and along the inside of the rim there is a small-toothed pattern. Down the rim and neck, passing onto the handle of the vessel, is a thick vertical stripe which changes below the handle into a thin wavy line that drops undulatingly towards the base. The spout is flattened at the sides and decorated with a network of triangles; the swelling at the base of the spout has a pattern of dots enclosed in a circle, from which three cross-hatched, extended petals radiate.
Bibliography:
Lukonin 1971, p.12; Maslenitsyna 1975, ill.4; Lukonin 1977b, p.44.

7. SPOUTED VESSEL.
8TH – 7TH CENTURY BC

Bronze, forged from a sheet (handle and spout cast and riveted). Height 11cm; diameter of body 9.5cm. The Hermitage, St Petersburg. Inv. No.19577. Donated 1971 by the scholar Krishna Riboud (France).

This "teapot" vessel is typical of Luristan culture. Of special interest is the spout, which terminates in a lion's jaw. Only very recently have such vessels begun to be found during the course of scientific excavations, as a result of which their exact date of manufacture has been determined.
Bibliography:
Lukonin 1977a, p.48.

8. FINIAL OF A VOTIVE
STANDARD. 800-750 BC

Bronze, cast by the cire perdue method, tooled with a chisel. Height 17cm. The Hermitage, St Petersburg. Inv. No.19574. Donated 1971 by the scholar Krishna Riboud (France).

This is a famous Luristan idol. Hundreds of similar finials were found by local inhabitants plundering the graves of Luristan. Such idols were very popular among collectors and many of them are now to be found not only in private collections but in the museums of Europe and the USA. It is probably with objects such as this (and also with bronze psalia, see Cat. No.10) that the concept of a Luristan style is most often associated. An idol is, as a rule, an anthropomorphic being with a number of human traits (male and female). Dragons with the heads of beasts of prey or birds grow from its torso. The figure is three-dimensional and can be observed from various angles. The idol was mounted on some sort of shaft (hence the frequent designation in specialist literature – "finial of a votive standard"). Until recently the exact date of manufacture of such objects was unknown, but in the early 1970s a

Belgian archæological expedition finally found the first such idol in an intact burial site at Tattulban (Chinan, Pusht-i Kuh, Luristan), where the material associated with it (pottery, weapons) enabled them to determine its date to around 800-750 BC. Even so the use of such standards and the rituals associated with them remain to be explained. Only one thing is so far clear – that they had no practical function.
Bibliography:
Lukonin 1977a, p.49.

9. Part of horse harness.
Late 2nd–early 1st millennium BC
Bronze, cast. Diameter 8.3cm.
The Hermitage, St Petersburg.
Inv. No.18613. Donated 1934 by the
Government of Iran.

The head of the moufflon with its enormous horns, and the two beasts of prey at the sides, are executed in a manner typical of Luristan bronzes. They undoubtedly had some sort of symbolical significance and many other details of horse harness are decorated with similar figures. It is usual to describe such pieces as "typical Luristan bronzes": they emerged suddenly in Luristan around the 12th century BC, replacing the local culture that had existed till then, and their manufacture ceases in the 7th century BC.
Bibliography:
Lukonin 1971, p.4; Lukonin 1977b, p.12.

10. Horse bit with psalia.
8th–7th century BC
Bronze, cast by the cire perdue method, engraved. Height 9.5cm; length 22cm.
Museum of Oriental Art, Moscow.
Inv. No.4465-II.

Horse bits with psalia in the form of real or mythical beasts or deities of the local pantheon are the most common Luristan objects found in museums and private collections. However, they have still not been found in any excavations supervised by specialists. There are a great number of images on these psalia, which catered for the tastes of a very varied clientele. Moufflons with solar signs and plant ornament engraved on their bodies are probably the image most frequently found on objects of this type.
Despite the great number of such objects, they remain fairly mysterious. The psalia and bit are too massive for use on horses and nearly all the known examples bear no traces of having been used.
It is also unclear why they have never yet been found during the course of scientific excavations, although numerous pieces of horse harness usually form part of the inventory of a grave's contents.
Bibliography:
Maslenitsyna 1975, p.71, ill.56; Lukonin 1977b, p.46.

11. Rhyton.
5th–4th century BC
Silver, embossed and chased. Height 20cm; weight 1600g.
The Erebuni Museum, Yerevan.

Rhytons, vessels for drinking and ritual libations, in the form of a horn or the head of an animal are known to have been in use on the territory of Iran from at least the 2nd millennium BC. Manufactured from precious metals, stone or clay, the rhytons came in two basic forms: goblet-rhytons and those in the shape of a curved horn. Goblet-rhytons sometimes had handles and in this case served as ritual vessels. Kings and rulers are depicted drinking from rhytons on Assyrian reliefs, like the 8th-century reliefs at Khorsabad. The wine was poured straight into the man's open mouth, and as such resembles *porrónes* in Spain, or the wineskins found in the Caucasus.
During the Achæmenid era in Iran, silver and gold rhytons became especially popular – such as the tributaries on the Persepolis reliefs, portrayed with rhytons in their hands.
Greek metalworkers also produced rhytons for the Persian nobility or for the satraps (governors of a province) of states in Asia Minor annexed by the Persians. This form of vessel became widespread throughout the entire Near, Middle and Far East and was widely used up until the 8th century AD. The rhyton was one of the attributes of power for some eastern rulers (among the Scythians, for example).
Rhytons with the protome of a horse are typical of Achæmenid metalwork. One is struck by the depiction of the horse's gear, the treatment of its mane and its muscles which are an exact replica of the horses depicted in the reliefs of Persepolis.

This rhyton, the rhyton with a rider (Cat. No.12) and two other silver rhytons, in the form of a goblet and in the form of a bull's head decorated round its rim with figures of a seated Dionysus and women playing instruments, were all found crushed (or, more likely, deliberately flattened) in a large clay vessel which was buried on the site of Erebuni (an Urartian town of the 8th–5th centuries BC). The vessel was discovered during building work in the courtyard of a private house and consequently it has not been possible to determine the character and date of the archæological layer.
The latest rhyton of this hoard (in the form of a bull's head) was in all probability manufactured in Ionia and dates from the 4th century BC.
As excavations of the Urartian citadel of Erebuni have shown, after the fall of the Urartian kingdom the headquarters of an Achæmenid satrap was apparently situated here. As a rule, satraps were only chosen from among the Persian and Median nobility.
Archæologists have discovered traces of the rebuilding of several Urartian buildings.
An *apadana*-palace with thirty wooden columns was erected on the hilltop of Erebuni, built according to the plan of the Achæmenid palaces of Persepolis and other buildings with a religious function. It is highly likely that all the rhytons were ceremonial and festal vessels of the Persian vicegerent of Armenia.
Bibliography:
Arakelian 1976, pp.41–47, pl.LVIII; Lukonin 1977b, p.80.

12. RHYTON.
5TH – 4TH CENTURY BC

Silver, embossed, chased and engraved. Height from horse's head to outer rim 42cm; height of rider 20.5cm; weight 1800g.
The Erebuni Museum, Yerevan.

This is the only known rhyton surmounted by the figure of a horse and rider. The rider wears the so-called Median dress with a short sword (*akinakes*) in his belt and a Median headdress with the figure of an eagle. The horse-cloth is interesting with its woven motif of ibexes and a bull and its fringe – characteristic of the Achæmenid age (for an example of a similar textile, see Cat. No.30).

Only one other free-standing Achæmenid sculpture of a riding warrior in such costume is known. This is the gold figurine (height 7.4cm) from the Oxus hoard of Achæmenid jewellery found in the late 19th century at the site of Takht-i Kuwat (on the banks of the River Vakhsh, now in Tajikistan). The figure subsequently found its way to India and from thence to the British Museum.

Although portrayals of Achæmenid riders are fairly rare in general, this is undoubtedly no ordinary rider on the rhyton but in all probability an important noble, possibly the governor of the province (satrapy) of Armenia, which formed part of the Achæmenid state. This is evidenced not only by the headgear (*kulah*) with its image of an eagle (according to Xenophon the royal Achæmenid standard was crowned with the figure of an eagle), and the ceremonial dress and special hairstyle and earrings (now lost), but also by the place where the rhyton was found (see Cat. No.11).

The portrayal is in typically Achæmenid "imperial" style, with details of the horse harness, *akinakes*, dress, etc. rendered with extraordinary precision. Apparently the rhyton served not only for drinking but for some sort of possibly ritual libations – there are small openings in the forelegs of the horse through which narrow streams of wine could have been poured.

Bibliography:
Arakelian 1976, pp.37–41, pls.LVI, LVII; Lukonin 1977b, pp.72, 76.

13. RHYTON.
5TH CENTURY BC

Silver, embossed, chased and engraved (ears and horns tooled separately and soldered on).
Length 21.2cm; weight 495.5g.
The Hermitage, St Petersburg.
Inv. No.S-274. Transferred 1864 from the Kunstkammer.

Every feature of this rhyton with the head of a moufflon, down to the minutest stylistic detail, is typical of Achæmenid art. The same devices were employed to portray the eyes and jaw of the animal, its wool and horns, not only in metalwork but also on stone reliefs and seals. Also typical is the decoration of lotus flowers around the rim of the rhyton; the same decoration, for example, adorns the capitals of Achæmenid stone columns.

The rhyton was found in Siberia, apparently in the late 18th century, but more precise information is not available.

Bibliography:
Smirnov 1909, No.17.

14. RHYTON.
5TH CENTURY BC

Silver, cast and forged, with traces of gilding. Length 50cm.
The Hermitage, St Petersburg.
Inv. SBr IV. 3.

This rhyton in the shape of a horn is probably more typical of Achæmenid art than is the goblet-rhyton. The protome of a winged goat at the end of the rhyton was a popular symbol in Achæmenid Iran; it is an incarnation of the god of victory, Verethragna. It is also encountered on engraved gems (see seal Cat. No.25) and in architectural decoration and reliefs.
The rhyton was found in 1876 in a Scythian barrow of the 5th–4th century BC (the "Seven Brothers" burial mound near the village of Verenikovskaya, Kuban province, in barrow 4).
Bibliography:
Smirnov 1909, No.15.

15. HANDLE OF A VASE,
IN THE FORM OF A STAG.
5TH–4TH CENTURY BC

Silver, cast and gilded. Height 16.5cm; weight 222g.
The Hermitage, St Petersburg.
Inv. No. S-273. Transferred 1859 from the Kunstkammer as part of Peter the Great's Siberian collection.

Handles of large silver vessels, in the form of animals (the overwhelming majority are ibexes, occasionally winged, or moufflons), have survived in large quantities. The lower plate which was fastened to the body of the vessel often bore engraved or even relief images of antique palmettes or heads of the Egyptian god, Bes, executed in the style of Asia Minor.

Several such vessels with handles have survived intact in various of the world's museums; their form is reminiscent of antique amphoræ. Vessels of identical form depicted, for example, in the hands of tributaries on reliefs decorating the Apadana at Persepolis have different handles, more like ancient oriental ones. Therefore similar vessels, although widespread throughout Achæmenid Iran, were possibly produced in Asia Minor for Persian clients. To date this is the only handle depicting a spotted stag.
An 18th-century drawing of objects from the *Kunstkammer* depicts the stag with branching antlers. Old inventories of the *Kunstkammer* note that the handle was found before 1734 in a barrow on the River Bukhtarma near Ustkamenogorsk.
Bibliography:
Smirnov 1909, No.18; *Oriental Jewellery* 1984, No.18.

16. PENDANT
TEMPLE ORNAMENTS.
4TH CENTURY BC

Gold, soldered and decorated with granulation. Length 12.95cm and 13.15cm; weight 100.73g and 101.07g.
The Janashia Museum of Georgia, Tbilisi. Inv. No.26. Acquired 1908.

Pendant temple ornaments formed part of the Akhalgori hoard, discovered accidentally in 1908, at the site of a female burial from the 4th century BC near the settlement of Sadzeguri on the left bank of the River Ksani.
More than a hundred objects survived including gold ornaments (torques, jewellery, earrings, parts of horse trappings, etc.), silverware and bronze objects (horse bits and pieces of harness).

These pendant ornaments are masterpieces of the goldsmith's art. The finest granulation is used, individual parts are created from fine wire and thin gold leaf. The bodies of the horses are formed of two crafted halves soldered together. The legs and ears are of gold leaf and the details in relief, even the horses' eyes are soldered on with fine wire.
The form of the temple pendants – a wide plaque surmounted by a large rosette with special springs for fastening – is not found among objects from Achæmenid Iran, whereas the figure of the horse, whith its horse-cloth ending in a toothed pattern and drop-shaped pendants, "plumes" and harness meticulously portrayed, is indisputably Achæmenid.
The technique employed is also Achæmenid, although ornamental jewellery found in Iran (such as, the so-called "Pasargadae treasure" or the women's ornaments found at Susa, dating from the mid-4th century BC) does not have such rich granulation.
The temple pendants of the Akhalgori hoard are an example of metalwork fashioned in the imperial Achæmenid, yet incorporating the achievements of the local metalwork schools, which can be seen in the details of the ornamentation.
Bibliography:
Smirnov 1934, pp.23–29 (detailed description), pl.III.

CAT N° 14

CAT N° 16

22. PERSIAN WARRIOR (FRAGMENT OF A GREY SANDSTONE RELIEF). 5TH CENTURY BC

22.3 x 20.2cm.
The Hermitage, St Petersburg.
Inv. No. S-461.

This is unquestionably a fragment of the relief decoration of a stairway in one of the palaces (in all probability, the Tripylon) of the Achæmenid capital, Persepolis. The warrior depicted on it, in Persian dress owing much to Elam, with a bow and quiver on his back and a spear in his hand (lost), is one of the regiment of "immortals" – the guard of the Achæmenid king of kings - recruited from among young members of the nobility, who accompanied the royal court during battle and on festive occasions and who stood guard at court.

Portrayals of the "immortals" were executed according to a strict canon which was not altered during the entire course of the Achæmenid period; they decorated the main staircase of many buildings at Persepolis.

It has not been possible to establish how the fragment came to be in the Hermitage. However, one could venture a suggestion. At the beginning of the 19th century a Scotsman, Robert Ker Porter, was invited to take up a post at the Russian court as a painter of battle scenes. He soon married a Russian girl, a relative of the president of the Academy of Arts in St Petersburg, Olenin. In 1818 the Academy sent Ker Porter to Iran to draw up plans and sketch the ruins of Persepolis and other antiquities. Ker Porter wrote an account of his journey and published it in

London. Here he mentions a number of times that he brought back to Russia several "objects of ancient art". Ker Porter died and was buried in St Petersburg, and there is an album of his sketches of Iranian (Achæmenid and Sassanian) monuments in the Hermitage.

The fate of those objects he brought back is unknown, but it is possible that it was he who brought back both this fragment of relief and several Achæmenid cylindrical seals.

Bibliography:
Lukonin 1971, pp.15, 16.

23. CYLINDRICAL SEAL. 4TH CENTURY BC

Carved sapphirine. Height 5.4cm.
The Pushkin Museum of Fine Arts, Moscow. Inv. No. 12B/254. Donated 1915 by V. Corbet.

The seal depicts the triumph of the king of kings Artaxerxes I over the rebellious Libyans (see also Cat. No.24). The Old Persian cuneiform inscription contains the name and title of Artaxerxes. Cylindrical seals came into use in the Near East as early as the 4th millennium BC. They were rolled onto clay tablets, the basic form

of written documents in the Near East, and onto the clay stoppers of vessels, etc. serving not only as the owner's or scribe's mark, but also as a type of amulet. Excavations of the Achæmenid capital, Persepolis, have revealed cuneiform documents from archives of economic affairs with imprints from similar seals. The scene depicted on the cylinder could be rolled off continuously as many times as one wished, thus forming a frieze similar, for example, to the sculpted friezes of Persepolis.

Cylindrical seals were used in the Near East up to the early centuries AD – essentially, for as long as clay tablets were in use.

Bibliography:
Shileiko 1925, No.1.

24. CYLINDRICAL SEAL. 5TH CENTURY BC

Carved sapphirine. Diameter 1.7cm; height 3.5cm.
The Hermitage, St Petersburg.
Inv. No. Gl. 849. Transferred 1925 from the museum attached to the former Stieglitz School of Technical Design.

The cylinder shows the king of kings Artaxerxes I or the Persian

commander Megabyze. In front of him is the kneeling figure of the Libyan satrap Inarus who led a revolt and attempted to seize the Egyptian throne in 456 BC. The revolt was cruelly suppressed. Behind Megabyzes' back are captive Libyans (see also Cat. No.23).

Bibliography:
Lukonin 1971, p.14.

25. SEAL. 4TH CENTURY BC
Carved agate. Height 2.6cm.
The Hermitage, St Petersburg.
Inv. No. Gl. 888.

Seals in the form of a truncated pyramid, together with cylindrical (see Cat. Nos.23 and 24) and scaraboid (see Cat. No.27) seals, are typical of the Achæmenid and early Hellenistic ages.

Cylindrical seals were traditional in the Near East and produced chiefly by local craftsmen in Mesopotamia and Iran; pyramids and scaraboids were made mostly by Greek craftsmen in Asia Minor. However, the designs were executed in the "imperial" style of Achæmenid art. This seal shows the Achæmenid king of kings and a winged goat - one of the incarnations of the Zoroastrian god of victory, Verethragna - in single combat. The scene had a symbolical significance: in this combat the king of kings acquired the qualities of the god of victory.

Bibliography:
Lukonin 1977b, p.73; *Oriental Jewellery* 1984, No.21.

26. SEAL. 4TH CENTURY BC
Carved sapphirine. Diameter 2.9cm.
The Hermitage, St Petersburg.
Inv. No. Gl. 892.

This conical seal also belongs to the group of Graeco-Persian carved gems. The "star" motif composed of the protomes or heads of various animals is characteristic of the glyptic art of both Asia Minor and Iran. The symbolism of this motif in Iran may possibly be linked with incarnations of the Zoroastrian deity of victory, Verethragna.

The seal came from the collection of L Ross, a 19th-century collector of antiquities.

Bibliography:
Lukonin 1977b, p.89; *Oriental Jewellery* 1984, No.23.

27. SEAL. 4TH CENTURY BC
Carved sapphirine. 3.4x3cm.
The Hermitage, St Petersburg.
Inv. No. Gl. 887.

The scaraboid form of the seal is typical of the group of Graeco-Persian carved gems produced by Greeks from Asia Minor to fulfill orders from Persian courtiers and kings. The twined gold ring of the seal is also of Asia Minor craftsmanship of the 4th century BC.

The scene on the seal is of a battle between a noble Persian rider and a Scythian warrior.

Depictions of a battle between Persians or Greeks and "barbarians" were very popular, not only on glyptics but on other objects of art, for example, on the metalwork manufactured by Greeks for Persian or Scythian clients.

Bibliography:
Lukonin 1977b, p.88.

28. SIGNET-RING.
4TH–3RD CENTURY BC
Carved sard set in a gold ring. Length of gem 1.7cm.
The Hermitage, St Petersburg.
Inv. No. Gl. 891.

The gold ring, judging by its shape, may also be assigned to the 4th–3rd century BC.

The monster depicted on the gem - a winged lion with horns - is reminiscent of the fantastic beasts of Median art and frequently appears on official Achæmenid objects, not only carved gems but also sculptures (such as the capitals of columns at Persepolis), metalwork and reliefs. The symbolic significance of this image, undoubtedly associated with the religion of Iran in Achæmenid times, has not been precisely determined.

The signet-ring came from the collection of L Ross, a 19th-century collector of antiquities.

Bibliography:
Lukonin 1977b, p.87; *Oriental Jewellery* 1984, No.20.

29. PILE CARPET.
5TH CENTURY BC
Coloured wool (360 knots/cm²).
189x200cm.
The Hermitage, St Petersburg.
Inv. No. 1687/93. Found 1949 in Pazyryk barrow V in the Altai.

The carpet formed part of the extremely rich burial inventory of a Saka chief.

All the iconographic details, as well as the technique employed, display evidence of Persian craftsmanship. This is the oldest known pile carpet. The portrayal of the riders on the fourth and " widest band" is of particular interest: the headgear is typical of Achæmenid warriors - pointed and apparently made of felt, like a bashlyk (hood) with its tip bent back.

Scythians, Bactrians and Saka, etc. were portrayed in such headgear on the reliefs at Persepolis. The horse trappings are also typically Achæmenid, with a horse-cloth decorated with a tooth-patterned border and a bridle decorated with plaques, etc. (see, for example, Cat. No.12).

Bibliography:
S Rudenko, "The Fifth Pazyryk Barrow", *KSIIMK*, 1951, XXXVII, pp.106-116 (in Russian); Artamonov 1973, pp.67-71, ill.81.

CAT N° 29

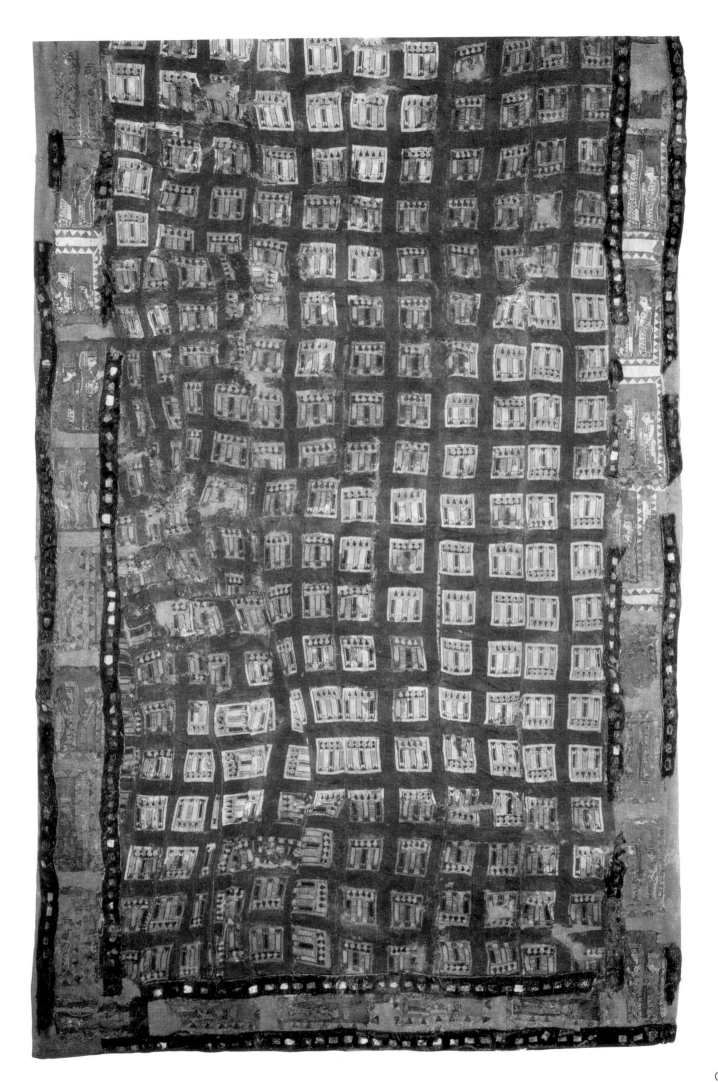

CAT N° 30

CAT N° 35

37. VESSEL. 2ND–3RD CENTURY
Clay, glazed. Height 20.8cm; diameter 12.3cm
The Hermitage, St Petersburg.
Inv. No. S-352. Donated 1935 by the Government of Iran.

The two-handled jar with relief mouldings is characteristic of the western regions of Iran; however, the absence of sufficient comparative material from excavations does not yet enable a precise dat-

ing. Vessels of various forms, covered with a dark green, yellow or blue glaze, are found in late Parthian and early Sassanian archæological layers.
Accompanying documents indicate that the vessel originated from Susa.
Bibliography:
Lukonin 1977b, p.134.

38. BELT BUCKLE.
4TH CENTURY
(GEM, 2ND–3RD CENTURY)
Gold, decorated with garnets and cornelian. Length 20cm; weight 92.5g.
The Hermitage, St Petersburg.
Inv. No. Z-346 1/3. Acquired in the 19th century from the Nelidov collection (purchased in Turkey).

The round buckle and two hasps of a belt are in the polychrome style characteristic of the 4th-early 5th centuries and decorated with garnets and small "pyramids" of granulation. The engraved cornelian gem on the buckle is most interesting of all: it depicts a rider at a hunt. The details of the depiction, especially the stylization of the horse's form, correspond exactly to frescoes found in the temple of Mithras in the Parthian town of Dura Europos on the Euphrates.
Bibliography:
Lukonin 1977b, p.135; *Oriental Jewellery* 1984, No.39

39, 40, 41. COINS:
TETRADRACHMA OF VAHUBARZ,
SOVEREIGN RULER OF PARSA
(LATE 3RD–2ND CENTURY BC);
DRACHMA OF DARIUS, SOVEREIGN
RULER OF PARSA (SECOND HALF
OF THE 2ND CENTURY BC);
DRACHMA OF ARTAHSHATR IV, KING
OF PARSA (EARLY 3RD CENTURY AD)
Tetradrachma of vahubarz Silver.
Diameter 2.9cm. Drachma of Darius
Silver. Drachma of Artahshatr IV
Silver. Diameter 2cm.
The Hermitage, St Petersburg.

The small kingdom of Parsa (region of Persepolis, Naqsh-i Rustam; capital Istakhr) preserved

a certain independence after the collapse of the Achæmenid monarchy. Here, in the Zoroastrian religious centre of the country, from the 3rd century BC to the 3rd century AD priest-kings of a local dynasty ruled. It was a king of Parsa, Papak, who was the father of Ardashir I, the founder of the Sassanid dynasty.
Parsa was one of the few provinces of Seleucid, and afterwards Parthian, Iran which had the right to mint its own coinage. The coins of this kingdom are the only source enabling us to reconstruct a few stages in its history.
On the obverse of early coins from Parsa the portrait of the ruler is represented in headgear which is Achæmenid (or "satrapian", just as on early Parthian coins).
On the reverse, the ruler is depicted full length in Median Achæmenid dress.
His right hand is raised in a gesture of veneration. He stands before a temple building (possibly the "Kaaba of Zoroaster" – the temple of Achæmenid times at the national shrine of Parsa, Naqsh-i Rustam). Next to the temple is the royal Achæmenid standard. Also on the reverse is an Aramaic legend with the ruler's name, his title – "divine ruler" –

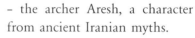

and the designation of the place where it was minted – "the fortress of Parsa".

The obverse of the Darius coin bears the ruler's portrait in an almost Seleucid helmet crowned with the figure of an eagle in place of the "satrapian" headgear of Achæmenid times. The image on the reverse is different (or more exactly, is deformed): the figure of the bird which, according to Xenophon, crowned the Achæmenid standard, is depicted on some sort of rectangle while the temple building becomes stylized and looks somewhat like a fire altar. The legends too are dis-

torted and the ruler's title changes, he is now "king of Parsa".

The coin of Artahshatr IV is one of the latest coins from Parsa. The first coins of the Sassanian dynasty can be traced back to this coin.

The lettering of the inscription changes on these coins and is already coming to resemble early Sassanian inscriptions in the form of the letters; possibly the language of the legend is already Persian instead of Aramaic.

The portrayal on the reverse also changes: instead of a scene before a temple or altar, there is a portrait of the ruler's father, or perhaps an anthropomorphic portrayal of the ruler's guardian-deity. The content of the legend, too, changes (here the obverse reads: "King Artahshatr"; the reverse: "Son of the king Mithridates").

The kings have complicated hairstyles with a "crown" of hair or a toothed crown with diverging rays; these crowns are the prototypes of the insignia of Sassanian shahanshahs.

42. DRACHMA OF ONE OF THE EARLY PARTHIAN KINGS. SECOND HALF OF THE 3RD CENTURY BC
Silver. Diameter 2cm.
The Hermitage, St Petersburg.

The drachma was the basic monetary unit of Parthian and Sassanian Iran. A portrait of the king in "satrapian" headgear occupies the obverse of early Parthian coins. The figure of a heroic ancestor of the dynasty appears on the reverse of all Parthian drachmae until the very end of their issue in the 230s AD

– the archer Aresh, a character from ancient Iranian myths.

This general type of depiction goes back to coins of the Achæmenid satraps of Asia Minor in the 4th century BC. On Parthian coins the legend was also generally fitted onto the reverse and written in Greek. In the 1st century AD the legend was occasionally stamped on the obverse in Aramaic script.

As a rule the legend on the reverse only indicated the ancestral name of Parthian rulers, Arshak, and their titles, sometimes very grand ones.

Around the middle of the 1st century BC a standard designation became established: "King of kings Arshak, beneficent, just, glorious, amicable towards the Hellenes".

43. TETRADRACHMA OF PHRAATES IV (38 BC–3 AD)
Silver. Diameter 2.9cm.
The Hermitage, St Petersburg.

The portrait of the Parthian king of kings is depicted on the obverse with the typical insignia of his power: a gold torque twisted into several rings and ending in the protome of a winged horse, rich dress decorated with precious stones and applied gold plaques. The figure of a Greek goddess is depicted on the dress (on the shoulder) and winged lions (on the breast).

On the reverse is the usual scene shown on Parthian tetradrachmae - the king of kings on a horse with the goddess of victory before him.

44. DENARIUS OF ARDASHIR I (224–241)
Gold. Diameter 2.4cm; weight 8.68g.

45. DENARIUS OF SHAPUR I (241–272)
Gold.

46. DRACHMA OF VARAHRAN II (276–293)
Silver. Diameter 2.7cm.

47. DRACHMA OF PEROZ (459–484)
Silver. Diameter 2.1cm.

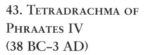
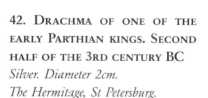

54. Seal. 5th–6th century
Carved amethyst. 1.6 x 1.5cm.
The Hermitage, St Petersburg.
Inv. No. Gl. 904.

The gem shows a head in profile portrayed schematically between two outspread wings. The hatched style of the image places the gem in the second half of the Sassanian period, but both style and inscription attest that the gem was made in the western provinces of Iran, where Hellenistic traditions endured for a long time: The inscription with the name of the owner, "Antioch", is written in Greek letters but with a grammatical error.
Bibliography:
Lukonin 1977b, p.157.

55. Seal. 6th century
Carved cornelian. 3.6 x 2.9cm.
The Hermitage, St Petersburg.
Inv. No. Gl. 884.

The gem shows the portrait of the Sassanian noble with the insignia of his power: he wears a headdress (*kulah*) with a patrimonial badge (*tamgha*), earrings and a necklace. The inscription on the gem, encircling the figure, indicates his name and title: "Papak, shahrab of the town of Khusraushad-Hormizd".

The title *shahrab* was bestowed upon the head of a town and a town district. The *shahrab* embodied both military and civil power in this district. The town and headquarters of Papak was called "Joy of Khusrau-Hormizd". It was founded in the west of Iran by the shahanshah Khusrau I (531–579) and thus named in honour of Khusrau's son, the future shahanshah Hormizd.
This gem was acquired from the Duke of Orleans for Catherine the Great's collection of gems.
Bibliography:
Borisov and Lukonin 1963, p.48, No.4; p.75, No.6; *Splendeur* 1993, No.133.

56. Ring-seal. 6th century
Carved chalcedony. Bezel:
1.5 x 0.9cm; ring: 2.9 x 2.7cm.
The Hermitage, St Petersburg.
Inv. No. Gl. 743. Acquired in the late 19th century from the Dom collection.

This ring-seal is of an unusual shape and depicts a recumbent moufflon – an incarnation of the god Khwarnah. The seal belonged to one Mah Hormizd.
Bibliography:
Borisov and Lukonin 1963, p.129, No.347.

57. Seal. 6th century
Carved brown-red jasper mottled with black. Height 1.9cm; bezel: 2.5 x 2cm.
The Hermitage, St Petersburg.
Inv. No. Gl. 833. Acquired in the 1920s; formerly in the collection of the Counts Shuvalov.

The seal shows a rider on horseback with a spear in his hand, piercing a seven-headed dragon at

the horse's hooves. A radiant halo surrounds the rider's head, to the left is a star, to the right the figure of a scorpion.
The image represents one of the ancient Iranian epic heroes of the *Avesta*. Nearly all these epic warrior-heroes (like their divine patron, the god of victory Verethragna) fought with dragons – the powers of the evil deity. For example, one of them named Krsaspa "by his virile strength slew the snake Srvara that devoured horses, that devoured men, down whose body poured a stream of yellow poison as thick as a finger". They slaughtered a great number of the so-called *khrafstra* engendered by the god of evil: scorpions, snakes, etc. The warrior-heroes were protected by the radiance of Khwarnah, the god of royal and heroic majesty.
It has been suggested that it was this image, so popular both in Iran and Mesopotamia, which served as the prototype for later depictions of St George.

Bibliography:
Borisov and Lukonin 1963, p.95, No.122.

58. Seal.
6th–early 7th century
Carved agate. 2.6 x 2.1cm.
The Hermitage, St Petersburg.
Inv. No. Gl. 861.

The portrait on the seal is executed in a generalized and fairly crude manner: the craftsman was striving to convey the signs of investiture of the individual portrayed with the maximum of accuracy - his *kulah*, hairstyle, ribbons, earrings and jewellery.
At the sides of the portrait are a many-rayed star and a crescent moon – symbolic signs which also appeared on late Sassanian coins. The inscription round the edge reads: Burznesh (?) magus priest, son of Burzengushnasp".
Bibliography:
Borisov and Lukonin 1963, p.49, No.13; p.83, No.47.

59. SEAL. 6TH–7TH CENTURY
Carved chalcedony. 2 x 1.7cm.
The Hermitage, St Petersburg.
Inv. No. Gl. 777.

Purchased in the early 20th century by the Armenian antique dealer, Mikhran Sivadzhan.

The seal belonged to the priest (magus) Bukhtakgushnasp, son of Burzator. A moufflon is depicted with a luxuriant ribbon bow – a popular incarnation of the god Khwarnah in late Sassanian Iran.
Bibliography:
Borisov and Lukonin 1963, p.128, No.337.

60. SEAL.
6TH–EARLY 7TH CENTURY
Carved chalcedony. 1.9 x 2.1cm.
The Hermitage, St Petersburg.
Inv. No. Gl. 407.
Donated in the late 19th century; for-

merly part of a collection of antiquities acquired in Seistan, Iran, by the Russian diplomat Cherkasov.

The dromedary depicted on the seal was a symbol (divine incarnation) of several Zoroastrian deities, but above all a symbol of the god of victory, Verethragna. Judging by the inscription, the gem served as a personal seal for one Datfarrukh, son of Barzushtan (?), who was perhaps a Zoroastrian priest (magus). In the inscription on the seal Datfarrukh uses a Zoroastrian religious formula – "may the Khwarnah [here success, happiness] of the seal's owner increase".
Bibliography:
Borisov and Lukonin 1963, p.49, No.12; p.186, No.753; Splendeur 1993, No.149.

61. BOWL ON A FOOT-RING DEPICTING VARAHRAN, KING OF KIRMAN (?), HUNTING BEAR.
3RD CENTURY
Silver, hammered from a sheet.
Diameter 28.5cm; height with stem 3.2cm; weight 1820g.
The Abkhaziya Museum of Local History, Sukhumi. Inv. No. 47-71.

Chasing was used to create a low relief image; the applied plaques form a high relief (individual details – the rider's face, the horse's crupper, etc. – are embossed). The vessel is incised.
Individual details were possibly gilded. The foot-ring was soldered on after the vessel had been polished. The production technique is characteristic of many objects of Sassanian metalwork.
This vessel, a festal bowl, is the earliest known Sassanian vessel with a hunting scene. Originally such vessels bore subjects which reflected the Zoroastrian symbolism of grandeur, might and victorious power: the ruler of Iran overcoming beasts in single combat, these animals being hypostases of the Zoroastrian deities Mithras, Khwarnah and Verethragna. In its first stage of development the main heroes of this theme were not Iran's shahanshahs but princes – sovereigns of large provinces. On this plate a prince is portrayed in official apparel, with the symbols of his rank – a specific type of headgear (*kulah*) with a precious diadem and a special badge, with a necklace, and in ceremonial dress with fibulae and a precious belt. These accessories, which altered during the course of the Sassanian epoch but always reflected

the owner's rank like a uniform, lead us to believe that the rider portrayed on the bowl was a sovereign prince and lived at the beginning of the Sassanian epoch (in the 3rd century). Both the badge on his *kulah* and the dotted Middle Persian inscription on the back (in the so-called Parthian script, of which in fact only the owner's name and the weight of the vessel can so far be read: "...Varahran. Weight 432 drachmas") may point to the fact that the prince portrayed on the vessel is the son of the shahanshah Shapur I, Varahran, king of the Kirman province, afterwards shahanshah of Iran, Varahran I (247–276). The bear is evidently a hypostasis of the god of victory, Verethragna, and consequently the entire scene symbolizes the victoriousness of the king. Executed in the Sassanian style, the hunting scene on this vessel is rendered purely canonically: the depiction represents its beginning and end simultaneously (the bear is caught in a lasso and the same bear lies under the horse's hooves) and the horse is shown at a flying gallop; the twist of the rider's body, however, is very original.
This bowl was produced by the same workshop as bowls Cat.

Nos.62, 64 and 65. Apparently this workshop existed at the royal court in the town of Bishapur.

The bowl was found in the village of Krasnaya Polyana (near Sukhumi) in a kitchen-garden, before 1946. Possibly it formed part of the burial inventory of a local nobleman's tomb (it seems a Roman provincial coin of the 2nd century BC was discovered with it and several other objects whose fate is at present unknown).

Bibliography:

Melikhov 1952, pp.71-79; Lukonin 1980, pp.35-38; Harper and Meyers 1981, pp.50-55.

62. BOWL WITH A GODDESS ON A PANTHER AND PROTOMES OF BEASTS. 3RD CENTURY

Silver, hammered from a sheet and gilded; low relief produced by hollowing the ground, high relief formed of separately tooled applied plaques; chased and punched. Diameter 23cm; weight 801.9g.
The Hermitage, St Petersburg.
Inv. No. S-74. Acquired 1886.

The bowl, undoubtedly an imitation of late Roman silverware, depicts a goddess of Asia Minor, Cybele, on a panther, Maenad blowing her horn and, round the rim, figures of gladiators fighting beasts. Analogies to individual elements of the bowl's decoration exist not only on Roman metalwork but also on late Roman glass vessels, coins, etc.

The style of the images, especially the protomes of beasts in the medallions, along with the nature of the medallions' frames, the plant ornament and so on, closely link this bowl to the early Sassanian court school of Bishapur in the late 3rd century (see Cat. Nos.61, 63).

But even without these links it is clear that the vessel was produced by an Iranian craftsman, albeit one who had served his apprenticeship under Roman masters. Within the confines of an alien theme, and not yet having any of his own Iranian devices to represent Zoroastrian symbols, the craftsman has nevertheless totally reinterpreted the scene shown round the rim of the bowl. The figures of the gladiators have become mere background decoration, while the observer's attention is concentrated on the protomes of beasts – a lion, a lioness, a horse, a wild boar, a bear and a zebu-like bull (the hypostases of the Zoroastrian deities) in the medallions.

Thus the bowl stands at the beginning of Sassanian metalwork: adopting foreign models, the craftsmen endowed them with a local, Iranian meaning.

On the reverse of the bowl there is a scratched Sogdian inscription in the so-called Sarnarqand script: "From [the property off Franch] (?)".

The bowl was part of a hoard discovered in 1866.

Bibliography:

Smirnov 1909, No.36; Livshits and Lukonin 1964, p.173; Lukonin 1980, pp.36-38; Marschak 1986, pl.97; Trever and Lukonin 1987, No.1; Splendeur 1993, No.72.

70. BOAT-SHAPED BOWL. 6TH–7TH CENTURY

Silver, hammered from a sheet, with applied high relief plaques. Underneath traces of solder of an oval base. Length 26cm; width 9.2cm; height 6cm.

The History Museum, Moscow. Inv. No. 83746. Acquired 1947.

The bowl was found in 1947 during the ploughing of a field near the village of Bartym in the Beriozovsky region of Perm province. Both before and after this find other silver vessels have been discovered within a limited area around the village. The distribution of the finds and their various datings have led to the assumption that they were once kept in some sort of shrine situated at this place.

At the sides of an altar are two very complex grylli – in this instance in the form of pheasants made up of a fantastic combination of human heads (body and chest), horns of a beast with an open jaw (rear part of the body) and fish tails and fish (legs).

Such fanciful combinations are found in late Roman and Sassanian glyptics. They are undoubtedly linked to some sort of complicated symbolism, possibly symbolizing all the fauna of the universe, but their exact significance has not yet been determined.

The dating of this bowl is based on its form and iconographic details.

Bibliography:

Bader 1949, p.85; Bader and Smirnov 1954, pp.17–19, ill.7.

71. BOWL DEPICTING BAHRAM GUR AND AZADEH. 6TH CENTURY

Silver, hammered from a sheet and gilded; low relief produced by hollowing the ground; chased and punched; foot-ring soldered. Diameter 21.7cm; weight 1155.6g.

The Hermitage, St Petersburg. Inv. No. S-252.

The bowl depicts a scene from the history of Prince Bahram – the future shahanshah of Iran Varahran V (420–438). Because of his hunting exploits he was given the nickname Gur – onager or wild ass. Firdawsi's poem *Shahnama* (10th century) relates that once he went hunting on a camel, accompanied by his beloved, Azadeh, a singer and musician (she played the *chang*).

Boasting to her of his skill, Bahram suggested that she herself should choose a victim from a herd of wild gazelles. However, Azadeh announced that real art would be to turn a female gazelle into a male and a male into a female. Bahram did this by means of arrows: with well-aimed shots he fired two arrows into the head of a female, thus causing her to grow "antlers", then, with a sickle-tipped arrow, he severed the antlers of a male. Firdawsi states that Azadeh took fright, exclaiming: "This art of yours is from the daevas [evil deities]", whereupon Bahram, enraged, trampled her beneath his camel and henceforth hunted without women.

The subject of Bahram Gur and Azadeh was depicted on Sassanian silver vessels of the 6th and 7th centuries (apart from this bowl, two others are known – one of them also in the Hermitage, the other in the Metropolitan Museum, New York) and also on late Sassanian stucco decorations and carved gems. They represent the entire story according to the rules of the Sassanian genre, blending the beginning and end of the action – with the figure of Azadeh cast beneath the camel's hooves.

This theme became popular in Iranian art again in the 12th century, when it was depicted first on ceramics (on bowls and tiles) and metal vessels (see Cat. No.126) and then in manuscript miniatures. It is interesting to note that the miniatures reproduced the very scene which had hitherto been known from Sassanian works of art.

Works of art from the Sassanian age indisputably attest that this story was already well known in Iran, at any rate in the 7th century. But was it already linked to the Sassanid shahanshah Varahran V? Ninth-century Arab historians (Tabari, Ibn al-Faqih), who used written sources from the Sassanian age and oral traditions of Varahran V, relate that he was nicknamed Gur as a prince and they mention that he loved to ride a camel and that he performed two exploits while hunting: with bow and arrows he shot down swift-footed ostriches and with a single arrow he transfixed a gazelle to a lion that was attacking it. There are also accounts that these exploits were illustrated in paintings on walls.

One late Sassanian plate featuring an ostrich hunt is known (from a private collection in Japan) and a Byzantine silk textile of the 8th century shows the second exploit – the impaling of deer and lion with a single arrow. It is interesting that these exploits were not subsequently illustrated. All these stories were brought together for the first time in Firdawsi's poem.

Firdawsi devoted 2600 distichs to the reign of Bahram Gur. In his poem Bahram Gur is represented as the model of a skilled hunter and knight. It is not known whether a "romance" of Bahram Gur already existed in Sassanian times, or whether various exploits and romantic adventures of different heroes, widely known through the oral art of the gosan, were united around the figure of this king, who was not famed for anything during his lifetime. But this only took place later, in the 8th-9th centuries, the age of Islam, when Arab, and in the 10th century Persian, books were composed on the history of the kings of ancient Iran on the basis of Sassanian historical works and oral traditions. One such book is the Large Shah-nama created at the demand of the vicegerent of the town of Tus in the second half of the 10th century, by four experts in the history of ancient Iran; it was used by Firdawsi as the basis for his poem. The Middle Persian inscription on the outside of the bowl was evidently engraved soon after its manufacture: "Property of Mihrbozed. 71 staters and 23 drachmae by weight".

The bowl formed part of a hoard found in the summer of 1927

near the village of Turushevo in Viatka province.

Bibliography:

Orbeli and Trever 1935, pl.11; Marschak 1986, pl.183; Trever and Lukonin 1987, No.13; *Splendeur* 1993, No.51.

72. JUG WITH THE FACE OF A GODDESS.
6TH–7TH CENTURY

Silver, moulded from a sheet, embossed, chased, punched and gilded (the neck produced separately, the join masked by a tooled relief rim). To judge from surviving traces of solder, the jug had a handle. Height 14.5cm; weight 358.3g.

The Hermitage, St Petersburg.

Inv. No. S-60. Transferred 1926 from the Moscow Kremlin Armoury.

Several small details of the ornament connect this jug closely with the lobed bowl decorated with goats (Cat. No.78). It is possible that both vessels were made in the same workshop.

The jug portrays a woman's face corresponding exactly with the Sassanian ideal of feminine beauty (of which a description survives in the late Sassanian work, *Khusrau, Son of Kavadh, and His Page*). The woman wears a complicated diadem and headdress composed of various plants. This, together with the frieze of Senmurvs (see Cat. No.69) on the neck of the jug, may be evidence that the image is that of the goddess of plants, Ameretat. Two medallions on the jug's body contain the history of some unknown hero, impaling a rampant tiger with his sword and tearing the jaw of

a wild boar. Although prototypes of the scene of a king's single combat with a beast go back to Iranian art of the Achaemenid age, at the early Sassanian "symbolical" stage of development in metalwork only the Iranian shahanshah was portrayed thus. This jug depicts neither the shahanshah nor a prince, but simply a noble knight. The symbolic genre has been reduced to that of the heroic exploit. The heroic genre (hand-to-hand struggle with a beast, lone hunt on foot for a beast, a battle of strength, etc.) is characteristic of late Sassanian metalwork of the 6th-7th centuries. The jug dates from this period.

Possibly the exploits of the hero depicted on this jug, as on other examples of late Sassanian metalwork, were illustrations of legends which have not survived but which would have been sung by Sassanian minstrels (*gosans*) at the courts of kings and nobles.

The original provenance of the jug is unknown. Before 1910 it was in the collection of Prince Vladimir Orlov, and then entered the Kremlin Armoury.

Bibliography:

Smirnov 1909, No.82; Trever and Lukonin 1987, No.28; *Splendeur* 1993, No.95.

73. JUG WITH DANCING WOMEN.
6TH CENTURY

Silver, moulded from a sheet and gilded (the neck is soldered); chased and punched.

Height 16cm; weight 871.3g.

The Hermitage, St Petersburg.

Inv. No. S-256. Purchased 1931 in Sverdlovsk.

Six women are portrayed beneath arches, each holding in her hands various attributes linked with the symbolism of fertility, wine and the festal banquet: a bunch of grapes, flowers (a tulip, a lily), fruit, a wreath or necklace, some type of vessel, a child. The jug may reproduce festal rituals, relating apparently to the feast of Mihragan. Vessels with dancers (not only jugs but also bowls) are perhaps the most commonly found articles of Sassanian metalwork. They were also produced in the early Islamic period, and their theme remained standard for illustrations not only on metal but also on ceramics for many centuries. On the neck of the jug is a deeply incised inscription in "Bukharan" script: "Sovereign of Mash (?) Charak. Weight 265. Repast forever!"

Bibliography:

Orbeli and Trever 1935, pls.46, 47; Livshits and Lukonin 1964, pp.167, 168; Marschak 1986, pl.188; Trever and Lukonin 1987, No.120; *Splendeur* 1993, pl.85.

74. BOWL WITH EAGLE CARRYING A WOMAN. 6TH CENTURY

Silver, hammered from a sheet of silver; low relief produced by hollowing the ground; engraved, chased, punched and gilded. Diameter 22.2cm; weight 828.6g. The Hermitage, St Petersburg. Inv. No. S-217. Acquired 1936.

The bowl is decorated with an illustration from an ancient Iranian myth, of which an extract is preserved in the Aban Yasht of the Avesta, the Yasht dedicated to the goddess Anahita. "Paurva, having suffered shipwreck, bore sacrifices to Ardvisura Anahita; because of the victorious warrior Thraetaona he flew off into the air in the form of a kite. He soared unceasingly for three days and three nights after this in the direction of his home but could not return to it". At dawn after the third night Paurva prays to Anahita to be merciful towards him and return him to his home, and then he will bear her the requisite sacrifices.

"And Ardvisura Anahita hastened to him
In the form of a beautiful maiden,
Strong and graceful
'With a high girdle (?),
Of noble birth, high-born,
From the ankles down she was shod in gleaming sandals
Laced with gold ribbons,
And she firmly seized him in her arms.
And thereupon it straightway came to pass
That he, with zealous striving,
Found himself in the land created by Ahura,
In his own house, alive and well,
Whole, in the form in which he was before."

An almost exact illustration of the text is reproduced on the bowl, even the moment mentioned there, of the "dawn, the rise of Ardvisura": the figures of the two children below are symbols of the day (a boy with a bow) and night (a boy with a pole-axe). In the surviving myth, it is true, there is no mention that Anahita feeds Paurva with fruit, if this is how we are to interpret the bowl of fruit in her hand. But the Avesta myth as such is not known to us. We do not know who Paurva was, why he suffered shipwreck, why the hero of Iranian mythology, Thraetaona (Faridun), turned him into a kite. It is also unclear why this particular composition should have been so popular: apart from this bowl, it is depicted on a gold jug of the 9th century from the hoard found at Nagyszentmiklos (Hungary), on the Iranian (?) printed cloth from the 11th-century Quedlinburg Schlosskirche reliquary, even on a 12th-century bowl from Rayy. However, the important fact is that the depiction on this bowl is one of the few examples of illustrations of the myths of the *Avesta*. Judging by all the facts, manuscript illuminations were not the prototypes for such illustrations. Transcribed in Iran up to the 9th century in a special "Avestan" script, the sacred Avestan texts, like other manuscript texts in Iran, probably did not have any illustrations. The ancient Iranian myths recorded in the *Avesta* are never quoted there in their entirety: there are only excerpts. Were the plots of these myths known in their entirety in Sassanian Iran in the 6th and 7th centuries when this bowl was manufactured? One can almost say for certain that they were not: all the didactic literature of Sassanian times, including the Sassanian "elucidation" of the *Avesta* - the *Zend* (commentary) - attests that even the priests were far from understanding everything in the ancient texts and were only interested in orthopraxy, the often senseless repetition of "holy words of prayer". Therefore, in all probability, the bowl's motif simply hints at the *Aban Yasht* - prayers to the goddess Anahita.

The bowl formed part of a hoard discovered in 1936 during the ploughing of a field near the village of Anikovskoye in Perm province.

Bibliography:
Trever 1937, pp.8-18, pl.III; Trever and Lukonin 1987, No.22; *Splendeur* 1993, No.74.

75. BOWL DEPICTING KHUSRAU II AND COURTIERS. LATE 6TH–EARLY 7TH CENTURY

Silver, hammered from a sheet and gilded; low relief produced by hollowing the ground; chased and punched. Diameter 26cm; weight 985.6g. The Hermitage, St Petersburg. Inv. No. S-520.

The scene on the bowl is fairly rare in metalwork, an official composition of a court reception seen mainly on rock reliefs.

On a throne supported by figures of winged horses (see also Cat. No.80) is the shahanshah of Iran, Khusrau II (591-628) (judging by details of his individual crown and other insignia) and his courtiers in official dress. Subsequently, under Islam, such illustrations became standard for scenes of court receptions. Of interest is the lower segment of

the bowl, showing a "hunting composition", no longer symbolical (see Cat. Nos 61, 65–67) but simply an ordinary genre scene of a royal hunt, possibly also showing Khusrau II (he wears a different crown), for moufflons in the mountains: the king shoots at the moufflons, twisting round in a "Parthian bend", and a frightened bird flies out from under the hooves of the horse.

The bowl was discovered before 1908 on the exposed edge of a river terrace above the River Sylva near the village of Strelka in the Perm region.

Bibliography:

Orbeli and Trever 1935, pl.7; Harper and Meyers 1981, pp.67, 68; Trever and Lukonin 1987, No. 9; *Splendeur* 1993, No. 61.

76. VESSEL.

6TH–7TH CENTURY

Clay, thrown on a potter's wheel, with sized polychrome decoration on a slip layer. Height 46cm.
The History Museum, Ashkhabad.

The form of the vessel is common. Certain details, such as the mouldings on the handles, enable us to assign this example to the 6th or 7th century.

There are four scenes on the vessel: a noble wearing a wedding garland and holding a fan and a bowl of fruit is seated on a *takht* next to his bride who has a flower in her hand; the same noble on horseback is seen shooting an arrow at a bird; mortally ill, he lies on a couch, accompanied by a mourner and a priest who, judging by the specific gesture of the right hand, is reading prayers; the noble, bound in a shroud, is borne on a litter to a Zoroastrian graveyard.

The painted decoration has many interesting details: the background strewn with red trefoils, the picture of a pomegranate, the garlands resting on a special stand, the jug, some kind of signs reminiscent of the letters of the Middle Persian alphabet, etc. Several details are indisputably similar to those of contemporary Central Asian Sogdian paintings, and faces, especially the eyes, depicted exactly like those on contemporary painted ceramics from Marv or early Islamic pieces. But it is undoubtedly a Sassanian noble who is portrayed. The banquet scene on the vessel is a standard element also found on silver bowls and particularly often on marriage gems (carved seals) with Sassanian texts wishing that the marriage will be happy. The hunting scene is also a standard element.

Thus, the bird at which the noble is shooting is portrayed exactly as on, for example, seals of the 6th and 7th centuries.

The funeral – although this is the only known depiction of such rites – is typically Zoroastrian: in accordance with Zoroastrian beliefs there is an even number of litter bearers and of accompanying mourners, the gesture of the priest singing the *Yasna* is characteristic, the shroud of the deceased is girdled with the Zoroastrian belt (*kustik*), and there is a wheeled litter. The entire life story of the noble is illustrated on the vessel in only four scenes. It unwittingly brings to mind four lines of a Persian *ruba'i* (lyrical quatrain), a literary genre widespread in the early Islamic period and most probably based on a prototype in Sassanian poetic texts.

They speak of the world's mortality, of the vanity of desires, of man's emergence from dust and return to dust, of the potter shaping a vessel from clay as god created man from clay.

Not a single genuine *ruba'i* has survived from Sassanian times, but here are several lines from a late Sassanian poem, *The Admonitions of Vehzat-i Frav-Peroz*:

"(22) When the body decomposes and the qalib [mould for a clay vessel] is broken, the soul has forgotten the body; just as when the potter finishes work, the qalib is of no use to anyone...

(23) When fate closes the eyes – the body of man is such that it cannot rise, and his heart is in such pain that it beats not, the hand is so broken that it cannot be raised, and the legs so shattered that they will not walk...

(25) And thus the body as flesh and bone on the funeral bier is borne to the graveyard, and the family mingles with strangers, and might and power pass to another owner, and the wife thinks of another husband and possessions pass to another.

(28) The soul is alone and the body, only a body as flesh and bone, lies apart... The dog and the bird sit next to it and quarrel over the prey.

(29) And the great and the small and the noble and the rich man and the beggar and the slave – even the very least of men will come to this."

The vessel was found in a Buddhist stupa at Marv. It was used by the Buddhists as a fine vessel to store holy relics – Buddhist palm-leaf manuscripts.

It was not, of course, intended for this purpose. In Eastern Iran Zoroastrians were buried in such vessels, and also in special clay ossuaries. According to Zoroastrian beliefs, the corpse defiled the sacred earth and the deceased were laid on couches specially carved into cliffs (or later in India, at the top of clay "towers of silence" – *dahma*) where birds devoured them. The bones were collected and buried either in clay vessels, or in ossuaries (mainly in Eastern Iran), or in specially carved niches in cliffs.

The images on the vessel are an extremely rare example of Sassanian painting (there is one single, small fragment of Sassanian mural painting found at Susa in Western Iran: it consists of the remains of a king's figure on a red horse).

Possibly such painting is yet to be unearthed by excavations of Sassanian towns, for it is surely with good reason that many early Islamic works, as well as sources contemporary with the Sassanids, describe the walls of reception halls and the *iwans* of Sassanian palaces as being decorated with paintings.

Bibliography:

Pugachenkova 1967, pp.91–95, pl.67; Lukonin 1977b, pp.214–217, 219–221.

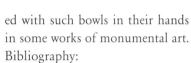

77. Bowl.
6th–7th century
Glass. Height 7.3cm, diameter 10.4cm.
The Hermitage, St Petersburg.
Inv. No. Kz 6247.

This is a typical example of a late Sassanian glass bowl. It was cast in an open mould and the facets were carefully polished. All the examples known at present are damaged, but in order to conceive the effect these vessels produced, one must imagine an almost colourless or slightly tinged glass covered with small and polished mirror-facets reflecting the light. Such vessels have been found during a number of excavations in Iran (for example, at Gilan) and in the Caucasus. One such vessel was found in the grave of the Japanese emperor Ankhan (*c.*535 AD), another has been kept at the Japanese temple treasury of Shosoin since the 8th century. Several examples have been found in Mesopotamia and Iraq.

This particular vessel was found in one of the graves near the village of Komunt (Northern Ossetia). All these vessels are amazingly uniform as regards their dimensions (7.6-9.7cm in height, 9.4-l2.2cm in diameter) and as a rule they have an identical number of rows of facets. This may indicate that they were produced in the same place or perhaps that they had a specific purpose.
First publication.

78. Lobed bowl.
7th century
Silver, hammered from a thick sheet and gilded; low relief produced by hollowing the ground.
Length 22.9cm; weight 869.2g.
The Hermitage, St Petersburg.
Inv. No. S-285. Donated 1940 by the Kiev Museum of Western and Oriental Art on the occasion of the 175th anniversary of the Hermitage (found in 1815 or 1823 in the Ostrozhsky district of Volynskaya province).

Goats at the sides of a tree constitute a very ancient figurative motif, dating back at least to the 2nd millennium BC. However, it is not known whether this motif had any sort of symbolical significance in Sassanian Iran, apart from in the usual benedictory sense.
All the illustrations on the bowl (goats at the sides of a tree; griffins with birds' heads and wings and the claws and bodies of a beast of prey; a recumbent lion) are represented here exactly as they are on Sassanian carved gems and stucco decorations.
It is this circumstance – the construction of the vessel's motif out of standard elements, each of which is found separately on other objects - which deters one from regarding the bowl's theme as a symbolical depiction of the universe, although it shows water and dry land, flowers, birds and beasts. The purpose of lobed vessels is also unclear. The participants in ceremonial banquets are represent-

ed with such bowls in their hands in some works of monumental art.
Bibliography:
Smirnov 1909, No.76; Trever and Lukonin 1987, No.33; *Splendeur* 1993, No.84.

79. Aquamanile.
6th–7th century
Bronze, cast, inlaid with light-coloured paste for the eyes and the necklace with four round pendants. The handle is hollow, soldered to the body; in the centre of the handle is a funnel with two rings for the attachment of a lid. Height 34.5cm.
The Hermitage, St Petersburg.
Inv. No. Kz 5765. Purchased in Daghestan.

Bronze sculpture of the Sassanian age is very rare. A few bronze busts are known, portraying the Iranian shahanshahs of the Sassanian era (although doubts have been expressed as to their authenticity), two or three bronze figurines also representing shahanshahs (*eg* the

incense burner, Cat. No.81) and finally this aquamanile. It forms part of a group of marvellous bronze aquamaniles, incense burners and vessels in the form of various birds and beasts, in which the art of Iran and its neighbouring lands was so rich during the early medieval period (see Cat. Nos 84, 87, 92, 93). A goat wearing a necklace is a widespread motif in Sassanian art, possibly as the symbol of one of the Zoroastrian deities.

Bibliography:
Trever 1959, p.324, pl.20; Trever and Lukonin 1987, No.47.

80. LEG OF A THRONE.
6TH–7TH CENTURY
Bronze, cast. Height 29cm.
The Hermitage, St Petersburg.
Inv. No. Kz 6267.

The zoomorphic legs of shahanshahs' thrones (*takhts*) are commonly represented on Sassanian objects (see, for example, Cat. No.75). However, only four

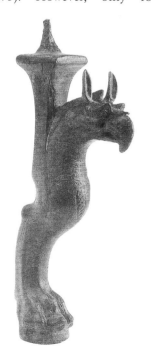

bronze examples have survived (two in the Metropolitan Museum, New York, one in the Hermitage and one in the Nizami Museum, Baku).

They all depict a protome – more exactly the head, body and leg - of a savage griffin with the beak of a bird of prey, a wolf's pricked ears, a "collar" of fur and a lion's claws. This terrible fantastic beast was a symbol in Sassanian Zoroastrianism of Verethragna, the god of victory, and its head appeared at the top of the crowns of Sassanian princes and queens (see Cat. No.46).

During excavations of the Sassanian town of Shush, a clay mould for the casting of such a leg was discovered.

Bibliography:
Lukonin 1977b, p.204; Trever and Lukonin 1987, No.49; Splendeur 1993, No.28.

81. INCENSE BURNER DEPICTING KHUSRAU II ON HORSEBACK.
LATE 6TH–EARLY 7TH CENTURY
Bronze, cast by the cire perdue method, details tooled with chisels. Height 35.6cm.
The Hermitage, St Petersburg.
Inv. No. Kz 5769. Purchased 1901 in Nakhichevan.

This object served as a censer: charcoal and incense were inserted into the rectangular orifice in the horse's side and smoke issued from the long slit running down the horse's mane and the openings in the rider's crown.

Khusrau II (591-628) is shown as on his coinage (the orb and crescent on the crown are missing). The body of the shahanshah is unnaturally small by comparison

with the head, and he has small, short legs shod in boots. The horse is decorated with a rich harness of phalerae (metal discs) alternating with tassels, plaques and ribbons. The image in its entirety is executed according to the typical canon of Sassanian monumental art.

In cast relief on the narrow front face of the rectangular stand there are two heraldic rampant lions and a leaping capricorn; on one of the side faces is a hunter with a dagger and shield, and a lion hurling itself at him, whilst on the other is a bough with bunches of grapes, an elephant and a fox.

Only the vine and the fox stretching towards it have analogies in other works of Sassanian art. The remaining motifs, although well known, are not depicted in genuinely Iranian style.

Bibliography:
Trever 1959, pp.327-330, pl.22; Trever and Lukonin 1987, No.48.

82. JUG WITH FLAUTIST AND FANTASTIC BEAST.
8TH-9TH CENTURY
Bronze, cast. Height 43cm.
The Hermitage, St Petersburg.
Inv. No. Kz 5725.

The jug has its origins in wine-jugs of this form which were typical of Sassanian Iran (see Cat. No.69). It is decorated with scenes that also have their origins in the repertory of Sassanian and Zoroastrian motifs.

The central scene consists of the figure of a flautist in a long pleated garment, standing next to a winged and horned dragon with

lion's claws, and it is found on a number of Sassanian objects, such as silver plates.

If it is based on a Sassanian iconographic scheme, then this fantastic creature evidently symbolized the entire animal and plant kingdoms; it has the head and claws of a carnivore, the horns of a herbivorous animal, the wings of a bird and plant shoots growing from its body. In that case the flautist standing next to it would represent the Zoroastrian deity of the animal and plant kingdoms, possibly the goddess Haurvatat or Ameretat. The rampant winged dragons represented on the neck of the jug are also Zoroastrian in their symbolism.

Judging by its shape, the style of the motifs and also by the fact that the central scene breaks the canonic rules, the jug was undoubtedly produced after the fall of the Sassanian state, when Sassanian compositions and forms were reproduced without any deep understanding of their symbolism, and yet were fashioned in a brilliant, traditional style, although one that was already becoming outfashioned.

Bibliography:
Marshak 1972, p.80; Trever and Lukonin 1987, No.50.

CAT N° 83

83. CAFTAN WITH SENMURVS. 9TH CENTURY

Silk (samite weave). Length 140cm; width 227cm.
The Hermitage, St Petersburg.
Inv. No. Kz 6584. Found in a ruined grave at Moshchevaya Balka (Northern Caucasus).

Clothes in such a good state of preservation are very rarely found in archaeological sites.

The cut of the caftan is indisputably local: all the men's caftans found at Moshchevaya Balka have a close-fitting top fastened with galloon ribbons and a wide skirt with slits for riding; however, they are usually made from ordinary textiles and only decorated with silk, which was as valued as gold during the early Middle Ages.

Thus the caftan in question is undoubtedly the costume of a chief of the local Adygo-Alan tribes. It was lined with squirrel fur; silk textiles of varied provenance (Sogdian, Chinese and Byzantine) were used for the trimmings and to reinforce the hems from inside.

Their variety was determined by the course of the trade route (the "Silk Road") which led over the north-western passes of the Caucasus near Moshchevaya Balka and linked Byzantium with Central Asia and the Far East by way of the Greek colonies on the Black Sea coast of the Caucaus.

This route was the reason why an enormous quantity of silk textiles accumulated in these parts of the Caucasus; caravans passing through were obliged to pay for the right of using a pass, for guides, porters, horses, etc. Usually in such cases the cloth was cut up and a small piece would be allotted to each person; in sewing garments one such piece would be joined to others. But this chief's caftan was entirely sewn from one piece of silk.

The silk is of marvellous quality, dense, heavy and lustrous, and decorated with a motif consisting of a right-facing figure of the fantastic Iranian beast, the Senmurv (see Cat. No.69), placed in a medallion surrounded by beading. Between the medallions are palmettes of intertwined lotuses, which were also frequently depicted on objects of art from Sassanian Iran.

This theme remained in the repertory of textile decoration for a particularly long period – until the 13th century, when its origins were, of course, long forgotten – and they helped spread this image throughout the world, as far as ancient Russia and Scandinavia. Silk was used to sew the ceremonial robes of the Iranian shahanshah and it is surprising that a garment of this precious material should have been found in a region so far from any large centres.

Bibliography:

Ierusalimskaya 1972; Jeroussalimskaja 1978; A A Ierusalimskaja, *The Caucasus on the Silk Road. Catalogue of the Temporary Exhibition*, St Petersburg, 1992, No.l (in Russian); *Splendeur* 1993, Nos 127, 128; *Great Art Treasures* 1994, No.448.

84. FIGURE OF AN EAGLE. BY SULEIMAN, 180 AW796-97 AD

Bronze (brass), cast, inlaid with silver and copper and engraved. Height 3 cm.
The Hermitage, St Petersburg.
Inv. No. IR-1567. Transferred 1939 from the Chechen-Ingush Museum, Grozny.

The vessel, in the form of bird of prey (most probably an eagle), was for a long time preserved and revered in the *aul* (village) of Erzi where it was seen during the last century. It is the oldest precisely dated bronze vessel made during the spread of Islam in the Near East.

It was previously thought that the vessel served as an incense burner, but there are too few openings for smoke in its upper part. It is more likely that this vessel, like a similar object in the Museum für Islamische Kunst in West Berlin, was an aquamanile (the opening in the lower part of the figure is of later origin).

The entire surface is richly ornamented and traces of silver and copper inlay survive in the outlines of the ornament and the letters of the inscription. It is possible that inlay once covered a larger area of the surface. The appearance of copper inlay in the 7th century was already well known. The vessel is evidence that at the end of the 8th century silver was also used as an inlay.

The inscription on the vessel is written in plain Kufic:

بسم الله الرحمن الرحيم بركة الله مما عمل
سليمن بمدينة العسر(؟)سنة ثمنن ومائة

"In the name of Allah the Merciful, the Compassionate!

Blessings from Allah. This is what Suleiman made in the town of al-F(q)... The year one hundred and eighty.".

The date (180 AH) was deciphered by L Gyuzalyan (1949) and afterwards by S Rice (1959).

Great controversy is aroused by the name of the town, insofar as the signs in this word permit several different readings. Rice read it as al-Fass, suggesting that an area of Nishapur is intended, and assuming that the letter "sin" has taken the place of the letter "za" (see Mayer 1959, pp.85, 92). Melikian-Chirvani considers that the name of the town should be understood as Kashan in Iran (with the initial letter as "qaf" and the "alif" omitted) or as Kasan in Central Asia; but with this version too the reading involves a number of difficulties. Above all, for the second letter to be read as "sin/shin", one stroke is lacking if the last letter is to be taken as a final "nun".

At the same time a correctly written "sin" occurs three times in the inscription. Apart from that, neither Kashan nor Kasan are mentioned in early Arab sources as centres of production for bronzeware. The town mentioned in the inscription has to date been sought in the eastern regions of Iran.

However, all the bronzeware of the 7th-8th centuries has analogies that come, on the whole, from the area to the west of Iran, possibly from Iraq (or Syria) where the centre of the Caliphate was situated. Evidently this town should be sought somewhere to the west of Iran.

Apart from that, it has now become clear that inlay on bronzeware appeared in Eastern Iran no earlier than the 11th century (see Ivanov 1985). This fact also casts doubt on the Eastern Iranian origin of the object under discussion.

Bibliography:

Kesati 1940; Gyuzalyan 1949; Dyakonov 1951; Melikian-Chirvani 1977b: Islam 1985, p.109, No.5; Masterpieces 1990, No.l ; Great Art Treasures 1994, No.403; Treasures 1994, No.4.

85. EWER. 8TH–9TH CENTURY

Bronze, cast, forged and punched.
Height 40.5cm.
The Hermitage, St Petersburg.
Inv. No. IR-2316. Transferred 1925 from the State Academy for the History of Material Culture; formerly in the A. Bobrinsky collection.

The ewer has a high neck and a spout in the form of a bird with wings folded across its back. It is decorated with relief designs on the neck and handle and fine vegetal ornament completely covering the surface of the body. Such luxuriant vegetal design totally subordinated to a classical harmony of form is characteristic of an entire group of similar bronze ewers. The entire group is usually assigned to the first half or middle of the 8th century, in accord with the stylistic features of the majority of the articles. The dated inscription on the figure of the eagle (see Cat. No.84) shows that such vessels were also produced in the late 8th and early 9th centuries.

The design reveals characteristics of Syrian and Iraqi art during the first centuries of Islam: these are seen in traditional stylistic elements from the former eastern provinces of Byzantium – which were by then vitally important regions of the Arab Caliphate – combined with isolated elements of Iranian and even Central Asian art (as in the ring-matted ground or the cast butterfly in the hawk's talons). The ewer can scarcely be of Iranian workmanship; in all likelihood it was made in Iraq.

But we can form some idea of how Iranian art developed during the 8th and 9th centuries, insofar as it is precisely on objects such as this that one sees features of the Sassanian inheritance together with the influence of art from the centre of the Caliphate.

Bibliography:

Marshak 1972, pp.80, 81; *Islam* 1985, p.108, No.l; *Masterpieces* 1990, No.3.

86. EWER. BY ABU YAZID.
8TH–9TH CENTURY

Bronze, cast and punched, with ring-matted ground. Height 64.8cm.
Art Museum of Georgia, Tbilisi.
Inv. No. V5.

This outstanding example of early Islamic bronzeware bears a dated inscription which includes the craftsman's name. In spite of that, however, the date remains disputed. The circular Arabic inscription round the crown, executed in plain Kufic with decoration on the tips of the, downstrokes of the letters "ra", "za" and "nun", reads as follows:

بركة مـن صنعه ابو يزيد عمل بالبصرة سنة تسع وستين

"Blessings. Of the works of Abu Yazid, of those made in Basra in the year sixty-nine".

In the original the last word of the inscription is "sixty". This word would not fit into the space left for it and its end is cramped, whereas the following word, "blessings", is written very freely, being the first of the inscription.

This is very important in dating the vessel insofar as it should be assigned to 60 AH/688-89AD according to the inscription, while its decoration suggests a date one or two hundred years later.

The complicated ornament of the bottom and sides of the foot, the neck and the widening of the handle at the top go back to the decoration of 8th-century Central Asian silverware, and in its almost abstract stylization it is close to 9th-century Mesopotamian stucco.

One can match the date on the inscription with the ornament if one assumes that the inscription was not finished owing to a miscalculation of its space.

In that case, after the word "sixty" the full text would have had the conjunction "and" followed by the word "hundred" or "two hundred".

The later dating – such as 269 AH/882-83 AD suggested in 1972 by Boris Marshak – was disputed by Géza Fehérvari, but supported by James Allan.

In the style of its decoration and the suggested later date of manufacture, the ewer is very close to one of the same shape in the Keir collection, England.

Several other ewers of analogous form are known, the decoration of which is sometimes similar to the ornament of the ewer in question, but more frequently of later date with counterparts among Khurasan and Central Asian bronzeware of the 12th century. In general, castbronze ewers of the 8th-13th centuries reveal an astounding stability of form coupled with a rapid evolution of the decoration.

This ewer was manufactured not in Iran but in Iraq, yet it relates to a number of pieces that in many ways defined the development of medieval Iranian and Central Asian bronzes. One observes in its form the combination of Byzantine and Sassanian traditions which is characteristic of early Islamic art.

Bibliography:
Dyakonov 1947a; Marshak 1972, p.72; Fehérvari 1976, pp.25-27, 32, pl.1a; Allan 1976; Melikian-Chirvani 1976b, p.291.

87. FIGURE OF A COCKEREL. 8TH–13TH CENTURY

Bronze (brass), cast, inlaid with copper and engraved. Height 41.5cm.
Museum of Ethnology, St Petersburg.
Inv. No. 2046/2. Acquired 1909 from von Peters.

It has not yet been precisely established what function was served by these early Islamic metal vessels in the form of birds or beasts. Apparently they were used either as aquamaniles or incense burners. The technique of this cockerel-shaped vessel is close to the figure of the eagle (Cat. No.84), although the latter is inlaid with silver and copper whereas only the eyes of the cockerel are inlaid with copper. Judging by the colour of the metal and the different ornamentation on the tail, the latter is a later addition.

Two holes in the body and neck suggest that a handle was attached here (as on the figure of an eagle in the Museum für Islamische Kunst in Berlin) and that the vessel was used to hold water, which would have been poured into it through an orifice in place of the tail or through a hollow handle. Near the left eye are traces of a word written in *naskhi* script. It is difficult to determine the vessel's place of manufacture. We must assume that this object, like the eagle figure (Cat. No.84), was made at the centre of the Arab Caliphate, in Iraq, or the western regions of Iran. First publication.

88. EWER. 9TH CENTURY

Bronze, cast and inlaid with copper. Height 44.5cm.
The Hermitage, St Petersburg.
Inv. No. IR-2314. Transferred 1925 from the State Academy for the History of Material Culture; formerly in the A Bobrinsky collection.

The ewer has an egg-shaped body and a handle crowned with a pomegranate; it is in many respects similar to the ewer Cat. No.85, but belongs to the following stage in the history of bronze ewer production in Iran and Central Asia. The relief design, copper inlay and other features are similar to the decoration of bronze ewers similar in form to Sassanian models.

Many peculiarities of form, such as the egg-shaped body, the high neck, the handle crowned with a pomegranate, etc., were to remain characteristics of cast bronze ewers up to the 13th century. The details of this particular ewer's vegetal ornament are no longer Sassanian but early Islamic.

All in all the combination of the foliate relief twining round the body and the smooth neck separated by a beaded relief pattern bring to mind the design of small, early Sassanian, silver jugs. All of this permits one to suppose that the ewer was made by an Iranian or – although this is less likely – an Iraqi craftsman.

Bibliography:

Orbeli and Trever, 1935, fig.74; Marshak 1972, p.81.

89. TRAY. 9TH–10TH CENTURY

Bronze, embossed and tooled with punches. Diameter 73.5cm.
The Hermitage, St Petersburg.
Inv. No. Kz-2321. Acquired 1926 from an inhabitant of the village of Kubachi, Daghestan.

In trays dating from the first centuries of Islam one can trace the same general tendency as in ewers (Cat. Nos 85, 88): early examples (7th–9th centuries) follow the traditions of the formerly Byzantine provinces of Syria and Egypt, whereas later examples (9th–10th centuries), while preserving their link with these traditions, display increasingly Iranian decorative motifs. This particular tray is tooled with a great variety of patterns, but the basic decorative motif is a medallion encircled by beads. The total absence of any sort of figural representation and the rhythmic division of the surface are less like Sassanian decoration than that of early Islamic architectural stucco work.

The tray is close to earlier examples (8th–9th centuries) in which the Iranian features are much less strongly expressed: the similarity is revealed in the rhythmical organization of the decorative surface and in a number of details (a vase with a plant in a medallion, shoots emerging from the sides of a vase, buds with petals curling outwards, small rosettes in the background, etc.).

Bibliography:

Orbeli and Trever 1935, fig.68; Marshak 1978, Marschak 1986, pl.206; *Masterpieces* 1990, No.8; *Great Art Treasures* 1994. No.408.

CAT N° 89

CAT N° 90

90. TRAY. 10TH CENTURY

Bronze, embossed. Diameter 58cm.
The Hermitage, St Petersburg.
Inv. No. IR-2322. Transferred 1925
from the State Academy for the History
of Material Culture; formerly in the
A Bobrinsky collection.

This tray is one of the very latest surviving early Islamic tray-plates. Many details link it to earlier examples of this group, but the general composition of its imagery is new and unlike the decoration of any other object. The mounted hunter (Bahram Gur), pairs of beasts confront or regard, a lion attacking another creature, are all frequently depicted on similar items. However, the motifs are portrayed here in another order than the usual, logical one: Bahram Gur is not sited in the centre but above, by the rim. The figures of the beasts are enlarged and more significant than that of the rider on his camel, who seems lost among them. Instead of the luxuriant foliage decorating other trays there remain only frail, hardly perceptible twigs.

The scene of the pouncing beast, the eagle carrying a woman, Bahram Gur and Azadeh (see Cat. No.71) are all of Iranian origin, already known to Sassanian art. The Iranian tradition has almost entirely forced out the traces of the Byzantine inheritance taken up in the 7th-9th centuries in early Islamic art. However, the plate's stylized images are closer to Islamic objects of the 10th-11th centuries than to Sassanian ones: the disposition of the motifs is haphazard; we have no

idea what Bahram Gur is shooting at; the gazelles are bigger than the lions; the figure of the woman on the eagle's breast is very small. All the themes have acquired a decorative rather than a symbolic significance.

Bibliography:
Orbeli and Trever 1935, fig.69; Marshak 1978; Marschak 1986, pl.204.

91. CUP. 9TH–10TH CENTURY

Bronze (brass), cast, turned and engraved. Diameter 11.8cm.
The Hermitage, St Petersburg. Inv.
No. IR-2 II 8. Acquired 1976.

This small, almost hemispherical cup is decorated inside and out with engraved details.

The nature of the decoration places this cup among a large group of items made between the end of the 8th century and the middle of the 9th century in the province of Khurasan, where the majority of objects from this group were found (see Melikian-Chirvani 1974), whereas hardly more than ten such pieces have been found in other regions.

There is neither inlay nor inscription on any of the pieces. Apparently they appeared only at a later stage of the group's evolution, no earlier than the 11th century. First publication.

92. FIGURE OF A HORSE. 10TH CENTURY

Bronze (brass), cast, turned and engraved. Height 36cm; length 42cm.
The Hermitage, St Petersburg.
Inv. No. IR-1984. Transferred 1925
from the State Academy for the History
of Material Culture; formerly in the
A Bobrinsky collection.

The figure of the horse once formed a main part of a complex sculptural group, for judging by the insert on the back and the lack of ornamention on the saddlecloth there was originally a rider. A shaft was fastened to the pintle fitted on the horse's crupper: in all probability this was the base of a lamp and the sculptural group once served as a lamp-stand.

The figure is richly decorated with engraved designs of people, birds, beasts and foliage. The ground is punched. Arabic inscriptions were engraved on the pendants of the crupper-strap under the tail, but only the text on the right pendant has survived (the script is Kufic):

بركة من الله لصاحبه

"Allah's blessings on the owner of this object".

From the form of the lettering one can confidently date the article to the 10th century.

Bibliography:
Orbeli and Trever 1935, fig.84; Dyakonov 1947b; *Islam* 1985, p.115, No.24; *Masterpieces* 1990, No.10.

93. INCENSE BURNER. 9TH–10TH CENTURY

Bronze, cast and chased. Height 39cm.
The Hermitage, St Petersburg.
Inv. No. IR-2324. Purchased 1935.

This incense burner in the form of a pheasant originally had a detachable tail so that incense could be inserted; this part was later soldered on and sealed up. In individual details, in particular the tooling of the feathers and the rosette on the breast, the vessel has a certain similarity to the incense

burner in the shape of an eagle of 180 AH/796-97 AD (see Cat. No.84). However, the stylization of the entire form of the pheasant has been taken a great deal further.

Bibliography:
Dyakonov 1947b.

94. JUG. 10TH CENTURY

Silver, chased and partly gilded.
Height 16cm.
The Hermitage, St Petersburg.
Inv. No. V3-795.

This jug is one of the very few silver vessels from the 10th century: judging by its Kufic Arabic inscription it belonged to a certain Abu Sa'id Iraq b al-Husain, client of the lord of the faithful. This was the title of vassal lords in Iran and Central Asia and of emancipated slaves of caliphs, or sometimes sons of emancipated slaves too. Although the caliph's clients in general lived in Iraq and Western Iran, estates belonging to the caliph survived in Khurasan, which in the 10th century belonged to the Samanids of Bukhara, and he had representatives there.

Pheasants or peacocks with twigs in their beaks take over from the pre-Islamic figures of birds carrying the royal necklace. From its decoration this jug could be assigned to Khurasan.

Bibliography:

Smirnov 1909, No.127; Marshak 1976, pp.155, 156: Marschak 1986, pl.128.

95. JUG. 10TH CENTURY

Silver, chased (handle, legs and soldered birds' heads on the body are cast). Height 17cm.
The Hermitage, St Petersburg.
Inv. No. V3-796. Acquired 1896 from the Imperial Archaeological Commission.

In the treatment of details this jug is close to the preceding one, but is distinguished by its fanciful form and luxuriance of decoration. The birds in relief on the body are similar to the birds on 12th-century Khurasan bronze vessels. Even the vessel's legs are made in the form of small birds. A Senmurv is depicted on the neck of the vessel; a peacock with a ribbon round its neck and a twig in its beak, and two other birds are also shown. The Sassanian motif is distorted: the position of the Senmurv's feet is unusual – it is not flying but standing. The background is ring-matted, which is traditional for works from both Central Asia and Khurasan, but the absence of any purely Central Asian features

obliges one rather to assign the vessel to Khurasan. Despite the extreme refinement of the decoration, the Kufic inscription, in 9th- or 10th-century script, is very simple both in its calligraphy and content: "Allah's blessings and prosperity and joy be upon al-Husain b Ali". The formula is typical of the 10th century. The name and patronymic referred to in the inscription are those of the famous Shi'ite martyr, son of Ali and grandson of Muhammad; no title or *nisba* is given.

The historian Ibn al-Athir relates an episode occurring in the 920s and involving al-Husain ibn Ali Marwarrudi. This was a man who had led a difficult life, a Shi'ite and rebel who had spent long years in prison. After being freed he joined the retinue of the Samanid Amir of Bukhara. Once al-Husain rebuked the son of the vicegerent of Nishapur (the capital of Khurasan) who had offered the Amir water in a plain ewer: "Surely your father must be able to send good, graceful ewers from Nishapur – My father sends such as you [*ie* rebels] and not ewers from Khurasan." And al-Husain bowed his head, compelled to remain silent.

Although it is impossible to prove, it is perfectly conceivable that it was this al-Husain ibn Ali from Khurasan who ordered this purposely graceful ewer.

Bibliography:

Smirnov 1909, No.128; Marshak 1976, pp.155, 156; Marschak 1986, pl.127.

96. SAUCER. 11TH CENTURY

Silver, tooled with punches, gilded and nielloed (king's eyes). Diameter 10.3cm.

The Hermitage, St Petersburg.

Inv. No. S-499. Acquired 1951 (discovered in a hoard of the 12th-13th century, near the village of Muzhi in the Yamalo-Nenetsky national region).

This saucer depicting a palace reception has been related to the art of Central Asia of the 6th- or 8th-9th century.

However, the peculiar two-horned hats of the courtiers and other peculiarities suggest a different attribution. Such hats were worn by courtiers and slave-guards of the Ghaznavids who ruled the territories of Khurasan and Southern Transoxiana in the 11th century, and the eastern part of these domains in the 12th century. The characters' footwear resembles that in paintings at the Ghaznavid palace in Lashkari Bazar in Afghanistan.

The composition on the saucer is very similar to that of a silver medal of about the 10th century, found at Nishapur, but many decorative details have their analogies among Khurasan 9th-century silverware. All of this compels one to assign the piece to the beginning of Ghaznavid rule in Khurasan in the late 10th- early 11th-centuries when the famous Mahmud Ghaznavi was proclaimed king. Possibly it is he who is portrayed on the saucer. The wide, Mongoloid face of the main figure lends full support to such an assumption.

Several features of the composition lead one to assume that the saucer was made within the tradition of late official Sassanian metalwork. But the iconography of the royal reception here is already of a later type, elaborated during the 9th-century in Khurasan and by the 13th century dominant throughout the world of Islam.

Bibliography:

Trever 1960; Marshak 1971, pp.66-68, fig.29; Marschak 1986, pl.33; Masterpieces 1990, No.19.

97. FRAGMENT OF TEXTILE. 11TH-12TH CENTURY

Silk (lampas weave). 38 x 16.5cm.
The Hermitage, St Petersburg. Inv. No. IR-2012. Transferred 1925 from the History Museum, Moscow.

In a large medallion (more than half a metre in diameter) the figure of a lion-clawed griffin rampant at the sides of the Tree of Life is symmetrically repeated. The Tree of Life is highly ornamented and below it there are plant shoots branching off to the right and left in the form of garlands of lotus flowers, filling the entire space within the medallion: the figures of the griffins are represented against this background. The medallion is framed by a two-line Arabic inscription (in Kufic script) against a ground of leafy stalks and palmettes, which is poorly preserved.

The inscription begins below, under the Tree of Life, from whence the words diverge to the right and left (half the text reads as a mirror image). So far only the first word has been deciphered – *barakat*, "blessing".

Only a part of the right-hand griffin figure has been preserved on this fragment of textile.

A larger fragment of the same textile, depicting the central part and right half of the medallion's design and giving one an impression of the image as a whole, is now in the Museum of Georgian History, Tbilisi.

Earlier it was kept in Svaneti (Georgia) in the Church of St George at the village of Syuti, from whence the Hermitage piece also came.

The textile is executed in the so-called *lampas* weave which appeared in Iran during the 10th and 11th centuries and heralded a new stage in the development of Near Eastern weaving.

Bibliography:

Meisterwerke 1912, vol.III, pl.179; Ketskhoveli 1972.

98. LAMP-STAND.
11TH–CENTURY

Bronze (brass), cast and engraved.
Height 44cm.
The Donish Institute of History,
Dyushambe.

Bronze lamp-stands consisting of a round base on three legs, with a figural shaft and a flat plate on top, were very wide-spread in Iran during the 10th-13th centuries.

Two types of base are known for these stands – lobed and circular. The earliest of them date from the

late 10th century, the latest from the early 13th century.

The stand in question was discovered in 1965 during excavations at the site of Khulbuk in the south of Tajikistan. The stand is fairly modestly decorated: on two of the four facets of its shaft the same benedictory Arabic inscription is engraved in Kufic script against a clear ground:

بركة من الله لصاحبه

"Allah's blessings on the owner of this".

The dating of this object to the first half of the 11th century is supported by archaeological evidence, since the site of Khulbuk was destroyed in the mid-11th century.

Such a dating is not contradicted by the epigraphic evidence – the intertwining letters, "sad" and "qaf", and also the somewhat archaic formula itself, "Allah's blessings" (later it would simply be "Blessings on the owner of this").

Bibliography:
Art of Central Asia 1980, ill.64; *The Antiquities of Tajikistan. Exhibition Catalogue*, Dyushambe, 1985, No.726 (in Russian).

99. INCENSE BURNER.
LATE 10TH–EARLY 11TH CENTURY

Bronze (brass), forged, pierced and engraved. Height 15.7cm.
The Institute of History of Turkmenian Academy of Sciences, Ashkhabad. Discovered at Serakhs in 1970.

Such vessels on a low foot with bodies widened at the top and with openwork ornamentation have only attracted the attention of scholars in the last decade. At present four sim-

ilar pieces have been published, three of which are decorated round the upper rim with Arabic inscriptions so close to each other in their lettering that the must surely be from the same workshop (see SPA 193, 8-39, vol.VI pl.1290a; *Arts of Islam* 1981, No.38). The upper part (lid?) of all these objects is missing, although one can assume that it was also openwork.

It is the openwork decoration and the small size of these pieces which lead one to assume that they served as incense burners.

The Arabic benedictory inscription is executed in lettering characteristic of the late 10th early 11th centuries:

بركة ويمن وسرور وسعادة . . . .

"Blessings and happiness and joy and prosperity...".

Bibliography:
Atagarryyev and Khodzhageldyyev 1972, p.28; Pugachenkova and Rempel 1982, p.253.

100. INCENSE BURNER.
BY ALI IBN ABU NASR.
11TH CENTURY

Bronze (brass), cast and engraved. Height 27.5cm; length 23.5cm.
The Donish Institute of History, Dyushambe. Inv. No. 571/1.

This incense burner in the form of a feline predator (a lynx, to judge by the ear-tips) was found during excavations at the site of Khulbuk (Southern Tajikistan) in 1978. Its construction differs slightly from that of similar objects – the head and neck are not detachable but fold forward on a hinge.

The incense burner is decorated with engraved and pierced ornaments. The decoration is especially luxuriant on the head and neck, where one should note the narrow strips filled with circlets dotted in the centre.

It is this design which links the incense burner to a large group of Khurasan objects of the 8th-9th centuries (see Cat. No.91). Engraved palmettes, rosettes and "knots" are found on the paws and the back of the body. Along the body, on both sides, there are cartouches with Arabic inscriptions in Kufic script:

عمل علي ابن ابي نصر

"Made by Ali ibn Abi Nasr";

كل عمل رجال

"To every work – [its] accomplishers..".

Insofar as the incense burner has an archaeological dating – not later than the mid-11th century (when Khulbuk perished) – it enables us to date other, similar incense burners more accurately (earlier they were assigned to the 11th-12th centuries). The palaeographical analysis of the inscription is entirely in accordance with this date.

Bibliography:
Art of Central Asia 1980; UNESCO *Courrier*, November 1980, pp.40, 41; *The Antiquities of Tajikistan. Exhibition Catalogue*, Dyushambe, 1985, No.716 (in Russian); *Oxus. 2000 Jahre Kunst am Oxus-Fluss in Mittelasien. Museum Rietberg*, Zurich, 1989, No.93.

CAT N° 100

CAT Nº 101

101. INCENSE BURNER.
11TH CENTURY
Bronze (brass), cast, inlaid with copper and silver and engraved. Height 45cm.
The Hermitage, St Petersburg.
Inv. No. IR-1565.

This incense burner in the form of a feline predator (in all probability a lynx, see Cat. No.100) belongs to a large group of similar objects, apparently widespread in their time. At least nine complete figures and five detached heads have survived. The breast and head of the lynx are inlaid only with copper discs. In the cartouche on the breast letters of a Kufic inscription are executed in silver:

علی بن محمد الطاجی (؟)

"Ali ibn Muhammad al-Tajji (?)".

The nisba of the person is still incomprehensible. The inscription does not indicate whether the name belongs to the owner or the craftsman. There are bands on the neck and body with engraved Arabic inscriptions, benedictory in their content, written in Kufic script. The text is repeated several times, beginning with the words:

"with happiness and blessings".

and ending as usual with:

"to the owner of this".

From the nature of the script, the ornament in the form of five-leaved palmettes and the modest inlay, this object can be assigned to the 11th century.

Bibliography:
Orbeli 1938; Dyakonov 1947b; Mayer 1959, p.37; *Islam* 1985, p.129, No.5; *Content and Context of Visual Arts in the Islamic World*, Philadelphia-London, 1988, p.42, fig.11; *Arts of Persia* 1989, p.172, pl.4; *Masterpieces* 1990, No.18; *Great Art Treasures* 1994, No.403.

102. INCENSE BURNER.
11TH - 12TH CENTURY
Bronze (brass), cast, inlaid with copper and silver and engraved. Height 20.7cm.
The Hermitage, St Petersburg.
Inv. No. IR-1669. Purchased 1958.

Among the various types of incense burner which were widespread during pre-Mongol times, one fairly frequently comes across similar examples, with a circular body on three legs and an open half-cupola with a bird on top. Along the rim of the half-cupola words of an Arabic inscription in *naskhi* script are fitted into two cartouches; it has not yet been possible to decipher it. On the body, between two guilloches, are three cartouches separated by medallions containing vegetal ornamentations. The cartouches contain an Arabic inscription in Kufic script, its ground tooled with punches:

بالیمن و * البرکة ولا * لتدمة

"Happiness and blessings and perfection".

(the third word is slightly deformed: "alif" in the middle is represented like "lam"). The letters "alif" and "lam" of the definite article are intertwined.

Next to the medallions of this band are engraved pairs of birds which were probably covered with silver leaf (traces remain on one bird). Silver inlay also survives on the figure of the bird on top of the incense burner. It is possible the silver inlay was added later than the copper inlay of the inscription. At the bottom a pacing beast (probably a lion) is depicted in a medallion. The ground here is also matt-tooled with a punch.
First publication.

103. INCENSE BURNER.
11TH CENTURY

Bronze (brass), cast and engraved.
Height 36cm.
The Hermitage, St Petersburg.
Inv. No. IR-2323. Purchased 1936.

This incense burner in the form of a cockerel, which now stands firmly on clipped claws and rests on its wing-tips, does not correspond to its original appearance. It clearly had long claws (like the eagle and cockerel – see Cat. Nos 84 and 87), projecting a little, which made the object unsteady. Therefore props were essential, of the type seen on the aquamanile in the shape of a hawk kept at the monastery of St Catherine in the Sinai Peninsula (see Weitzmann 1964, p.122). The oval holes on the reverse of the wing-tips are the traces of these props (the hole below in the centre of the body is apparently of later origin). Insofar as there are no traces of a handle on the upper part of the object, one can confidently assume that it served as an incense burner.

The treatment of the plumage on the legs and wings links this vessel with earlier ones. The human figures in the large medallion on the cockerel's breast and in the small one on its back have their counterparts among silver medallions of the Buyid period; hence one can assign this particular incense burner to the late 10th – early 11th century.
Bibliography:
Orbeli and Trever 1935, fig.82; Dyakonov 1947b; *Content and Context of Visual Arts in the Islamic World*, Philadelphia-London, 1988, p.42, fig.9.

104. EWER. BY AL-FADL.
LATE 10TH - EARLY 11TH CENTURY

Bronze (brass), cast, forged, engraved and inlaid with copper. Height 37cm; diameter 22.5cm.
Museum of Georgian History, Tbilisi.
Inv. No. MS 134.

The ewer is decorated with benedictory Arabic inscriptions executed in Kufic script (on the neck, the shoulders and the fluting of the body) and in *naskhi* script (on a flute, but the text is incomprehensible). On another flute under the pouring lip the craftsman's signature is written in Kufic script:

عمل ا * الفضل

"Made by al-Fadl".

(although the name could also be read as "Ba Fadl").

The intertwined letters "alif-lam" and other factors, as well as some ornaments, allow one to assign the fabrication of this ewer to the late 10th-early 11th century.
Bibliography:
Collections 1902, p.199, pl.XIV.

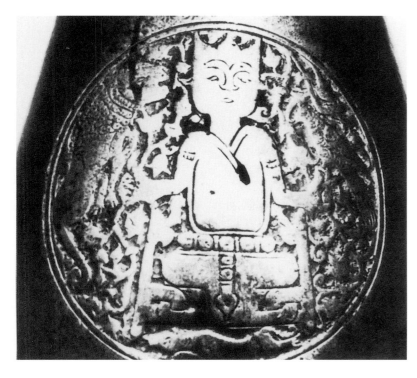

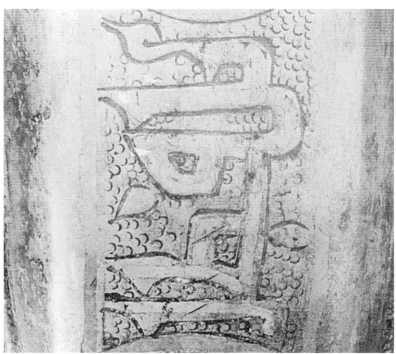

105. CAULDRON.
11TH CENTURY

Bronze (brass), cast and engraved.
Height 53.4cm.
The Hermitage, St Petersburg.
Inv. No. TP-161. Transferred 1925 from the State Academy for the History of Material Culture; formerly in the A Bobrinsky collection.

The cauldron was cast in a mould consisting of two halves (the souldering is visible under the rim). The ornament on the upper part consists of relief arcs but the everted rim is more richly decorated, with two rosettes and two cartouches with an Arabic inscription in Kufic script:

اليـمن واليركة و * البركة ولصاحبه

"Happiness and blessings" and
"blessings and to the owner of this".

The inscription, standard in the first cartouche, is unusual in the second one where the word "blessings" is repeated with the conjunction "and" after it, unnecessarily in this particular instance. The ground of the inscription is decorated with twigs and palmettes. The words:

السعاد مرد سلامـة

"happiness... prosperity"

are also engraved on the cauldron in plain Kufic.

It is not clear when this shape emerged. Only a small number of cauldrons with spherical bodies is known. One of them, completely analogous in form and decoration, is in the Archaeological Museum in Tehran. The rim of that cauldron also bears rosettes and three inscriptions in "floriated" Kufic:

بركة لصاحبه * مـحـمـد بـن اسـحاق * لكل احل كتاب

"Blessings to the owner of this Muhammad ibn Ishaq II to all times - their duty".

From the nature of the script one can date the cauldron to the 11th century.
There is one more cauldron in the Archaeological Museum in Tehran, also with a spherical body and two massive handles, but its everted rim is narrow and has two small, horizontal projections. The dating of this cauldron is hindered by the absence of ornament and inscription. The third, smaller cauldron with a spherical body (height 29.5cm) on three legs and with two massive handles is in the Linden Museum, Stuttgart and originates in the Ghazni region (see Kalter 1982, D 48).
The everted rim and upper part of the body are richly decorated with ornament and an inscription with silver inlay. This object dates from the second half of the 12th century. Thus, from the nature of their script, the earliest examples of these cauldrons date from the 11th century. Their place of manufacture remains unclear.

Two more cauldrons, of a shape akin to these three items, also exist; one of them is in the Art Museum of Georgia in Tbilisi (see Cat. No.106) and the second was in a private collection in Tehran.
They are also on three legs, with two massive handles and an everted rim, but unlike the above mentioned cauldrons they have a long pouring lip.
First publication.

106. CAULDRON.
LATE 10TH CENTURY
Bronze (brass), cast and engraved.
Height 70cm; diameter 64cm.
Art Museum of Georgia, Tbilisi. Inv.
No. 1/1.

It is the only one of its form in the collections of the former Soviet Union (there was another cauldron with a pouring lip in a private collection in Tehran). The cauldron was cast in a mould consisting of three parts: two hemispherical halves (the souldering is visible under the lip and on the inside) and a lower round part with legs and relief ornament.
The ornament on the lowest part of the cauldron is unique insofar as, at the time, if part of the object was

not visible to the observer, it was left undecorated.
The everted rim is adorned with an undulating tendril with long leaves, which is similar in style to early Islamic objects. There is a short inscription on the lip:

بركة لصاحبه

"Blessings on the owner of this object".

The character of the Kufic script, with split apices on several letters, dates the cauldron to the late 10th century.
First publication.

107. MIRROR. 10TH CENTURY
Bronze (brass), cast. Length 20.6cm;
diameter 14.2cm.
The Hermitage, St Petersburg.

Inv. No. SA-12689. Acquired 1899 (?) from the Imperial Archaeological Commission.

During the early Middle Ages bronze (brass) mirrors became widespread throughout the Islamic world. They were always of the same shape: round and flat with a polished face and a reverse ornamented in relief. In the centre of the reverse side was a pierced boss through which a string passed to serve as a handle. In some instances the rim might be thicker or the mirror might have a handle.
This particular mirror is one of the earliest examples of a bronze mirror made in Iran. It bears a hunting motif in the central cir-

cle and an Arabic inscription executed in Kufic script and repeated four times:

امن من امن بالله

"He is safe who has faith in Allah".

The plain character of the Kufic script, the bend in the top extension of the letter "lam" and the winged crown on the rider's head enable one to assign the mirror to the Buyid period, that is, the 10th century.
Bibliography:
Balashova 1940.

110. FLASK.
11TH - 12TH CENTURY
Blown glass. Height 14.8 cm.
The Hermitage, St Petersburg.
Inv. No. IR-2115. Acquired 1893
from the Yu. Lemme collection.

From its shape and the decoration with glass of a different colour, the flask can be assigned to the 11th-12th century.
First publication.

108. INCENSE BURNER.
12TH CENTURY
Bronze (brass), forged, pierced and engraved. Height 21cm.
Institute of History, Ashkhabad.
Found 1970 at Serakhs.

This openwork incense burner apparently had a handle on one side. The upper part folds sideways on a hinge.
Its shape attests to the variety of incense burners in existence during the pre-Mongol period.
Bibliography: Atagarryyev and Khodzhageldyyev 1972, p.32.

109. LAMP-STAND.
11TH CENTURY
Bronze (brass), cast and engraved.
Height 89.5cm.
The Hermitage, St Petersburg.
Inv. No. IR-1449. Transferred 1925 from the State Academy for the History of Material Culture; formerly in the A Bobrinsky collection.

This stand is possibly formed from the parts – the base and the shaft – of two different, although roughly contemporary, objects, insofar as the diameter of the base at the top is a little wider than

that of the shaft. Both parts are decorated with engraved and pierced ornament. The edge of the base is badly damaged and not all its decoration is clearly visible, but it is possible to make out imitation feathers as on early figural vessels (see Cat. No.103): there were evidently bird's heads here, as on other similar objects. The palmettes on the shaft are also of an archaic form. All these indications enable one to date the article to the 11th century.
Bibliography:
SPA 1938–39, vol.VI, pl.1283a.

111. FLASK.
11TH–12TH CENTURY
Blown glass. Height 11cm.
The Hermitage, St Petersburg.
Inv. No. IR-2114. Acquired 1898 from the Urfalidis collection.

This flask of blue glass was blown into a mould; two small handles imitate animal figures. Similar objects are usually dated to the 11th-12th centuries when, to judge by surviving examples there was an increase in the production of glassware in Iran.
First publication.

112. BUCKET. LATE 11TH–FIRST HALF OF 12TH CENTURY

Bronze (brass), cast, forged and engraved.
Height (without handle) 17.5cm.
Museum of Ethnology, St Petersburg.
Inv. 16260. Transferred 1948 from the Museum of the Peoples of the USSR, Moscow.

The outer surface of the bucket's body is decorated with five bands of engraved details. The second band is filled with an Arabic inscription in Kufic script:

باليمن والبركة لصاحبه والتـامـة والسلامة
والسعادة

"with happiness and blessings to the owner of this and perfection and prosperity".

The letters "alif" and "lam" of the definite article are intertwined (this is fairly seldom encountered, see Cat. Nos 102, 104); the word "salamat" contains a mistake ("waw" instead of "mim").
The inscription is an ordinary benedictory one, but its word order differs from that of dozens of similar texts. The fourth band is divided into five parts; each part contains large medallions with figures of birds and, above them, small medal-

lions also with bird figures and depictions of plants.
The group of objects with a matt-tooled ground is assigned to Khurasan in the 11th–early 12th centuries but their centre of production has not been determined. First publication.

113. MORTAR. 12TH CENTURY

Bronze (brass), cast, engraved and inlaid with copper. Height 13.6cm.
The Hermitage, St Petersburg.
Inv. No. IR-1465. Transferred 1925 from the State Academy for the History of Material Culture; formerly in the A Bobrinsky collection.

A fair number of such mortars have survived (more than fifty are known). They are usually cylindrical in shape, but the external surface of the body is sometimes rounded or faceted, and the top and bottom edges may be wide and everted. However, the decoration of the outer walls can be varied and a typology of these objects' forms and decorations has not yet been established.
All the mortars known at present, date from pre-Mongol times – 12th–13th centuries. However, it is difficult to imagine that during the 14th–18th centuries mortars fell into disuse and were no longer manufactured (though it is true that early mortars might remain serviceable for a very long time).
The Hermitage mortar is very richly decorated both with copper inlay and with various designs and inscriptions.
Above, on the everted rim, are six cartouches separated by medallions. The cartouches contained

Arabic inscriptions which are badly damaged.
The decoration of the external surface of the sides consists of three bands: on the first there are six cartouches with an Arabic inscription in *naskhi* script:

العز الد * ائم والاقبا * ل والدولة و * الدوامة
و * التاييد و * البقا لصاحبه

"Long fame and happiness and power... and constancy and support and length of life to the owner of this".

The second band bears ornaments. The third one resembles the first in its decoration, but the Arabic inscription – its exact counterpart as regards content – is written in Kufic script.
At the base there are six cartouches along the edge, separated by medallions containing palmettes.
The ornament in the cartouches

is faint. In the centre is a large six-leaved palmette, the ground is tooled with a punch.
One peculiarity of the Kufic inscription must be pointed out – the intertwined letters "alif" and "lam".
On this evidence, and also that of the punched ground, the mortar can be assigned to the group of articles (see Cat. Nos 104, 112) manufactured in the province of Khurasan in the 11th–12th centuries.
First publication.

114. INK POT.
SECOND HALF OF 12TH–EARLY 13TH CENTURY

Bronze (brass), cast, engraved and inlaid with silver and copper. Height 10.5cm; diameter 8.2cm.
The Hermitage, St Petersburg.
Inv. No. IR-1533. Transferred 1925 from the State Academy for the History of Material Culture; formerly in the N Veselovsky collection.

Evidence of widespread literacy in the Muslim world exists in the form of hundreds of manuscripts and in the numerous names of calligraphers and painters known from historical sources. The multitude of ink pots and *qalamdans* (pen-cases) that have survived tell the same story. These objects were manufactured from a wide variety of materials. This is a typical example of a richly decorated bronze ink pot. Judging by its construction (the presence of loops on the body and edge of the lid), such ink pots were carried tied to the belt by string threaded through the loops. The shape is characteristic of ink pots in pre-Mongol times.

The decoration of the lid consists

of six bands: the first four are ornamental, the fifth bears an Arabic inscription in *naskhi* script against a background of spiral stalks with palmettes:

العـز والاقبـال والدولة والتـامـة والدوامـة
والسعـادة(؟)والرياد (؟) والكـرامـة والثنا والبقا
لصاحبه!

"Glory and happiness and power and perfection and constancy and success and... generosity and praise and duration of life to the owner of this";

on the vertical edge of the sixth band there are three cartouches with Arabic inscriptions in Kufic script against a ground of spiral stalks:

باليمن والبركة والسلامة * والتامة والكرامـة
والشكرة وا * لطاعة والكرامة والصاحبه

"Happiness and blessings and prosperity and perfection and generosity and gratitude and obedience to the owner of this"

(in the final word there is a superfluous "alif' and "waw").
Inside the body is a wide flange scalloped around the opening. It has a band with an Arabic inscription in *naskhi* script against a ground of spiral stalks with palmettes:

العز والاقبـال والدولة والسلامة والدوامـة والبقا
لصاحبه

"Glory and happiness and power and prosperity and constancy and duration of life to the owner of this".

The rich finish and the nature of the background worked in scrolled tendrils permit an attribution of this ink pot to master craftsmen active during the late 12th-early 13th centuries. It is

curious to see the punched ground, which is usually found on more modestly decorated pieces.
Bibliography:
Masterpieces 1990, No.29.

115. QALAMDAN (PEN-CASE).
BY UMAR IBN AL-FADL IBN YUSUF AL-BAYYA.
20 DHU-I-QA'DA 542 AH/11 APRIL 1148 AD

Bronze (brass), cast, engraved and inlaid with silver and copper. Length 18.8cm.
The Hermitage, St Petersburg.
Inv. No. SA-12688. Transferred 1925 from the former Asiatic Museum of the USSR Academy of Sciences.

This *qalamdan* is one of the most famous items among a group of 12th-century Khurasan bronze items.
The inclusion of the name of the craftsman and customer and also

the exact date of production place it in the same class as such articles as the Herat bucket of 1163 (see Cat. No.116).
A detailed comparison of the *qalamdan* with the Herat items leads one to assume that it was produced in a different manufacturing centre in the province of Khurasan.
Bibliography:
Mayer 1959, p.87; Giuzalian 1968; *Masterpieces* 1990, No.28.

116. BUCKET.
BY MUHAMMAD IBN ABD AL-WAHID AND MAS'UD IBN AHMAD AL-NAQQASH.
HERAT, MUHARRAM 559 AH/DECEMBER 1163 AD

Bronze (brass), cast, engraved and inlaid with silver and copper. Height to rim 18.5cm; diameter 22cm.
The Hermitage, St Petersburg.
Inv. No. IR-2268. Transferred 1925 from the State Academy for the History

of Material Culture; formerly in the
A Bobrinsky collection.

This bucket (or, more exactly, bath-house pail – *satl*) is one of the most famous products of Khurasan bronze (brass) ware of the 12th–early 13th centuries. N I Veselovsky devoted a monograph to it and it is mentioned in virtually every work on pre-Mongol Iranian art or in studies of Islamic art. This bucket is a sort of touchstone to determine articles of Khurasan (and above all Herat) provenance. An indication of the exact place and date of production, the names of the craftsmen, the customer (Abd-al Rahman ibn Abdullah) and the owner (Rashid al-Din Azizi ibn Abu-l-Husain al-Zanjani) – all make this object outstanding in terms of its historical documentation (in this respect only the aquamanile in the form of a zebu (Cat. No.127) bears comparison with it, but the latter item has no indication of its place of manufacture).

On the external surface of the bucket are three bands of Arabic benedictory inscriptions written in various scripts and two bands containing court and hunting scenes. The entire decoration is executed in silver and copper inlay.

Bibliography:

Veselovsky 1910a; Mayer 1959, p.61; *Arts of Islam* 1976, No.180; *Arts of Persia* 1989, p.175, pls 8–9; *Masterpieces* 1990, No.30; *Great Art Treasures* 1994, No.406.

117. Ewer. By Mahmud ibn Muhammad al-Harawi. Herat, Sha'ban 577 AH / 10 December 1181–7 January 1182 AD

Bronze (brass), forged and inlaid with silver and copper. Height 38.5 cm.
Museum of Georgian History, Tbilisi. Inv. No. MS 135.

This famous ewer, by the master craftsman Mahmud ibn Muhammad al-Harawi, bears an inscription indicating that it was made in the town of Herat; its importance in scholarly terms is equal to that of the bucket of 559 AH / 1163 AD (see Cat. No.116).

There are a fairly large number of articles of similar form in various collections around the world. The ewer has suffered damage during its long life and now bears the marks of a previous restoration: the upper part of the neck and handle plainly come from other objects and the wide side of the foot has been added; on the lower part of the body are numerous rivets, evidently holding an internal patch in place.

The inscriptions on the neck, in Kufic script, consist of the usual benedictions. The body has twenty-four flutes ornamented and inscribed in *naskhi* script, running from top to bottom. Ten flutes contain a Persian verse inscription (in *hazaj* metre, each flute has one line – *bait*). The eleventh flute has an Arabic inscription with the name of the craftsman and the date:

مـــــــائنـدة ایـن بـدهـر امــــروز کــواست
هرکس کــه ورابـدیـد کـفت نیک زیبـاست *
هم بـاش نـدیـد کـس کـه ایـن بی همـاست
افـــتـابه (به) ایـن کـه روح ازیـن بغـزایـد *
وایـن آب دیـــــــاتـسـت کی زوهی آیـر
هـی آب کی زوبـدسـت مـن بـرایـد *
هی سـاعـت رادت دیگی بنمــایـر
افـتــابه (به) بیـن کس همه کس بسـتایـد *
در خـدمت جـون تـو مـعـتـریـن شـایـر
هی دیـده بدیـداد کـه می کـشـایـر *
نتـوانـد کـفت هیـچ کـه بـه زیـن (باشـرا)
ایـن جـــامـــة آب در هی اتـش ســازد *
مـــــائنـدة ایـن بـدهـر کی بـردانـر
هغت اخـتـر چرخ اکـروجه سی افی ازنـد *
انکس کی جنیـن ســازد بـاو ســازنـد
رهـــمـت بـادا بـران کی جنیـن ســازد *
سـیـم زر بخـــشـــدـه (و) جـنیـن بـرادرد
بخـــتش آیـر بـدوســـتـی بنـوازد *
مـدنـت بـرنمــود بـدشـمـنـش ســازد
العمل النقش محمود بن محمدالهروى * بتاریخ
شعبان سنة سبع وسبعین وخمسمائة

"A beautiful ewer – most beautiful – I possess,
Who has its like in the contemporary world?
Everyone who has seen it said "It is very graceful."
And nobody has seen one [a ewer] that was its equal.
Look at the ewer – it animates the spirit,
And this is the water of life that flows from it.
Each drop of water that flows from it onto my hands
With every hour brings some new delight.
Look at the ewer – everyone will praise it,
[It] is worthy to serve such a great man as you.

Any eye which sees it will open wide
And will be unable to say if there is anything better!
This is the garment of water [*ie* the ewer] – it is made in Herat,
Who in a hundred years will make its like?
The seven lamps of heaven, though they are proud,
Are on good terms with those who make such ewers.
Let there be favour for him who creates such things,
Uses pure silver and produces such things.
In happy times he [the craftsman] will give the ewer to a friend,
In misfortune he will make it for an enemy.
The work and engraving of Mahmud ibn Muhammad al-Harawi
In the month of Sha'ban the year five hundred and seventy-seven."

Bibliography:
Collections 1902, p.199, pl.XV; Gyuzalyan 1938.

The lamp-stand has six lobed depressions and is decorated with engraved inscriptions and ornaments with silver and copper inlay. At the top of the base is a projection – a lock to fasten the shaft. Lower down, on the neck, is an Arabic inscription in Kufic script in three cartouches; the ground to the inscription is formed of spiral stems with palmettes:

باليمـن والبـركـة * والدولة والتـا * مـة والبقـا لصاحبه

"Happiness and benediction and power and perfection and duration of life to the owner of this".

On the shoulder of the base there is an Arabic inscription in *naskhi* script on a clear ground:

عـمل بـايدار بن مـزربان * القـايـنى والبـركـة * والدولة والسلامة

"Made by Paydar ibn Marzban al-Qaini and blessings and power and prosperity".

Inside each depression there is a medallion decorated with plants and a narrow band containing an arabesque– *islimi* around the edge. On the edge of the base are six cartouches with Arabic inscriptions on a ground of spiral stalks with palmettes (in *naskhi* script):

العـز والاقبـال و * الدولة والسعادة * والسلامـة والنعمة والنصرة والتاييد*والبقا والثنا لصاحبه

"Glory and happiness and power and success and prosperity and well-being and victory and support and duration [of life] and praise to the owner of this".

This work by Paydar ibn Marzban al-Qaini can be assigned to the late 12th-early 13th centuries, in view of the high quality of the inlay and the

background design of spiral stems.
Bibliography:
Giuzalian 1968, p.107, fig.7.

123. BASE OF A CANDLESTICK.
LATE 12TH–EARLY 13TH CENTURY
Bronze (brass), forged, engraved and inlaid with copper. Height 20cm.
The Hermitage, St Petersburg.
Inv. No. IR-1458. Transferred 1925 from the State Academy for the History of Material Culture; formerly in the A Bobrinsky collection.

Despite the fact that a number of pre-Mongol Khurasan bronze (brass) items have survived, there are few candlesticks among them, although various oil lamps are well represented. It is interesting that from the 13th century until the early 15th century it was candlesticks, of the most varied form, which became most common throughout the Muslim world.
One type of 12th- and 13th-century Khurasan candlestick has a thin-walled, bell-shaped base decorated with Arabic benedictory inscriptions and relief depictions of seated lions and birds. Analogous motifs are found on ewers from Herat (see SPA

121. BUCKET.
FIRST HALF OF 12TH CENTURY
Bronze (brass), forged and engraved, with a cast handle. Height 22.5cm.
The Hermitage, St Petersburg.
Inv. No. IR-1485. Transferred 1925 from the museum attached to the former Stieglitz School of Technical Design.

This thin-walled bucket has a flat base and a massive cast handle; it is decorated with three bands of engraved ornament.
In the first band is an Arabic inscription in *naskhi* script on a ground of spiral stems with two palmettes:

العـز الدائم والاقبـال والسـعـادةا والسـلامـة والسلطانى؟.... والرقعة

"Long fame and happiness and success and prosperity and supremacy and... and... and a high standing".

The choice of blessings is unusual, two words are undecipherable. It is possible that this bucket served as a bath-house pail (satl).
Bibliography:
SPA 1938–39, vol.VI, pl.1291A.

122. BASE OF A LAMP-STAND.
BY PAYDAR IBN MARZBAN AL-QAINI.
LATE 12TH–EARLY 13TH CENTURY
Bronze (brass), cast, engraved and inlaid with silver and copper. Height 19cm.
The Hermitage, St Petersburg.
Inv. No. IR-1545. Transferred 1925 from the museum attached to the former Stieglitz School of Technical Design.

1938-39, vol.VI, pls 1325, 1326). In earlier pieces the shape of the base differs from that of the candle socket, whereas in later candlesticks these shapes are the same, to judge by those complete examples that have survived (see SPA 1938-39, vol.VI, pl.1321; Mahboubian 1970, No.556; Arts de l'Islam 1971, No.131; Davids-Samling 1975, p.71; Melikian-Chirvani 1976c, pls IV–VI). Bibliography: Meisterwerke 1912, vol.II, pl.144.

124. EWER. BY NASIR.
11TH–EARLY 12TH CENTURY

Bronze (brass), cast, forged, engraved and inlaid with copper. Height 37,5cm The Hermitage, St Petersburg. Inv. No. SA-12680. Transferred 1930 from the former Asiatic Museum of the USSR Academy of Sciences.

This ewer, with a large pumpkin-shaped body and a long, upright neck, once had a handle, flat at the top and decorated with a row of beads in the middle. The neck is now wrongly soldered and its

pouring lip turned towards the side of the body where the handle was fixed. On the neck there are three bands of ornament. The first has an Arabic inscription in *naskhi* script against a ground of scrolled tendrils with two palmettes at the centre:

العز والاقبال والدولة والنعمة

"Glory and happiness and power and prosperity";

the third contains a hare and two dogs against a ground of scrolled tendrils with three palmettes at the centre.

There are five bands on the body. The first is filled with an Arabic inscription in Kufic script:

باليمن والبركة والتامة والسر (؟) والسعادة (؟)
و ....

"Happiness and benediction and perfection and... and success and...".

In the second band there is an imitation of a Kufic inscription. The third band has an Arabic inscription in large *naskhi* script:

العز الدائم والاقبال وا * السلامة والسعادة والر

"Long fame and happiness and prosperity and success and...".

This band is interrupted in the middle by a cartouche with two roundels at the ends; there is a lozenge in the centre of the roundels and in the cartouche itself the craftsman's signature in Kufic script:

عمل ناصر

"Made by Nasir".

The ground of the roundels and the cartouche is tooled with punches; next to the letters there are two bird's heads.

The fourth band occupies the greater part of the body's surface; at the front (under the craftsman's signature) is a decorative scalloped medallion with scrolled tendrils, and at the sides two large roundels with Sirens and fine bands with an undulating stem and leaves. The place where the handle was fixed is without orna-

ment, but lower down there is a horseshoe-shaped cartouche with scrolled stems and three palmettes in the centre (beneath it is a vegetal ornament engraved at a later period).

The fifth band contains an undulating stem. No other works by Nasir are known. From the character of the ornament and inscriptions such objects are usually assigned to the 12th-early 13th centuries and linked to the province of Khurasan.

But in this particular case the style of some of the letters in the Kufic inscription (for example, the intertwined "qaf") enables one to speak of a somewhat earlier date for the ewer's manufacture (the second half of the 11th century). This ewer should be included in the class of objects bearing inscriptions on a punched ground (see Cat. Nos 102, 112 and 113).

First publication.

CAT N° 124

CAT Nº 126

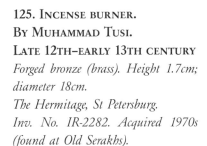

125. INCENSE BURNER.
BY MUHAMMAD TUSI.
LATE 12TH–EARLY 13TH CENTURY

Forged bronze (brass). Height 1.7cm;
diameter 18cm.
The Hermitage, St Petersburg.
Inv. No. IR-2282. Acquired 1970s
(found at Old Serakhs).

This small, thin-walled plate
stands on three cast legs and has
an everted rim; it probably
served as an incense burner.
Inside on the bottom there are
designs and inscriptions in
naskhi script; three cartouches
contain the benediction – "Glory
and success and happiness and
prosperity" – and the fourth had
the craftsman's signature: "Made
by Muhammad Tusi". There is a
similar object by the same craftsman in the Archaeological Museum of Tehran.
Muhammad Tusi is a new name
among Iranian coppersmiths.
Recently another craftsman has
become known who has the same
nisba – Khwajagi Tusi. However, it
would be difficult to assert on the
basis of two names alone that
during the 12th century the production of bronze (brass) wares
took place in the town of Tus.
Bibliography:
Ivanov and Orazov 1984, No.7;
Masterpieces 1990, No.36.

126. BUCKET.
BY MUHAMMAD IBN NASIR IBN
MUHAMMAD AL-HARAWI.
LATE 12TH–EARLY 13TH CENTURY

Bronze (brass), cast, inlaid with silver
and copper, engraved and gilded. Height
to rim 18.8cm; diameter 21.5cm.
The Hermitage, St Petersburg.
Inv. No. IR-1668. Purchased 1955.

In form and function this bucket
is very close to the Herat bucket
of 559 AH/1163 AD (see Cat.
No.116). However, one is immediately struck by a number of differences. The edge of the rim is
broken into twelve facets, the decoration of the outside surface
forms twelve sections, and there
are relief figures of animals on the
base. The bucket is richly gilded.
One can assume that the gilding
was not original, since traces of
matt-tooling are visible through it
in several places; such tooling is
often found on 12th- and early
13th-century Khurasan bronzes.
The history of the bucket can
only be traced back as far as the
mid-19th century when it was in
the collection of L Fould in Paris;
after that it came into the possession of the Petersburg jeweller,
A K Fabergé. The bucket has been
described in an article by
L Gyuzalyan (in which there is a

reading of all the inscriptions);
nevertheless a number of questions remain unanswered.
The script on the rim, which contains the owner's name, is very
careless and is consequently hard to
decipher. It could be assumed that
it was added later, although a thick
layer of gilding impedes the detec-
tion of traces of any earlier inscription. The reading of the word *li-
tajir* ("for the merchant") arouses
suspicion: the ligatures here are
imprecise, although the analogy of
the Herat bucket inevitably comes
to mind. It is strange that the merchant has the epithet *bahadur al-
Islam* (hero of Islam), although
bahadur is usually applied to military ranks. Moreover the epithet
only occurs during the Mongol era,
which also argues for the fact that
the inscription was added later. The
reading of the owner's *nisba* "al-
Bistami" has also remained hitherto problematic.

The striking difference between
the bucket's decoration and that
of all other similar objects can
hardly be explained by the influence of the client's taste, as
Gyuzalyan suggests.
Bibliography:
Mayer 1959, p.71; Gyuzalyan
1978; *Islam* 1985, p.137, No.2.

127. AQUAMANILE. BY ALI IBN
MUHAMMAD IBN ABU-I-QASIM AL-
NAQQASH. MUHARRAM 603 AH /
AUGUST–SEPTEMBER 1206 AD

Bronze (brass), cast and inlaid with
silver. Height 35cm.
The Hermitage, St Petersburg.
Inv. No. Az-225. Acquired 1929.

This bronze water vessel (aquamanile) with its rich ornamentation and Persian inscription is, by
date of manufacture, the latest
known Iranian figural vessel. The
creation of such a configuratively
complex object was a great
achievement for the craftsman,
who, in his inscription, under-
lines the fact that the entire
sculpture was cast at the same
time: "This cow, calf and lion –
all three were cast at once with
the help of the just, all-powerful
god, thanks to the endeavour [i.e.
the order] of Ruzbih ibn Afridun
[ibn] Burzin. Blessings to the
owner of this – Shah-Burzin ibn
Afridun ibn Burzin. Made by Ali
ibn Muhammad ibn Abu-I-
Qasim al-naqqash."
This inscription mentions three
people – the customer, the owner
and the craftsman (the customer
and owner were brothers). But
one word before the customer's
name has given rise to various
readings and interpretations. In

the opinion of F Rozenberg (1929) and L Gyuzalyan (1968) the first mentioned person – Ruzbih ibn Afridun ibn Burzin – participated in the making of this item as an amateur founder (judging by his name he was of aristocratic Iranian origin), whereas Ali ibn Muhammad ibn Abu-1-Qasim al-naqqash was its decorator, that is, was responsible for the engraved patterns and silver inlay.

In the opinion of M Dyakonov, the Ruzbih referred to was only the customer. This opinion seems better founded. A division of labour did exist at that time between founders and inlayers (although one can only deduce this from the basis of a single example - the Herat bucket of 559 AH/1163 AD, see Cat. No.116); however, the moulding and casting of such a complex sculpture in one go, as the inscription notes, would have posed serious problems even for an experienced professional. The place of manufacture of this unique sculpture has not yet been established. Dyakonov suggested that the object was most probably made in the "feudal environment" of Shirvan rather than in Tabaristan or Dailaman, although he did not present any solid evidence. In the last fifty years not a single bronze vessel has been discovered (let alone one of comparable quality) the manufacture of which could be connected with Shirvan (Northern Azerbaijan) of the 12th-early 13th centuries. There is also no information from written sources as to the existence of

bronze production in Shirvan during the period in question.

At the same time the inlay technique, the motifs of the depicted scenes and the vegetal ornament have direct analogies among Khurasan bronze items of the 12th-early 13th centuries. It is to the products of this province that the aquamanile should be assigned.

Bibliography:
Mistetstvo 1930, p.114, No.390; Dyakonov 1936, 1938 and 1939; Mayer 1959, p.36; Giuzalian 1968, pp.102–05; *Masterpieces* 1990, No.39; *Great Art Treasures* 1994, No.405; *Treasures* 1994, No.6.

128. EARRINGS.
LATE 12TH–EARLY 13TH CENTURY
Gold, forged and decorated with filigree. Length 3cm.
The Hermitage, St Petersburg.
Inv. No. IR-1682. Transferred 1958 from the Museum of Ethnography of the Peoples of the USSR, Leningrad.

The earrings, together with coins of the early 13th century, formed part of a hoard found in the

ruins of ancient Gurgan (North-Eastern Iran). We can therefore assume that they were made no later than the early 13th century.
Bibliography:
Oriental Jewellery 1984, No.45.

129. RING.
LATE 12TH–EARLY 13TH CENTURY
Silver, cast and engraved, with carved cornelian. Height 2.5cm.
The Hermitage, St Petersburg.
Inv. No. IR-1678. Transferred 1958 from the Museum of Ethnography of the Peoples of the USSR, Leningrad.

The ring is decorated with engraved vegetal ornament. The hexagonal cornelian is fixed in place with claws. The names of the prophet Muhammad and the Shi'ite imams are carved on the stone in *naskhi* script.

The ring formed part of a hoard found in the ruins of ancient Gurgan (see Cat. No.128) and was made no later than the early 13th century. Since the majority of articles of jewellery from the pre-Mongol period have come from unsupervised "looting" or from

chance finds rather than scholarly excavations, the Gurgan hoard is important in dating them. The fixture of the stone with claws is characteristic of a number of pre-Mongol rings found during excavations in Central Asia.
Bibliography:
Oriental Jewellery 1984, No.44.

130. VASE.
EARLY 13TH CENTURY
Faience, pressed in a mould. Height 28cm.
Museum of the History of the Peoples of Uzbekistan, Tashkent.

The vase is in the form of a cylinder on three short legs, with a conical neck. This shape is found in early 13th-century ceramics, albeit infrequently. The dark blue glaze is characteristic of many examples of 13th-century faience. The body of the vase was made in a ceramic mould and decorated with human figures standing in arches. Similar motifs are also fairly often found on 13th-century ceramics, although a dancer is usually depicted in such scenes (see SPA 1938-39, vol.V, pl.770; Bahrami 1949, pl.VII; Mahboubian 1970, No.196).
First publication.

131. JUG.
LATE 12TH–EARLY 13TH CENTURY
Clay, modelled from two halves (upper and lower) stamped in a mould. Height 14.2cm (the neck and handle are missing).
The Hermitage, St Petersburg.
Inv. No. SA-15422. Found in 1960 at the site of Khauz-khan in Turkmenistan (on the old road between Serakhs and Marv).

The upper part of the jug is decorated with an arcade with eight arches. Four of the arches contain a royal banquet: a king, two servants, one of whom is holding a jug and bowl, a queen and a servant with an incense burner. Under two of the arches we see the same figure in a short garment and patterned stockings; in the first scene he is carving, bowed over a stone, and in the other he carries on his shoulders a horse together with the girl mounted on it.

Two more scenes are fitted onto the most damaged part of the jug: here the scenes of the servant with the incense burner and the man carrying the horse and girl are repeated.

The vessel could have been made in some outlying town or other from matrices brought there, in all probability moulds manufactured in Nishapur, for excavations of workshops there have unearthed very similar examples.

On the edge of the fragment of one of them, part of a composition has been preserved in which a man in patterned stockings carries on his shoulders a horse and a girl. In the L A Mayer Memorial Museum in Jerusalem there is a jug with the scene of a royal banquet, the matrices of which were made with the help of imprints from the same original that served for the Hermitage jug. The mould in the Hetjens Museum, Düsseldorf, with a scene of a royal banquet, is a replica of the same model.

The subject depicted on the Hermitage jug is an illustration to the legend of the Sassanid king Khusrau Parwiz, his wife Shirin and the general Farhad who loved her and whom Khusrau destroyed.

In miniatures to manuscripts of Nizami's poem *Khusrau and Shirin* from the end of the 14th to the 17th centuries, artists often depicted the scene of Farhad carrying Shirin's horse together with its rider. In the poem this occurred when Farhad was breaking a path across the mountain of Bisutun (Behistun), and Shirin came to look at his work. The horse slipped, but the stonemason stopped it falling, lifting it onto his powerful shoulders.

The potters' quarter of Nishapur was destroyed in the Mongol invasion of 1220–21. However, the vessel was already broken when found (thrown on a rubbish tip), i.e. it arrived at the site of Khauz-khan appreciably earlier than 1220.

Nizami finished his poem in 1180, but it was only at the very end of the 1180s that he presented it to Qizil Arslan, one of the Seljuk rulers of Iraq.

Therefore the interval between a possible prototype, a miniature which supposedly existed in the original manuscript of the poem, and the mould for the vessel is too short – no more than twenty years. It is also unexplained how a manuscript from the library of Qizil Arslan in Ganja could have turned up in

Marv, especially in view of the complicated political situation in Iran at the time.

The first miniatures illustrating Nizami's poem *Khusrau and Shirin* and repeating in detail the vessel's subject, date from the late 14th century.

It is well known that from the 8th century onwards in Iran, oral tales of the past were widespread, in particular those about the shahanshah Khusrau Parwiz, his wife Shirin and the general Farhad.

Thus, the author of the *Fars-nama* (a work undoubtedly written before Nizami's poem) informs us that on the Sassanian relief of Taq-i Bustan, Khusrau is depicted and his horse Shabdiz, Shirin and the general Farhad, and that Farhad broke through the mountain of Behistun which is next to Taq-i Bustan – that is, he knows those same tales which are missing from Firdawsi's *Shah-nama* but are found in Nizami's poem and depicted on the vessel from Khauz-khan.

In this case it is possible that it was not the miniatures which influenced the composition on the vessel, but the reverse – such vessels (or more likely metal ones which, as has been proved, they imitate) had an influence on the formation of the canonical composition of later miniatures.

Bibliography:
Balashova 1972.

132. JUG.
SHA'BAN [5]90 AH / JULY–AUGUST 1194

Faience, painted in lustre; double firing. Height 16.5cm.
Museum of the History of the Peoples of Uzbekistan, Tashkent. Inv. No.192/17.

Lustreware is justifiably considered the acme of Iran's ceramic production and the height of its development occurred in the 13th century, even though the first lustre articles only appeared in Iran itself in the late 12th century (see Grube 1966, pp.71, 72; Watson 1975, p.65).

This jug seems to be one of the early examples of lustreware. Its shape is typical of 13th-century pieces; its surface is richly decorated. Two bands contain Persian verses and the band in the middle of the body also contains the date of manufacture: "the month of Sha'ban, year five hundred and ninety" ("ninety" is written legibly but the word signifying the hundreds is very cramped, though the first letter "kha" is clearly delineated, hence it must be "khamsarniatun" – "five hundred").
First publication.

133. BOWL.
LATE 12TH–13TH CENTURY.

Faience, painted in enamels and gilded; double firing. Height 8.7cm; diameter 18.5cm.
Museum of Oriental Art, Moscow. Inv. No. 729 II. Acquired 1920 from the K. Nekrasov collection.

The bowl has a strict hemispherical form and a slightly conical foot. Its external surface is deco-

rated with a band of ornament, while inside it is decorated with figural designs against a light ground. A narrow strip with an inscription and ornamental motifs completes the decorative composition (the inscription has not been deciphered).
Bibliography:
Maslenitsyna 1975, p.178, No.26, pl.12.

134. BOWL. 13TH CENTURY

Faience, painted in enamels; double firing. Height 7.8cm; diameter 18cm.
The Hermitage, St Petersburg. Inv. No. IR-1301. Transferred 1925 from the museum attached to the former Stieglitz School of Technical Design.

The bowl is richly decorated inside: next to the rim there is a narrow band with an Arabic inscription in Kufic script:

العز الدائم والاقبال الزايد والنصر الغالب والعز
القايم والدولة... العز الدائم العز الدائم العز
الدائم والاقبال الزايد... واليمن (؟) البركة
(؟)....والبقا لصاحبه

"Long fame and growing happiness and complete victory and steady fame and power... long fame, long fame, long fame and growing happiness... and happiness (?) and benediction (?)... and duration [of life] to the owner of this".

The figure of a rider is placed in the central medallion.
On the outer wall next to the rim there is an inscription in *naskhi* script:

الاعز الدائم والاقبال الزايد والنصر الغالب والعز
القايم والعمر (؟) السالم والدولت والسعاد (؟)
والسلامة والدولة والبقا....

"[Long fame] and growing happiness and complete victory and steady fame and

prosperous life (?) and power and success and prosperity and power and duration [of life]...".

The painting and inscription are restored in several places along the rim and consequently the inscription cannot be deciphered in full. First publication.

135. GOBLET. 13TH CENTURY

Faience, painted in enamels; double firing. Height 11.5cm
The Hermitage, St Petersburg. Inv. No. IR-1311. Transferred 1925 from the museum attached to the former Stieglitz School of Technical Design.

The goblet is decorated with polychrome enamels. On the outer walls there are banqueting figures and along the outside rim there is an Arabic inscription in Kufic script on a blue ground (the inscription is carelessly written and not all the words are clearly legible):

اليـمـن والبـركـة (؟) والدولة والسـعـادة
والسلامة.... والعز الدائم والاقبال الزايد
والنصر الغالب والعز [و] البقا(؟)

"Happiness and benediction and power and success and prosperity...and long fame and growing happiness and complete victory and fame and duration of life (?)".

Along the inside rim there is also a band with an Arabic inscription in Kufic script on a ground of intertwined stems:

العز الدائم والاقبال الزايد والنصر الغالب والعز
القايم والبد الصاعد والدولة

"Long fame and growing happiness and complete victory and steady fame and increasing endeavour and power".

Bibliography:
Kverfeldt 1947, fig.XV; *Islam* 1985, p.133, No.44.

136. Tile.
Safar 624 AH / 21 January–18 February 1227 AD

Faience, painted in lustre. Diameter 21cm.
Museum of Western and Oriental Art, Kiev.
Inv. 704 PR/BV.

This is a fairly early example of a dated tile with Persian verses. Its inscriptions have been published by Bahrami and Gyuzalyan. The authors of the verses have not yet been determined.

Bibliography:
Mistetstvo 1930, No.37; Bahrami 1937, pp.58, 69; Gyuzalyan 1956.

137. Tiles.
Dhu-i-hijja 660 - Rabi' al-akhir 661 AH/October 1262–March 1263 AD

Faience, painted in lustre; double firing.
The Hermitage, St Petersburg.
Inv. Nos IR-1046-1056. Transferred 1925 from the museum attached to the former Stieglitz School of Technical Design.

From the late 12th century cruciform or star-shaped tiles were widely used in architectural decoration, covering large areas of wall. The tiles were painted in lustre and many of them bore inscriptions (Koranic or secular). One very rarely comes across tiles painted in enamel: only in the second half of the 13th century do tiles with gold and enamel painting appear.

The Hermitage possesses over a thousand whole tiles and fragments from the mausoleum of imamzade Yahya in the town of Varamin (see Wilber 1955, pp. 109-111). Among them are sixty accurately dated examples, which allow one to state that the entire set of tiles was produced between the month of Dhu-1-hijja 660 AH/17 October–14 November 1262 AD and the month of Rabi' al-akhir 661 AH/12 February–12 March 1263 AD.

The overwhelming majority of the inscriptions on these tiles consists of extracts from the Koran.

This can probably be explained by the fact that they decorated a mausoleum. However, in the same set one also comes across entirely secular inscriptions – one of the tiles of the published panel bears verses from Nizami's *Laila and Majnun* (see Gyuzalyan 1953). First publication.

138. Vase.
Second half of 13th century

Faience, painted in lustre; double firing. Height 80cm.
The Hermitage, St Petersburg.
Inv. No. IR-1595. Acquired 1885 from the V. Bazilevsky collection.

The making of a large, thick-walled vase has presented numerous difficulties to potters of all periods. In this particular instance all the technical difficulties have been overcome and we see a genuine masterpiece of the ceramic art of 13th-century Iran. The vase is richly decorated with figures of people, animals, birds and vegetal ornament, executed in high relief. There is a large drop of light blue glaze on one of the figures of musicians in the uppermost band. The craftsman may have added this in order to show that it alone separated this article from the perfect work of art whose creation was the prerogative of Allah.

Bibliography:
Yakubovsky 1938; SPA 1938-39, vol.V, pl.701.

CAT Nº 138

148. VESSEL.
FIRST HALF OF 14TH CENTURY
Copper, forged, tinned and engraved.
Height 12cm; diameter 23.5cm.
The Hermitage, St Petersburg.
Inv. No. IR-2167. Purchased 1938.

A number of bronze vessels, of the same shape and decorated with gold and silver inlay, are known. Their function, however, is not clear, although they were probably water containers.

The decoration consists of four bands: in the first and third is an animal chase against a ground of scrolled tendrils, while the second band is decorated with twelve roundels containing the signs of the zodiac, between them there is plant ornamentation and the words of an Arabic inscription (the first eight words form a line of verse written in the *basir* metre):

العز [و] النصر [و] الإقبال والنعم [و] الجد والمجد [و] الإفضال والكرم [و] العادل (؟)

"Glory and victory and success and prosperity and grandeur and glory and honour and generosity and..."

(the final word is incomprehensible). The fourth band contains geometrical ornament.

It is important to note that the vessel is made of copper which was not used in the manufacture of pots before the first half of the 14th century (before this copper alloys - brass and bronze - were used). It has not yet proved possible to determine the exact period when copper articles appeared in Iran, since very few early examples have survived. In the Syro-Egyptian region the earliest copperware also dates from the 1330s. First publication.

149. GOBLET.
FIRST HALF OF 14TH CENTURY
Bronze (brass), forged, engraved and inlaid with silver. Height 14cm.
Art Museum of Georgia, Tbilisi.
Inv. No. 1/106.

In its shape this small goblet is typical of 14th-century wares; it has lost almost all its silver inlay. The cartouches along the edge and on the foot bear Persian verses which it has not proved possible to read in full. Large medallions on the body display riders or vegetal ornament.
First publication.

150. BOWL. 811 AH/1408–09 AD
Copper, forged, tinned and engraved.
Height 12cm; diameter 23.9cm.
The Hermitage, St Petersburg.
Inv. No. IR-2173. Acquired 1890 from the Imperial Archaeological Commission.

This is probably one of the very earliest metal bowls of this form, although ceramic bowls of similar form date from the 13th–14th centuries.

The external surface of the bowl is richly decorated. Unlike analogous bowls of a later date this one bears a cartouche on the inside of the rim with the name of the owner and a date: "The owner and possessor of this is Imam-Quli.. 811", and also an extract from a *ghazal* of Hafiz (in *thuluth* script, the *mozari* metre; the order of the hemistichs is not upheld):

"Morning has come. O cupbearer, fill the bowl with wine.
The turning of the heavens does not tarry, hasten!
Before the destruction of this transient world
Shatter [i.e. inebriate] us with a bowl of red wine!
If you seek delight, then cast off sleep !"

Six cartouches on the outside bear extracts from other ghazals of Hafiz (in *thuluth* script and in the metre *mojtass*):

"You will be able to perceive the mystery of Jam's bowl When you can turn wineshop dust into antimony for the eye.
Be not without wine and a musician, for under the dome of heaven
With this melody you can banish sadness from the heart.
But ever since you have yearned for your lover's lips and a bowl
Do not claim there is any other business you can perform."

In the second band six cartouches contain extracts from yet another of Hafiz's ghazals (in nastaliq script and in the metre ramal):

"What will be better than thought of wine and the bowl
Until we see what the end will be.
How much can the heart mourn that nothing remains of the days,
Tell me: if heart and days disappear, what is left?
Drink wine, do not grieve and do not heed the buffoon's admonitions,
What faith can one have in the words of the multitude?"

The remainder of the surface is decorated with vegetal ornament. The background to the ornament and inscriptions is filled with widely spaced cross-hatching, which from the end of the 14th

century was a characteristic feature of Iranian copper and bronze (brass) ware. Here the cross-hatching is widely spaced, which is evidence of its early manufacture (later the hatching becomes finer). The *thuluth* script also indicates an early dating for the bowl, although on the second band there is already a different script – nastaliq – which is unusual on 15th-century wares. *Nastaliq* takes its definitive form during the second half of the 14th century, but is only used in copying manuscripts. It is used for inscriptions on objects from the mid-16th century.

This bowl is also unusual in that it bears extracts from various ghazals of Hafiz: as a rule one object will bear extracts from a single *ghazal*.

Bibliography:

Ivanov 1960b (presents the texts of the inscriptions in the Arabic script); Arts of Persia 1989, p.183, pl.26; Masterpieces 1990, No.75; Komaroff 1992, No.29.

151. Frontispiece of a manuscript (left half). 1330s

25 x 21cm.

Manuscript: The Revival of the studies on Faith of al-Ghazzali.

The National Library of Russia, St Petersburg. Inv. No. Dom 255, f.2a.

The art of manuscript illumination attained a very high standard in the 14th century in Iran.

Usually the first two pages and the end of the manuscript would be richly decorated, although the contents were also illuminated with ornament around the chapter titles and in the margins etc.

The 14th century was evidently a turning point in the development of manuscript illumination, for during this period new forms of composition were created and their palette changed.

The manuscript of al-Ghazzali's *The Revival of the Studies on Faith* belongs to this transition period, to judge from similar and accurately dated manuscripts. The left half of the double frontispiece is reproduced here (the right half is

in a poor state of preservation). The illustration betrays the influence of an earlier period: the composition still divides into two separate parts not linked by the common frame; medallions with ornament are depicted in the left margins. But at the same time new features appear, such as vertical cartouches which connect the upper and lower parts of the page decoration. The floral ornament is large. The interlace in the corners of the cartouches is very characteristic of the 14th century. The palette - gold, dark blue, green, white and brown (red?) – is traditional.

Bibliography:

Akimushkin and Ivanov 1979, p.36, ill.19.

152. Miniature:
Rustam Besieges the Castle of the Ogre Kafur. 1330s

21.5 x 13cm.

Manuscript: Shah-nama of Firdawsi. Calligrapher: Abd al-Rahman ibn al-Hasan ibn Abd al-Rahman ibn Ahmad ibn al-Zahir. Date of comple-

tion of copy: 30 Jumada 1733 AH /16 February, 1333 AD.

The National Library of Russia, St Petersburg.

Inv. No. Dom 329, f. 123b

The poem *Shah-nama* was completed by Abu-1-Qasim Firdawsi in the early 11th century. The two earliest copies of it (plus an Arabic translation) date from the 13th century. But from the early 14th century on, during the rule of the Mongol dynasty in Iran, the poem became very popular. Many copies made during this period have been preserved, and several of them are illustrated. It is possible that this return to an ancient national epic had its political causes in the growth of anti- Mongol feelings and the creation of independent states.

It has been suggested that the miniatures of the very earliest *Shah-nama* manuscripts, the so-called *"Small Shah-namas"*, were executed in Baghdad.

The miniatures of this manuscript (as also another six manuscripts of the poem illuminated with miniatures) were produced in Shiraz in the second quarter of the 14th century, during the rule of the Inju dynasty. They are characterized by rather crude draughtsmanship, large and somewhat clumsy human figures and a colour scheme in which red, yellow and gold predominate.

Bibliography:

Gyuzalyan and Dyakonov 1934, No.1; Akimushkin and Ivanov 1968, p.6.

153. Miniature: Bahram Gur Falls into the Pit. 1370s–1380s
8.7 x 12.8cm.
Manuscript: Khamsa of Amir Khusrau Dihlawi. The Biruni Institute of Oriental Studies, Tashkent. Inv. No. 3317, f.344a.

In Shiraz during the second half of the 14th century a new style of miniature painting took over from that of the so-called Injuid school (see Cat. No.152). During the early 1370s miniatures appear which betray the influence of Chinese painting, but with their own idiosyncratic treatment of individual elements such as the horizon, water and vegetation. Chronologically this style appears during the rule of the Muzaffarid dynasty (1356-93): it is reflected in the miniatures of a small group of manuscripts (see Robinson 1982, pp.18, 19) which include the manuscript of the Tashkent *Khamsa* of Amir Khusrau Dihlawi. Though their format is small, the miniatures are more richly coloured than works of the second quarter of the 14th century; movement is more skilfully portrayed here and elements of the landscape are treated with more subtlety.
Bibliography:
Pugachenkova 1953; Oriental Miniatures 1980, No.6.

154. Miniature:
Parrot and Raven in a Cage. Mid-1420s
8.2 x 4.2cm.
S Khanukayev collection, St Petersburg.

In the collection of the late S Khanukayev there are seven odd sheets of works by various authors: around the edges of each page are written verses (*ghazals*) of Humam Tabrizi; the middle section has extracts from the poems of Imad Faqih-i Kirmani; in the centre is the text of Sa'di's *Gulistan*. The final folio of the manuscript has been preserved and we know the exact date when the copy was completed – "the last days of the month of Rajab 829 [AH; early June 1426 AD]".
All the miniatures illustrate the Gulistan. Their small size and sparse scenery and the colour range dominated by yellowish-brown tones indicate that they belong to the Shiraz school of the first half of the 15th century, although they are not by the leading masters of that time. The manuscript's Shiraz origin is also indicated by the layout of the text on the page and the triangular medallion with plant ornament in the margins.
First publication.

155. Book binding. Early 15th century
Leather, tooled, fretted, painted and gilded. 51.2 x 26.6cm.
The Hermitage, St Petersburg.
Inv. No. VR-84. Transferred 1924 from the museum attached to the former Stieglitz School of Technical Design.

This leather binding, which has survived intact, consists of two covers and a flap. The design of the outer covers demonstrates the increase in decoration during the course of the 14th century. A new feature appears in the design – openwork in the corners and the central medallion. This decorative device was to be further developed during the 15th century.
A new colour, dark blue, has also been added to the combination of gold and dark brown leather. In verse Persian blessings are tooled on the spine next to the flap:

جهان افرینت نکه باد * جهانت بکام وفلک یار باد

"May the creator of the world be your protector

And may the world be as you desire it, and heaven your friend."

The decoration of the inside surface of the covers and flap is more restrained: surrounding a small tracery medallion there are four medallions formed from a fourfold repetition of Ali's name (there are only two such medallions on the flap); around the edges there are bands of geometrical ornament.
Judging by its decoration and the lettering of the inscription, the binding can be assigned to the early 15th century.
First publication.

156. Miniature:
Farhad Carrying the Horse and Shirin. 1430s
16 x 12,1cm.
Manuscript: Khamsa of Nizami. 835 AH/1431 AD.
The Hermitage, St Petersburg.
Inv. No. VR-1000. Transferred 1924 from the museum attached to the former Stieglitz School of Technical Design.

The Hermitage copy of Nizami's *Khamsa* is widely known, for apart from its high artistic merit it contains a colophon with detailed information about the manuscript. It was copied for Shah Rukh at his court workshop in Herat by the calligrapher Mahmud. The work was finished on the 10th Rabi'II, 835 AH, *ie* 16th December 1431 AD. The 38 miniatures illustrating the copy convey a vivid impression of the Herat school of painting during the first half of the 15th century. The miniature reproduced here is an illustration to the poem *Khusrau and Shirin*. It depicts the meeting of Farhad and Shirin in the mountains. This episode is one of the most popular among illustrators of the story of king Khusrau, the beautiful Shirin and the stonemason Farhad. It appears on the 12th-century jug (see Cat. No.131), in the earliest known illuminated manuscript of Nizami's poem (Baghdad, 1386–88) and in a multitude of later copies.

In its depiction of the basic group of figures the miniature in the Hermitage manuscript closely resembles the relief on the 12th-century jug, which points to the persistence of tradition in the portrayal of the most popular themes. The miniature corresponds exactly in showing characters against a background of steep, inaccessible mountains with sharp peaks, which take up almost the whole sheet and even overlap the margins. The posture and movements of a man carrying a heavy load on his shoulders are conveyed with great mastery.

Bibliography:
Dyakonov 1940; Balashova 1972, p.100, fig. 8; Timur 1989, Cat.38.

157. MINIATURE:
THE SHAH'S HUNT.
1460s–1470s

27 x 37.5cm and 25.5 x 37.8cm.
Manuscript: Silsilat al-Dhahab of Jami. Date of completion of copy: 1 Sha'ban 956 AH/25 August 1549 AD. Calligrapher: Shah-Mahmud al-Nishapuri.
The National Library of Russia, St Petersburg.
Inv. No. Dorn 434, f. 816-82a.

This large-format double composition is glued into a later manuscript of the mid-16th century in which it occupies the final pages. It is possible that it was cut into two parts at that time.

Its palette of dark grey and brown tones is unusual in 15th-century miniatures of the schools known to us. The treatment of plants, clouds and mountains links it to Herat miniatures of the 1460s.

It is of interest to note that another double miniature of a Hunt with a similar composition has recently been published and this was indisputably painted in Herat at the end of the 1490s (see Lukens- Swietochowski 1979, p.210, pls.LXIII, LXIV).

Some are of the opinion that the miniature in question should be associated with Uzun-Hasan Aq-Qoyunlu, *ie* with the western regions of Iran (see Robinson 1979b, p.241, ills 140, 141).

G Pugachenkova attributes the origin of this unique miniature to Mavera al-Nahr during the rule of Khalil-Sultan (1405–09) or the young Ulugh-Beg. The grounds for such an attribution are that the banner supposedly carries Timur's heraldic emblem – a lion and the sun – and that the flora and fauna are typical of the Kashka Darya region in Southern Uzbekistan (see Pugachenkova 1979, p.51, and Pugachenkova 1980, pp.72–74). In our view these arguments are totally unfounded (see Ivanov 1977, p.154; Ivanov 1980b, pp.68, 69).

Bibliography:
Martin 1912, pls 60, 61; Akimushkin and Ivanov 1968, p.13, pls 18, 19.

158. FRONTISPIECE
OF A MANUSCRIPT. 1490s

35 x 24.5cm (opening).
Manuscript: Khamsa of Nawai. Calligrapher: Sultan-Ali. Date of completion of copy: 898 AH / 1492-93 AD.
The National Library of Russia, St Petersburg.
Inv. No. Dorn 560, f. 2a-3b.

On the first page of this splendidly designed copy there is a postscript, added at a later date to judge by the handwriting, attesting that it was copied by Sultan-Ali Mashhadi, illustrated by Yari- mudhahhib, and that the binding was the work of "the wonder of the age" Sultan-Ali mujallad Harawi.

It is in no way surprising to find such famous names in this copy – the calligrapher Sultan-Ali Mashhadi (his name is in the colophon) and the gilder Yari Harawi (Shirazi) – for the quality of the writing and design of the copy are magnificent.

The leather binding, tooled and painted in gold, is also beautiful and some parts of it are lacquered. There are two frontispieces, which is rarely encountered even in particularly sumptuous manuscripts. The manuscript was undoubtedly decorated at Herat; evidence of this is shown by the medallions and cartouches with a gold ground, above which scrolled stems are painted with flowers, leaves and arabesques of various colours (this device is found in almost all Herat manuscripts).

First publication.

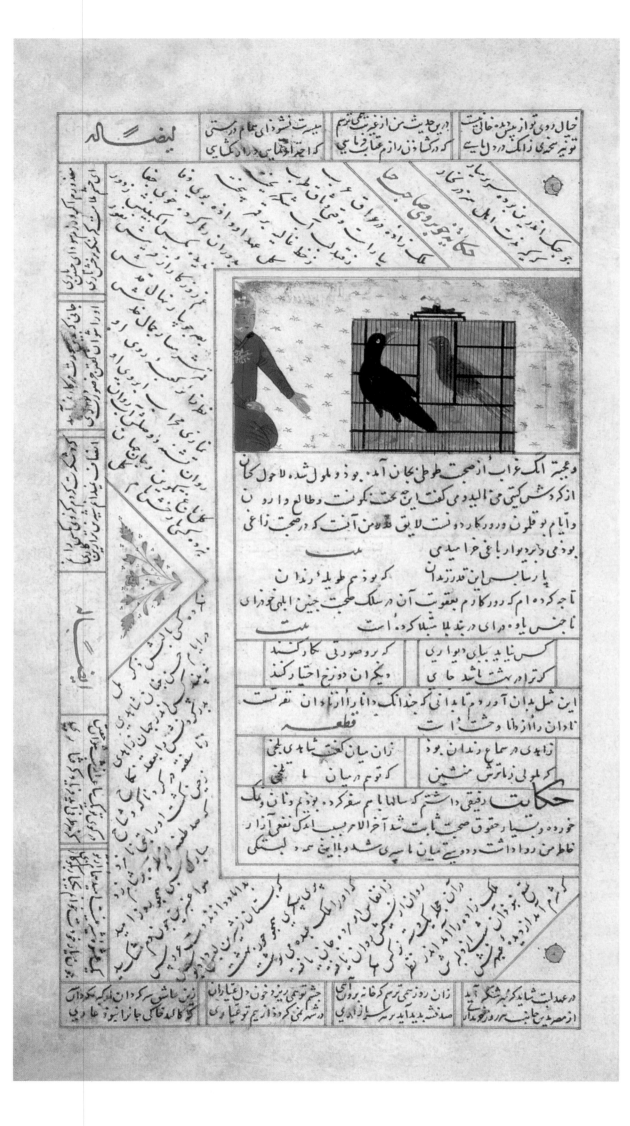

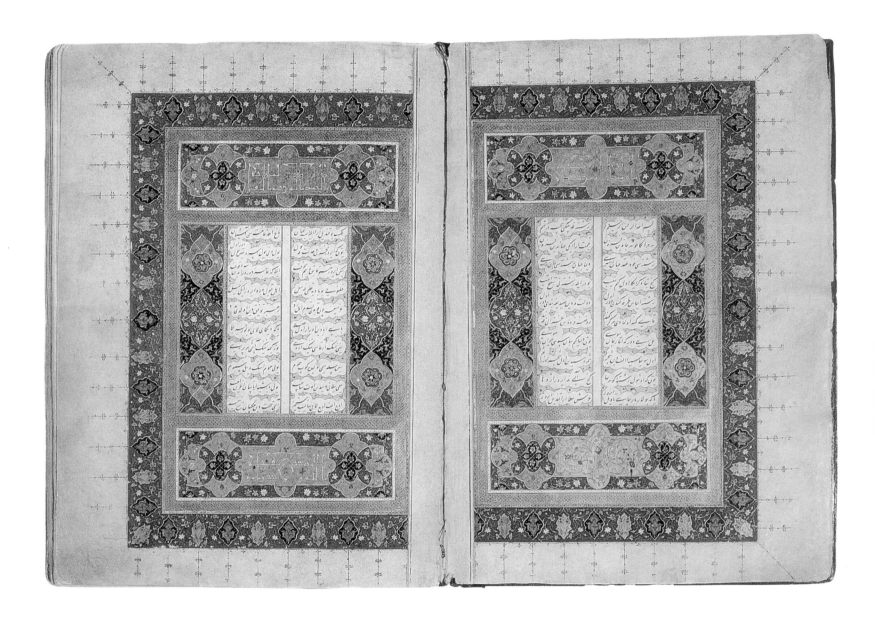

167. Basin.
Early 16th century

Copper, forged, tinned and engraved.
Height 11.3 cm; diameter 26.2 cm.
Museum of Oriental Art, Moscow.
Inv. No. 1751-II. Acquired 1942.

The shape of the basin, with its flat base, rounded body and thickened rim, is characteristic of analogous articles of the late 15th-early 16th centuries.

In its treatment of the foliate ornament, this basin can be attributed to the workshop of Shir-Ali ibn Muhammad Dimashqi, during its later period (see Ivanov 1969a). This craftsman was a descendant of Syrian (Damascene) coppersmiths brought by Timur to the East; he worked in Khurasan in the late15th-early 16th centuries.
First publication.

168. Bucket (satl).
Second half of 15th century

Copper, forged and engraved. Height
12.3 cm.
The Hermitage, St Petersburg.
Inv. No. IR-2177. Purchased 1926
from S. Magomedov (Kubachi).

In shape the bucket resembles 14th-century objects (see, for example, the bucket of 733 AH/1333 AD – Cat. No. 146). A Persian inscription in four cartouches decorates the top of the bucket (metre *ramal*, *thuluth* script):

چون بحــمــام در آید مــه مـن پیـوسـتـه *
قــرص زریـن فلک سطل و مــه نو دسـتـه
تا بحــمـام در آیـد مه مـن پیـوسـتـه *
سطل آبیـسـت مـرا دیده و ابرو دسـتـه

"Always when my moon [i.e. beauty] enters the bath-house, The golden disc of the heavens [becomes] a bucket, the crescent moon is the handle.

So that my moon should always enter the bath-house,
My eye will become a bucket of water, my eyebrow the handle."

This poetic excerpt gives us the object's name – satl – and at the same time indicates its purpose – a bath-house pail. These objects are well represented at various stages of the development of Iranian metalwork.

It is of interest to note that the second line of the quoted excerpt is found in the memoirs of the Herat writer of the late 15th-early 16th centuries, Zain al-Din Wasifi (see Wasifi, vol.2, p.227).
The large foliate ornament assigns the bucket to a group of objects (see Cat. No.166) which date from the second half of the 15th-first half of the 16th centuries. It has not yet proved possible to determine their exact place of manufacture.
Bibliography:
Masterpieces 1990, No.79; Komaroff 1992, No.26.

169. Book binding.
By Muhammad-Zarnan ibn Mirza beg Tabrizi.
Early 16th century

Leather, tooled and decorated with gold. 33.8 x 23.5cm. Manuscript: Kulliyat of Nawai. 1001/04 AH/1592-96 AD.
The National Library of Russia, St Petersburg.
Inv. No. Dorn 558.

The two identical covers of black leather (the flap is missing) belong now to a fairly modestly decorated manuscript of Nawai's *Kulliyat*. The contrast between the magnificent binding and the modest manuscript is very striking and leads one to suspect that the binding belonged to some earlier and more sumptuous manuscript. The signature on the lower part of the binding, hardly noticeable now, names Muhammad-Zaman, the son of Mirza beg Tabrizi, and undoubtedly an outstanding craftsman in his day. Apparently this is his only surviving work.
The Turkish writer of the second half of the 16th century, Mustafa Ali, mentions Muhammad-Zarnan among the craftsmen who left Iran for Turkey.
First publication.

170. MINIATURE:
THE LOVERS' MEETING. 1520s

7.3 x 12.8cm. Manuscript: Diwan of sultan-Husain Baykara.
Branch of the Institute of Oriental Studies of the Russian Academy of Sciences, St Petersburg.
Inv. No. V 284, f. 20a.

This small manuscript is a masterpiece of Persian book design during the early years of the 16th century. It is very probable that it was produced for some important person, which would explain such a high artistic level of calligraphy, illumination and binding.

Although collections of lyric poetry – *diwans* – were fairly seldom illustrated, in this particular case there are five miniatures, one of

them reproduced here. The colour scheme and the treatment of figures and landscape are evidence that the present work belongs rather to the Herat school of the 1520s than to that of Tabriz.
Bibliography:
De Bagdad à Ispahan 1994, No.37.

171. MINIATURE: THE FIRST SERMON OF HASAN IBN ALI. BY QASIM IBN ALI. DHU-L-HIJJA 932 AH/SEPTEMBER 1526 AD.

21 x 15.8cm. Manuscript: Ahsan al-Kibar of Muhammad al-Husaini al-Varamini. Calligrapher: Khizr-shah. Date of completion of copy: 4 Rabi' 1837 AH/19 October 1433 AD.
The National Library of Russia, St Petersburg.
Inv. No. Dorn 312, f. 373b.

The miniatures in this manuscript were executed over ninety years after the copy had been completed. There are 39 miniatures in the manuscript, four of them added later, possibly in the 18th-19th century. One of the 16th-century miniatures bears the signature of Qasim-i Ali, *ie* Qasim ibn Ali. This artist was a contemporary of Bihzad and not inferior

to him in his artistry. Very little is known of his life, but judging by the less vivid palette of this copy's miniatures by comparison with those of Tabriz in the 1520s, one can assume that Qasim-i Ali worked in Herat and was still alive in the mid-1520s.
Bibliography:
Akimushkin and Ivanov 1968, pp.15, 16, 21, 36 (reading of the inscription to the miniature), No.35.

172. MINIATURE: ISKANDER SETS OUT IN SEARCH OF THE WATER OF LIFE. MID-1520s

20.5 x 24cm. Manuscript: Shah-nama of Firdawsi. Calligrapher: Muhammad al-Harawi. Date of completion of copy: 5 Muharram 931 AH/2 November 1524 AD, Tabriz.

Branch of the Institute of Oriental Studies of the Russian Academy of Sciences, St Petersburg.
Inv. No. D 184, f. 338a.

In the miniatures of this manuscript one can trace the process of consolidation of the Tabriz school of miniatures, which took place during the mid-1520s. In the early 16th century Tabriz already had its school of miniatures, whose most brilliant representative was Sultan-Muhammad Iraqi. Around 1520 Bihzad came to Tabriz, together with the future Shah Tahmasp, and he became the head of the court library – *kitabkhanah*. Apparently other artists from Herat also arrived with him. In the mid-1520s a new style of the Tabriz school appeared, which was soon to produce such masterpieces as the miniatures of the *Khal-nama* (see Cat. No.173), the *Shah-nama* from the former Houghton collection and the *Khamsa* of Nizami (British Library).
Bibliography:
Gyuzalyan and Dyakonov 1934, pp.27–30; De Bagdad à Ispahan 1994, No.39.

CAT N° 169

173. MINIATURE:
POLO GAME. LATE 1520s

13.8 x 10.4cm.
Manuscript: Khal-nama of Arifi.
Calligrapher: Tahmasp al-Husaini
(Shah Tahmasp I). Date of completion
of copy: 931 AH/1524-25 AD, Tabriz.
The National Library of Russia,
St Petersburg.
Inv. No. Dom 441, f. 26b.

One can assume that the miniatures in this manuscript copied by the young Shah Tahmasp I were executed by the best artists of his court workshop. Judging by the different styles, the miniatures were executed by various artists, although all were from the same school.

The artist who produced this miniature painted two others with a similar theme (18a and 39a). The particular treatment of landscape and faces - small, rounded, with bushy eyebrows - is characteristic of his style. He also conveys movement with great skill.
Bibliography:
Akimushkin and Ivanov 1968, No.31.

174. BOOK BINDING AND FLAP.
LATE 1520s

Papier-mâché and leather, decorated with
painting and lacquered. 29.6 x 18.8cm
(each cover), 29.6 x 9.2cm (flap).
Manuscript: Khal-nama of Arifi. Cal-
ligrapher: Tahmasp al-Husaini (Shah
Tahmasp I). Date of completion of copy:
931 AH/1524-25 AD, Tabriz.
The National Library of Russia,
St Petersburg. Inv. No. Dom 441.

The binding resembles leather ones in the layout of its decoration (division of surfaces into

borders and medallions). Both covers and the flap are identically painted. The inside of the binding is of dark red leather. Two frames surround the central field. On a wide frame, in the corners and in the middle of the central field, cartouches and medallions are displayed, decorated with a fine tracery of black foliage on a dark blue ground.
First publication.

175. FRONTISPIECE
OF A MANUSCRIPT.
LATE 1520s–EARLY 1530s

35 x 24cm (opening). Manuscript:
Khusrau and Shirin of Nizami.
Calligrapher: Sultan Muhammad
Nur. Date of completion of copy: 937
AH/1530-31 AD, Herat.
The National Library of Russia,
St Petersburg.
Inv. No. Dom 346, f. 1b-2v.

This manuscript was copied at Herat by the famous early 16th-century calligrapher Sultan-Muhammad Nur. Apparently the illumination was also executed in this town. The text of this magnificent manuscript is on paper of various colours, with beautiful headpieces at the beginning of the sections of the poem and gold-mottled margins, but the decoration was not completed for empty spaces have been left on several pages, probably for miniatures.

The text opens with a double frontispiece in which dark blue and gold dominate. The form of its decoration is very close to that of late 15th-century frontispieces (see Cat. No.158). But in the 1520s several differences are noticeable: to the left and right of the first frame large, triangular, scalloped medallions containing ornament have appeared, the foliate decoration has become finer and the number of borders round the central field has increased.

All in all the Herat tradition is apparent as much in the composition and colour range as in the use of coloured arabesque-islimi on a gold ground in the medallions of the central field.
First publication.

176. MINIATURE: SHAH'S HUNT.
MID-16TH CENTURY

21 x 31.7cm (each). Manuscript:
Silsilat al-Dhahab of Jami.

Calligrapher: Shah-Mahmud al-
Nishapuri. Date of completion of
copy: 1 Sha'ban 956 AH/25 August
1549 AD, Ardebil.
The National Library of Russia,
St Petersburg.
Inv. No. Dom 434, f. 1b-2a.

This large-format double composition is glued at the beginning of Jami's poem, but does not illustrate it.

In its bright palette and treatment of figures this miniature belongs among the late products of the Tabriz school. It is possible that the treatment of the mountains already displays features which were to reach their full development in the workshops of Qazwin and Mashhad around the late 1550s–1560s.

This work by a talented, unknown artist is a true masterpiece of the Persian miniature.
Bibliography:
Ashrafi 1966, pp.6, 7; Akimushkin and Ivanov 1968, Nos 42, 43; Bretanizki 1988, pl.VIII.

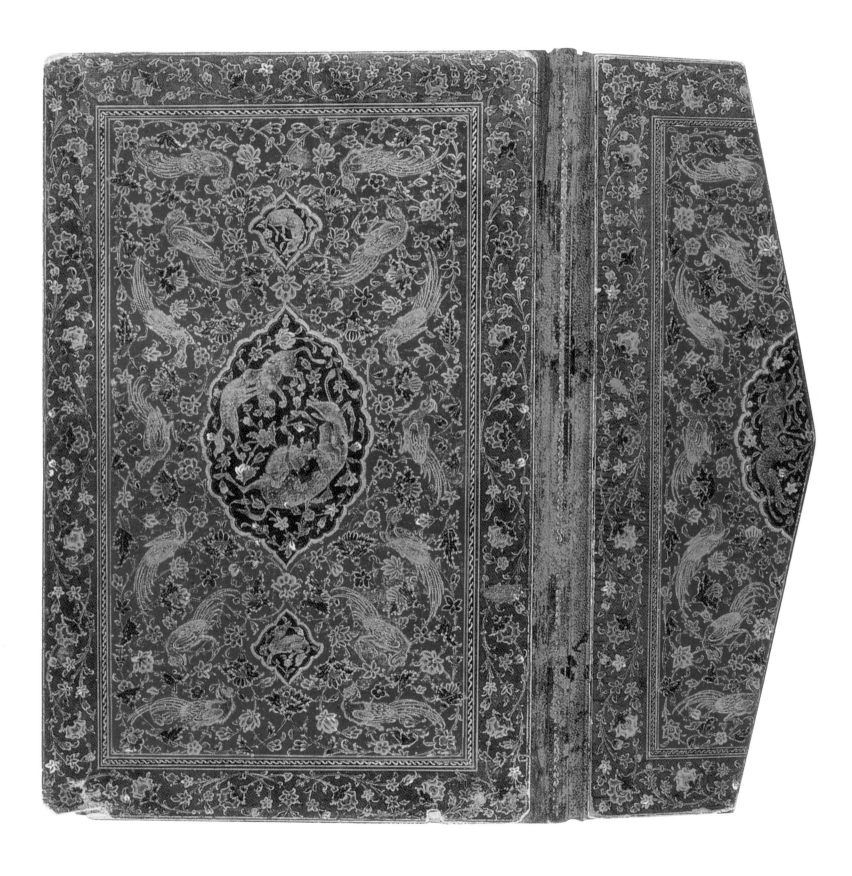

CAT N° 174

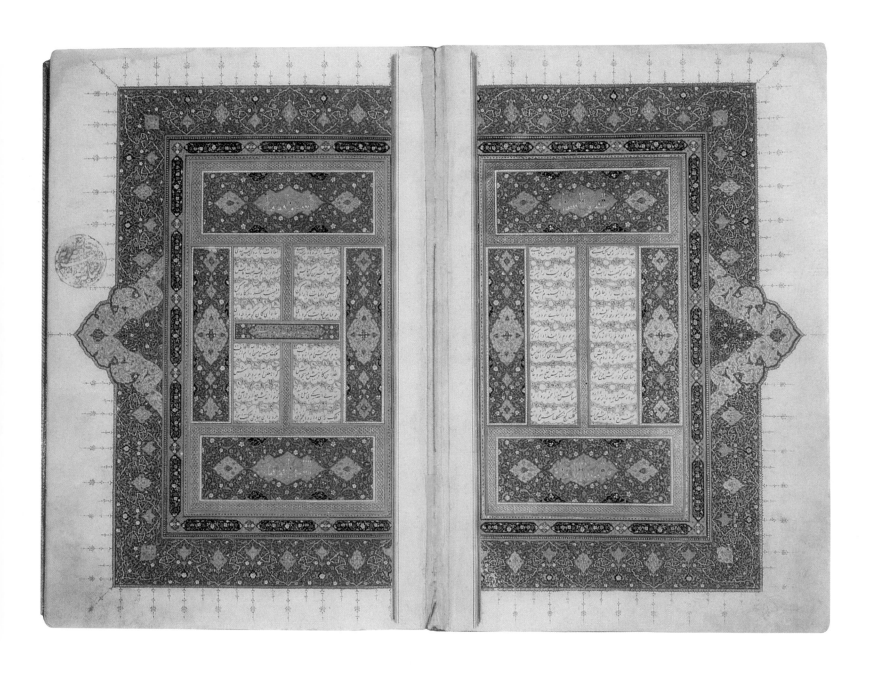

CAT N° 176

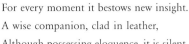

177. BOOK BINDING.
983 AH/1575–76 AD

Papier-mâché and leather, decorated with painting and lacquered. 41.6 x 26cm (each cover), 41.5 x 14cm (flap).
Manuscript: Silsilat al-Dhahab of Jami. Calligrapher: Shah-Mahmud al- Nishapuri. Date of completion of copy: 1 Sha'ban 956 AH/25 August 1549 AD, Ardebil.
The National Library of Russia, St Petersburg.
Inv. No. Dom 434.

The binding of the manuscript *Silsilat al-Dhahab* provides us with the rare opportunity of proving that bindings existed separately from the manuscripts, which apparently only preserved their original bindings in extremely rare instances. This binding bears the precise date of manufacture on the flap, 983 AH, *ie* it was made 27 years after the book itself had been completed.

The covers and flap are decorated with painting, supplemented with ground mother-of-pearl, against a black ground. In the first, and fairly wide, border, Persian verses (metre *hazaj*) are written in cartouches, in white point, but today only the text on the flap can be fully deciphered:

انیس کنج شـــهـابی کــتابی است *
فــروغ صـبح دافـانی کـــتابست
بود بی مـــزد و منت اسـتادی *
زدانش بخـشـدت هردم کــشادی
ندیمی مــغنی داری پوشت پوش *
بسرکار گـویانی نــــــموش
فی شهور سنه ثلث وثمانین وتسعمایه

"A book is a bright treasury and a companion.
A book is the gleaming of the dawn of knowledge.
A master [mentor] will be unnecessary,

For every moment it bestows new insight.
A wise companion, clad in leather,
Although possessing eloquence, it is silent,
In the months of the year nine hundred and eighty-three."

The themes of the illustrations are a banquet, a battle and a fairy-tale garden. The treatment of plants and clouds is evidence that all the compositions were done at the same time. The various types of headgear in the scenes on the covers are somewhat surprising, although it is possible that the making of the binding coincided with those years when the fashion for the turban crowned with a cone was waning.
The inside is of dark red leather and is decorated with cartouches and medallions with tracery foliage against a dark blue, turquoise and yellow ground, and also with cartouches and medallions containing tooled ornament on a gold ground.
First publication.

178. ARCHERY RING.
16TH CENTURY

Carved ivory. 2.8 x 4.1cm
The Hermitage, St Petersburg.
Inv. No. IR-2095. Transferred 1925 from the museum attached to the former Stieglitz School of Technical Design.

This type of ring was worn on the thumb of the right hand. The bowstring was drawn with the thumb, locking it with the index finger. When the bowstring was released, the projection on the ring protected the thumb from injury. In Persian such rings were called *zehgir* or *shast*. Persian verses are engraved on the outside of the ring (metre *khafif*, *nastaliq* script):

دلقــــه دیده باد زهگیــــرت *
تارسـد گـــاه گــاه هر تیرت

"May the ring of your eye be your zehgir,
That each of your arrows may always attain [the target]."

On the projection an exclamation is engraved in a small medallion:

یاعلی صارد

"O Ali! Sublime one!"

The Hermitage collection includes archery rings of ivory, steel and cornelian, and several ceremonial rings of nephrite and gold decorated with gems.
First publication.

179. KNIFE AND SHEATH.
FIRST HALF OF 16TH CENTURY

Steel, gold, wood, textile; forged, inlaid with gold, engraved and decorated with gemstones. Length 33.8cm.
The Moscow Kremlin Armoury.
Inv. No. OR-3831. Transferred 1810 from the Rüstkammer.

The knife's blade is of damask steel, with a slight curve towards the cutting edge. It is decorated all over with gold inlay forming two longitudinal bands of different widths, with stylized flowers, buds, leaves and arabesque-islimi. Along the blunt edge runs an inscription with verses in praise of Ali:

"Call Ali – performer of miracles,
You will find him a support in sorrow.
All care and grief will vanish
With your protection, o Ali, o Ali, o Ali!"

The knife's hilt is straight, thickened at guard and pommel, and fitted with a double mount: the

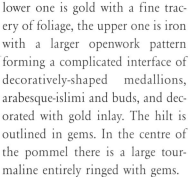

lower one is gold with a fine tracery of foliage, the upper one is iron with a larger openwork pattern forming a complicated interface of decoratively-shaped medallions, arabesque-islimi and buds, and decorated with gold inlay. The hilt is outlined in gems. In the centre of the pommel there is a large tourmaline entirely ringed with gems. The sheath is in an iron mount faced with an openwork tracery of interlaced decoratively-shaped medallions in the centre of which small emeralds are fixed. The reverse of the mount is smooth with two medallions inlaid with gold. The sheath is tipped with a ring of small gems.
The knife is a marvellous example of Iranian art of the first half of the 16th century.
Bibliography:
Treasures of Applied Art 1979, p.21, No.11.

180. BROADSWORD AND SCABBARD.
BLADE: IRAN, EARLY 16TH CENTURY;
MOUNT: TURKEY (?), 17TH CENTURY

Steel, silver, wood, textile; forged, inlaid with gold and silver, gilded and decorated with turquoises. Length 104.5cm.
The Moscow Kremlin Armoury.
Inv. No. OR-4440. Mentioned in an inventory of the Great State Treasury in 1687.

The blade of the broadsword is two-edged damask steel, decorated on the right side with gold and silver inlay depicting the battle of a dragon and a phoenix.
The hilt and scabbard are in silver-gilt mounts with fine foliate decoration and turquoises in raised settings. Similar sword and

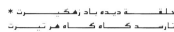

sabre mounts are known on a large number of pieces. The traditional attribution connecting the production of silver-gilt mounts with the work of 17th-century Turkish craftsmen may be mistaken. Examples of similar mounts are known, produced in the Moscow Kremlin Armoury during the 17th century by Russian craftsmen working from oriental patterns.

Bibliography:
Treasures of Applied Art 1979, p.21, No.10.

181. Fragment of a carpet.
Early to mid-16th century
Pile-woven wool. 258 x 250cm.
The Hermitage, St Petersburg.
inv. No. VG-994. Transferred 1925 from the museum attached to the former Stieglitz School of Technical Design.

The composition and design of the carpet are characteristic of patterns attributable to Tabriz. It should be noted that designs with a large central medallion are typical of North-Western Iranian carpets; they were also very popular in the decoration of book bindings and illuminated pages of manuscripts. In its ornamentation and composition the carpet resembles miniatures of the Tabriz school during the first half of the 16th century.

Bibliography:
SPA 1938–39, vol.VI, pl.1204a; Shandrovskaya 1960, p.153.

182. Velvet chasuble.
16th century (cloth)
Silk, woven in silver thread, with appliquéd velvet design. Stitched from 24 pieces (size of largest piece 80 x 60cm).

Height 136cm.
The Hermitage, St Petersburg.
Transferred 1930 (?) from the History Museum, Moscow.
Inv. No. IR-2327

The best Iranian textiles of the Safavid period were thematic, ie they depicted characters from miniature paintings, illustrating various literary works. On this velvet, an episode from the poem *Laila and Majnun* is shown. The textile design consists of repeated scenes of the young Majnun sitting in the wilderness among the beasts, with a deer on his lap.

The movements of the figures are free and the poses natural, secondary figures are skilfully placed around the central figure of Majnun.

Bibliography:
Meisterwerke 1912, pl.195; Kverfeldt 1940, pl.III; Treasures 1994, No.26.

183. Fragment of silk textile.
16th century
Silk, woven in silver thread (satin weave). 118.5 x 33cm.
Museum of Oriental Art, Moscow.
Inv. No. 616 II. Transferred 1919 from the History Museum, Moscow (before 1919 in the P Shchukin collection; textile purchased 1887 in Istanbul from the antique dealer, Kelekian).

The long, narrow fragment of cloth has a vertical composition. The light-coloured design stands out in contrast against a dark red ground. The pattern on textiles with figure subjects is based on a repetition of the motif and does not have a compositional centre, since these textiles were intended for clothing and woven as a whole piece. This textile fragment was possibly part of a robe.

Bibliography:
Maslenitsyna 1975, p.91, ill.81.

184. Fragment of textile.
Mid-16th century
Silk (twill weave). 47 x 26cm.
The Hermitage, St Petersburg.
Inv. No. VT-1010. Transferred 1925 from the museum attached to the former Stieglitz School of Technical Design.

This is one of the finest examples of 16th-century textiles with figural compositions. The decoration of the cloth consists of vertical stripes with four repeated scenes set in rectangular frames: a garden scene, a musical scene, "reading" and "preparing dinner". The design employs the traditions of 16th-century textiles, with a skilful arrangement of scenes and a free disposition of the figures, a "classical" treatment of the characters with an exact rendering of everyday details and a high standard of technical execution. The period of the textile's manufacture, the mid-16th century, can be established by means of a comparative analysis of the costumes reproduced on textiles and on dated miniatures. The basic means of dating is the characteristic headgear, in the form of a turban crowned with a cone, which was worn in Iran under the first Safavid shahs during the second and third quarters of the 16th-century.

Bibliography:
Kverfeldt 1940, fig.II; Pirverdian 1969.

CAT N° 181

CAT N° 182

CAT Nº 184

185. CAFTAN.

LAST QUARTER OF 16TH CENTURY
Silk (satin weave). Length 140cm.
The Moscow Kremlin Armoury.
Inv. No. TK 2845.
The caftan is made of light blue silk
with a repeat motif on the yellowish-
green lining and trimmed with grey-
blue cotton.

An article of precious cloth which has not been refashioned and is in a good state of preservation is a highly unusual phenomenon. This caftan must take its place among other such unique works of applied art. One might conjecture that it was made in Iran and brought to Moscow as an ambassadorial gift. In Russia as a rule such textiles were termed kamka kizylbashskaya (Kizylbash damasks). It is possible that this is that very caftan of "Kizylbash damask" which can be traced through the inventories of the Tsars' possessions (clothing) beginning with Tsarevich Ivan Ivanovich (late 16th (century).

Bibliography:
Meisterwerke 1912, pls 196, 197; Treasures of Applied Art 1979, p.27, No.34.

Iranian seals and talismans of the Islamic period remained for a long time beyond the scope of research. To all intents and purposes the tradition of their study, established in the 19th century, was interrupted and a renewal of interest in this material has only been observed in very recent years. There are sizeable collections of these objects in the museums of Yerevan and Samarkand. However, the largest collection is probably that of the Hermitage, with more than 750 items.

There are as yet no objective criteria for distinguishing early Iranian seals and talismans with inscriptions in Kufic script from the general run of pieces. The names of their owners are engraved on the overwhelming majority of seals, without any titles, ranks or even nisbas, which makes it completely impossible to associate them with specific individuals. Consequently they are not represented in this catalogue. In the 14th century Kufic script was already falling into disuse. Seals of historical personalities "have survived, albeit very few". However, from the 14th century on, many documents have been preserved from succeeding centuries which bear indications of where they were written and imprints of seals, thus allowing one to approach the problem of localization on the basis of fully objective evidence.

186. SEAL.

LATE 13TH–14TH CENTURY
Carved nephrite. 1.2 x 1.4cm.
The Hermitage, St Petersburg.
Inv. No. HP-2035. Acquired 1925
(?) from the Shuvalov collection.

The seal is a flat oval representing a lion. Around the edge runs a band with a Persian verse inscription (metre *motaqareb*) in *naskhi* script. The ground of the inscription is clear:

بکام تو باد همـــــه کـــارتو *
خـــــــداوند باد نگه دار تو

"May all your affairs be as you desire!
And may the Lord be your protector!"

This verse fragment was first noted on a tile of 669 AH/ 1270–71 AD (see Kühnel 1931, p.230, fig.10). Therefore one should assign the seal to a later period. This is the only example among later seals (apart from 19th-century seals) bearing the figure of an animal. First publication.

187. SEAL.
802 AH/1399–1400 AD
Carved chrysolite, mounted in silver.
Height 2.4cm.
The Hermitage, St Petersburg.
Inv. No. SA-8481.

The seal is flat and almond-shaped. There are two lines around the edge. The centre of the seal is entirely filled with the inscription in *thuluth* script against a clear ground:

اميــر الامـراء اذربايجـان ميـرانشاه بن اميـر
صاحبقران امير تيمور كوركان ٨٠٢

"Amir of amirs of Azerbaijan Miran-Shah ibn Amir Sahibkiran Amir Timur Gurgan, 802".

This is the earliest seal with an exact date. Subsequently, especially from the 16th century on, dates on seals became the rule. It is possible that the seal in question was made in Azerbaijan

(North-Western Iran) during the reign of Miran-Shah.
Bibliography:
Veselovsky 19 lob; Timur 1989, Cat. No.127.

188. SEAL.
FIRST HALF OF 15TH CENTURY
Carved nephrite. 1.6x2.2cm.
The Hermitage, St Petersburg.
Inv. No. SA-13650.

The seal is almond-shaped, with a flat face and convex reverse, into which one long and two short leaves are carved. Around the edge of the face are two incised lines, the centre is occupied by an inscription in *thuluth* script on a clear ground:

كــوهر شــاد بنت غـيـاث الديـن تـرخـان

"Gouhar-Shad, daughter of Ghiyath al-Din Tarkhan".

This seal belonged to the wife of Timur's son, Shah Rukh, and the mother of such outstanding public figures of the 15th century as Ulugh-Beg, Baysunghur and Muhammad-Juki.
Gouhar-Shad played an important role in the political life of the Timurid state in Khurasan and was famed for her part in furthering the construction of build-

ings. She was executed on 9th Ramadan 861 AH/31 July 1457 AD, on the order of Sultan Abu Sa'id. The seal may have been made at Herat.
Bibliography:
Ivanov 19716; Timur 1989, Cat. No.128.

189. SEAL.
SECOND HALF OF 15TH CENTURY
Carved lapis lazuli. Diameter 1.8cm
The Hermitage, St Petersburg.
Inv. No. IR-2102. Acquired 1975 from the S Yurenev collection.

In the two halves of the seal there is an inscription in *thuluth* script against a clear ground:

الواثق بالمنان بير محمد شمس الدين

"Relying upon a merciful [Allah]. Pir-Muhammad ibn Shams al-Din".

The lettering, the seal surface filled with the inscription alone, the absence of any decorative element in the inscription's ground and the circular form of the seal itself, are all typical features of the 15th century.
It has not been possible to determine who the owner was from historical sources, since this combination of names occurs frequently. First publication.

190. SEAL.
926 AH/1519–20 AD
Carved cornelian. Diameter 2.4cm.
The Hermitage, St Petersburg.
Inv. No. IR-1871. Acquired 1964 as part of the G. Lemmlein collection.

There are two lines around the edge of the seal. The script of the inscription is *thuluth*, the background is clear. In the centre there is a square with the name (?) of the owner which has not yet been deciphered and the date 926 AH/1519–20 AD. In the segments around the edge are the names and epithets of Muhammad and the Shi'ite imams:

المصطفى وحيدر ... وسجاد وباقر وبعفر
و موسى ورضا والتقين والعسكري ومهدى

"...al-Mustafa and Haydar, Sijjad [i.e. Zain al-Abidin] and Baqir and Ja'far and Musa and Riza and al-Taqiyin and al-Askari and Mahdi".

The shape and lettering of the seal continue the 15th-century tradition, but the letters are becoming smaller and fill the space allotted to the inscription more densely.
First publication.

CAT N° 197

198. Plate. 17th century
Faience, with underglaze painting.
Diameter 33.5cm.
The Hermitage, St Petersburg.
Inv. No. VG-634. Purchased from
A Pashayev (Kubachi).

The use of a combination of cobalt and olive paint, in which cobalt plays the dominant part, is characteristic of a large number of Kubachi wares of the 16th century (see Cat. No.161). Even the ornament decorating the sides and rim is often found on ceramics of this type. The same can also be said of the decoration on the bottom of the plate, of birds painted in cobalt amid rocks and flowers.

As in the majority of Kubachi wares of the 17th century, radial bands and three circles are drawn in cobalt on the outside of the plate. First publication.

199. Dagger and sheath.
Blade: second half of 16th century; hilt and sheath: 17th–century Turkish
Work Steel, nephrite, silver, gold, gemstones; forged, engraved, inlaid and nielloed. Length of blade 21.5cm.
The Hermitage, St Petersburg.
Inv. No. OR-504. Acquired 1924 (?) from the former Paskevich collection.

The blade of the dagger is straight and two-edged with two grooves and a thickened tip. On the ricasso there are medallions with foliate ornament on a gold ground, surrounded by gold ornament on a dark (steel) ground. Further down the blade there are eight cartouches with Persian verses, and towards the tip four cartouches with gold vegetal orna-

ment. The verses are written in *nastaliq* script on a ground with elements of foliate ornamentation. Three separate excerpts appear in the cartouches:

a) on the obverse (metre *ruba'i*):

"Every time your dagger spoke of vengeance
It brought confusion upon the times with its bloodshed.
In the grace and purity of the damask steel,
It is like a willow-leaf covered with dew."

b) on the reverse (metre *hazaj*):

"Stab my breast several times with a dagger,
Open in my heart several doors of delight."

c) on the reverse (metre *hazaj*):

"Pull out the dagger and draw the heart from my breast,
That you may see our heart among the lovers."

At present four blades of this form are known. They are all decorated with Persian verses; on one of them, in the Kremlin Armoury, the name of the craftsman, Muhammad ibn Mas'ud, is cited. All these blades are unlikely to have been produced by a single craftsman (or workshop). Rather, one could speak of a single centre of production, since they are linked by their form and by the content and script of their inscriptions.

The *nastaliq* script of the inscriptions and the appearance of elements of vegetal ornament in their ground permit the dating of the blade to the second half of

the 16th century. The exact place of its manufacture and the names of the authors of the verses remain unknown (however, it should be pointed out that the beginning of the second excerpt coincides with one line of a little-known poet of the second half of the 15th century, Bayazi Hisari – this line is quoted in the poetry anthology of Mir Ali-Shir Nawai *Majalis al-Nafais*).
Bibliography:
Ivanov 1979a, pp.66–68, No.7 (the article includes the Persian text of the inscriptions); Masterpieces 1990, No.86.

200. Shield.
By Muhammad-Mumin zarnishan.
Last quarter of 16th century
Damask steel, forged, engraved, inlaid with gold, decorated with filigree, rubies, turquoises and pearls.
Diameter 48.8cm.

The Moscow Kremlin Armoury.
Inv. No. OR-176.

The shield is circular, convex, forged from a single sheet of damask steel and tooled with fluted grooves which divide the external surface into separate bands and create a whirling effect. Each alternate band is inlaid with gold and widens slightly from the centre outwards towards the rim. A particular refinement is achieved through the use of two types of gold in the inlay – bright (pure) gold for the basic designs and greenish gold (an alloy of gold and silver) for the secondary details.

The medieval artist portrayed 89 figures of people and animals on the shield. On one of the bands a half-bear, half-man is represented with a stone lifted above its head. A figure of a bear appears in another scene at the edge of the

shield, where it has a camel on a lead. Beneath the bear is a stamp into which the name of the craftsman is incised – Muhammad-Mumin zarnishan.

A gold boss with gemstones is fixed to the centre of the shield. The edge is decorated with a gilded steel band into which small rubies and turquoises are set amid foliate ornament.

The shield formed part of the "Sovereign's grand attire" of Tsar Mikhail Fiodorovich (1613- 1645). Documents attest that it originally belonged to Prince Fiodor Mstislavsky who served as a commander for Tsars Ivan IV (the Terrible) and Boris Godunov, and who was head of the boyar government of 1610-11. The shield ended up in the sovereign's armoury after the death of the prince in 1622.

Bibliography:

Mishukov 1954, pp.122-125; Bretanizki 1988, pl.69.

201. SABRE.

SECOND HALF OF 16TH CENTURY

Damask steel, forged and inlaid with gold. Length of blade 80cm.
The Hermitage, St Petersburg.
Inv. No. OR-2839. Transferred 1886 from the Tsarskoye Selo Arsenal.

The blade of the sabre is widened at the tip. The hilt and sheath are of later workmanship (they may have been made in Moscow during the 19th century).

The blade is richly ornamented with gold inlay. On the obverse, next to the guard, there is vegetal ornament. Along the blunt edge of the blade are three cartouches with vegetal ornament

separating twin cartouches with three lines of different Persian verses. After the first cartouche the entire width of the blade is occupied by a scalloped medallion containing gold vegetal ornament and four rubies (?). To judge by the ornament in the form of leaves and rosettes around the stones, this addition was made in Turkey.

One can assume that this cartouche once contained the name of the original owner, which was masked with ornaments by the new owner.

On the reverse, next to the blunt edge, there are cartouches with ornament in the form of stylized "Chinese clouds" and two cartouches with a fine verse.

The script of all the inscriptions is nastaliq, stems and leaves from the ground of the inscriptions.

The verses on the obverse of the blade are as follows (in order from the hilt to the tip of the blade):

a) metre *ramal*:

تیغ خون ریز که شد روی زمین گلگون ازو *
چون زنیغت نوی ابرو که بارد خون ازو

"Bloodthirsty sword, which has made red the face of the earth,

[And] also from your sword, [concealed] in your brows, blood flows."

b) metre indeterminable since a variable number of syllables fall in the hemistich, but there is a radif (rhyme):

شمشیر برهن کشاید ان حبیب نازنین *
کفتمش چرابزد شمشیر حبیب نازنین

"A coquettish beauty bared her sabre against me, I said to her: 'Why do you strike [me], coquettish beauty?"

c) metre *ramal* but not sustained in the first *misra'* (hemistich):

"I said: 'That word of my beloved damascened the sabre, The sword grew a watered pattern and an inlay of gold."

d) On the obverse there is only one line, in *ramal* metre:

سر نمیتایم ز شمشیر حبیب * هرجه میابد سر
من بانصیب

"I shall not bow my head before my beloved's sabre,

[Although] all this will fall on my head together with fate."

It has not been possible to establish the authors of these lines. By the character of the script (*nastaliq*) and the appearance of vegetal ornament in the ground of these inscriptions, one can assign this blade to the second half of the 16th century.

First publication.

202. THRONE.
LATE 16TH CENTURY

Gold, rubies, tourmalines, turquoises, pearls, velvet, wood; stamping, filigree and chasing. 90 x 62.5 x 51.5cm.
The Moscow Kremlin Armoury.
Inv. No. R-28. Brought 1604.

The outline of the throne is severe, precise and graceful. One detects features characteristic of Iranian furniture of that period in the form of the low back passing into the downward-sloping armrests and in the openwork side-walls that blend into the decoratively-shaped legs.
This throne was presented to Tsar Boris Godunov by Shah Abbas in 1604. In preparing the throne for a coronation in 1742 the worn Iranian velvet on the back, seat and armrests was replaced with French velvet.
Bibliography:
Goncharova 1964, p.260.

203. LAMPSTAND-TORCH.
1560s–1580s

Bronze (brass), cast and engraved.
Height 60.5cm.
The Hermitage, St Petersburg.
Inv. No. IR-2202. Transferred 1925 from the museum attached to the former Stieglitz School of Technical Design.

A new type of lighting appliance appeared in Iran during the first half of the 16th century. It consisted of a base in the form of a hollow shaft with a widened lower section and a reservoir for oil set on top of the base and secured to it by means of a flange. The reservoir could also be used separately from the base as a torch. In such a case it would be mounted on a stick by means of a special socket in the lower hemispherical section of the reservoir. At a later period these objects were used as candlesticks. Consequently, in the specialist literature they have for a long time been described as candlesticks (see Ivanov 1960).
The reservoir and base of almost all the known pieces are richly decorated with vegetal ornament and Persian verses. In this particular case two poetical extracts are to be found on the reservoir. By the rim there is an extract from a *ghazal* of the 15th-century poet Katebi Torshizi (metre *mojtass*, script *nastaliq*):

"On that night when the moon of your countenance became the lamp of our solitude,
The candle melted, [for it] could not bear the fire of our converse!

That instant when you throw the veil from your moon-like face
Will be the sunrise of our happiness."

On the vertical edge of the flange there is an extract from a *ghazal* by a poet of the late 15th–early 16th centuries, Ahli Khurasani (its authorship has been determined by Melikian-Chirvani; the metre is *hazaj*, the script *nastaliq*):

چراغ اهل دلرا روشن از روی تو می‌بینم *
همه صاحب دل نرا روی دل سوی تو می‌بینم
توئی مقصود عالم کم مبادا زسر موی *
که عالم را طفیل یک سر از موی تو می‌بینم

"Thanks to you I see the lamp of the magnanimous lit,
I see the heart of all the wise turned towards you.
You are the world's aspiration, let no hair of your head grow less,
For I see the world hanging from the end of your hair."

The base is distinguished by its large size; it is made up of five parts (and not of three, as is usual) – two circular, two faceted and one with spiral fluting.
The first part bears verses from the *Bustan* of Sa'di (metre *motaqareb*, *nastaliq* script):

شبی یاد دارم که دشم نخفت *
شنیدم که پروانه با شمع گفت
که من عاشقم گر بسوزم رواست *
تراگربه و سوز باری چراست

"I remember once at night, when my eyes did not sleep,
I heard a moth speaking to the candle:
I am in love, and if it is fated I should burn,
Why should you also weep and be consumed?"

Engraved in the middle of the second section is the same extract form a *ghazal* of Ahli Khurasani

as appears on the flange of the reservoir (see above), plus an extract from a *ghazal* of Amir Khusrau Dihlawi (metre *hazaj*, script *nastaliq*; part of this inscription is covered by the handles):

زمانی نیست که عشق توجان من نمیسوزد *
کدامین سینه راکان غمزه [یرفر نمیسوزد]
زغیرت سوختم جانا .... آتش مه *

"There is no instant when your love does not inflame my soul,
Whose soul would not be burnt by this artful coquetry.
I am burnt, o soul, by ardour..."

The third section contains a short inscription – the name of the owner: sayyid Muhammad ibn sayyid Jan Shirvani. Judging by the tooling of the ground, the inscription was executed at the same time as the lampstand.
The fourth section bears a long inscription made up of three different poetical extracts. The first (metre *ramal*) of them is by a poet of the first half of the 16th centu-

ry – Hayrati Tuni, the third line is from one of Hafiz's *ghazals* (metre *mojtass*), while the author of the last two lines is unknown (script of all the extracts is *nastaliq*):

که دل از عشق بتان که دکرم میسوزد *
عشق هر لحظه بداغ دکرم میسوزد
همجو پراونه بشمع سروکارست مرا *
که اکریش روم بال او ابرم میسوزد
خوشست خلوت اکربار یار من باشد *
نه [من] بسوزم او او شمع انجمن باشد
عشق بایر در دل تاربک تاروشن شود *
شمع اکر آتش نبیند که کجا روش شود
گر فروز صدهن [ا] ران شمع بن زخسارتو

"When the heart is full of love for the idols who set fire to my soul,
Then love each moment brands me with another mark.
I am in the same state as the moth and candle,
For if I strive forward, my wings will be burnt."
"Pleasant is solitude, when my lady friend is my friend indeed.
I will not be burnt and she will not be the candle of society."
"Love should be [preserved] in the depths of the heart, until [it] flares up.
How can the candle be lit, if it does not see a flame!
If a hundred thousand candles should flare, [yet] without your countenance,
Which [one] of those thousands will set light to my heart?"

On the fifth and last section are engraved the same verses of Katebi Torshizi as on the rim of the reservoir.
Thus verses by seven different poets are represented on this lampstand, six of whom it has been possible to trace – Sa'di, Hafiz, Amir Khusrau Dihlawi, Katebi Torshizi, Ahli Khurasani and Hayrati Tuni. Does this indicate the craftsman's literary culture? Probably, but one finds these same

excerpts on dozens of similar objects of various periods. Hence their use is to a certain extent traditional, and their content – candle, moth, the theme of burning – linked to the object's function. Possibly the quotations also have a mystical (Sufi) meaning.
The ground of all the ornaments and inscriptions is finely cross-hatched, as on accurately dated objects of the 1560s–1580s.
This allows one to assign the Hermitage lampstand to the same period.

Bibliography:
SPA 1938–39, vol.VI, pl.1382; Propyläen Kunstgeschichte 1977, fig.358.

204. FRAGMENT OF A CARPET. LATE 16TH CENTURY
Pile-woven wool. 120x295cm.
The Hermitage, St Petersburg.
Inv. No. VT-997. Transferred 1925 from the museum attached to the former Stieglitz School of Technical Design.

The carpet belongs among the so-called vase carpets, which are distinguished by their large size, variety and intensity of colour and large design of stylized flowers and palmettes.
One of the most characteristic designs on vase carpets is the network pattern seen on this carpet. Carpets of this type are thought to have been produced in the province of Kirman.

Bibliography:
Shandrovskaya 1960, p.155.

CAT Nº 204

CAT N° 205

**205. FRAGMENT OF A CARPET.
SECOND HALF OF 16TH CENTURY**
*Pile-woven wool. 88 x 150cm.
The Hermitage, St Petersburg.
Inv. No. VT-966. Transferred 1925
from the museum attached to the former
Stieglitz School of Technical Design.*

This example belongs to one of
the types of vase carpet from
Kirman, whose characteristic pattern is a network of indented
leaves. This piece has supplementary pile on the reverse.
First publication.

**206. CLOUD COLLAR OF A ROBE.
MID- TO LATE 16TH CENTURY**
*Silk, with linen lining, embroidered in
gold thread. Length 154cm; width 93cm.
The Moscow Kremlin Armoury.
Inv. No. TK 3117.*

The Cloud collar of the robe has
a rounded upper section, two
straight bands along the skirts and a hem partly preserved as a
small rectangle. The collar has a
smooth neckline and four flaps
along the outside border at the
shoulders, chest and back.

At present the original ground of
the embroidery, a scarlet satin,
can only be discerned through
worn patches or at folds, since it
is sewn over entirely with green
silk thread imitating the texture
of serge. In all probability this
was done during its restoration in Russia in the 17th century.
Definite evidence of this is provided by the use of rough linen
as a supplementary lining to the
new embroidery: this is a traditionally Russian fabric, widely
used in Russian embroidery of
the 17th century.

Bibliography:
Treasures of Applied Art 1979, p.27,
No.32; Timur 1989, Cat. No.116.

207. MINIATURE:

THE SHAH LISTENS TO THE TEACHINGS OF A SUFI. 1570s

9.3 x 16.3cm. Manuscript: Lavaih of Jami. Calligrapher: Ahmad al-Husaini al-Mashhadi al-katib. Date of completion of copy: 978 AH/ 1570-71 AD.
The National Library of Russia, St Petersburg. Inv. No. Dom 256, f. 10b.

This sumptuously decorated example of the *Lavaih* was copied by the famous calligrapher of the second half of the 16th century, Ahmad Mashhadi, for the ruler of Mazandaran, Murad Khan.

Apparently the artistic merits of this manuscript were so great that Qazi Ahmad Qumi, the well-known biographer of artists, mentions it in his work, which is an extremely unusual occurrence.

There are three miniatures in the manuscript, and they are clearly painted by a single artist. They are all beautiful examples of the style of miniature painting which was developed at the courts of

Qazwin and Mashhad. The artist was obviously trained at these centres, but this manuscript of the *Lavaih* was apparently illustrated at Mazandaran.
Bibliography:
Akimushkin and Ivanov 1968, pp.23, 24, No.38.

208. MINIATURE:

YOUTH WITH A LUTE. BY SHARAF AL-HUSAINI AL-YAZDI. 1003 AH/1594-95 AD

14 x 22.4cm.
The Hermitage, St Petersburg. Inv. No. VR-701.

During the 16th century, together with traditional illustrations of literary works, Persian painters began producing miniatures on separate sheets. Unconnected with literary subjects and depicting characters and scenes from real life, these miniatures took on the significance of easel paintings.

It was in Qazwin – from 1548 to 1585 the capital of Iran – that miniatures on separate sheets flourished.

Delicacy of draughtsmanship, the brilliance of pure colours – albeit somewhat muted by comparison with the previous stage, a specific "Qazwinian" treatment of figures involving attenuated proportions, long necks, small, round heads and dynamic curves – these are some of the features of this school which played an important role in the formation of the following century's style of painting.

The miniature *Youth with a Lute* belongs to the Qazwin school. The figures of the youth and the white horse are set against the clear ground of the paper, this being characteristic of Qazwin miniatures on separate sheets.

At the bottom of the miniature is the artist's not entirely decipherable inscription:

"Painted by a poor man, who trusts in the mercy of Allah Sharaf al-Husaini al-Yazdi, in the year 1003."

No other work by this artist is known.
Bibliography:
Akimushkin and Ivanov 1968, No.52.

209. MINIATURE:

PORTRAIT OF A GIRL. BY RIZA-I ABBASI. 1011 AH/ 1602-03 AD

Indian ink, paints and gold on paper. 14.8 x 8.4cm (19.3 x 16.9cm with borders).
The Hermitage, St Petersburg. Inv. No. VR-705. Acquired 1924 from the museum attached to the former Stieglitz School of Technical Design.

In the late 16th–early 17th centuries new trends appeared in Persian painting, linked above all with the endeavour to convey a visual impression of the surrounding world.

One of the artists who dealt with these problems was Riza-i Abbasi, considered the founder of the so-called Isfahan school of painting formed in the early 17th century.

The artist's full name was Aqa Riza ibn Ali-Asghar Kashani. His date of birth is not known. In the early 17th century he adopted the *nisba* "Abbasi" in honour of Shah Abbas I, under whom he became head of the library-workshop and leading master of the Isfahan school.

Riza-i Abbasi died in the month of Dhu-l-Qa'da 1044 AH/ between 18 April and 17 May 1635 AD.
Bibliography:
Akimushkin and Ivanov 1968, No.61.

210. YOUTH HOLDING A JUG. BY RIZA-I ABBASI, 1037 AH/ 1627-28 AD

12.5 x 22.3cm.
Museum of Western and Oriental Art, Kiev. Inv. No. 449 GRV.

211. Four miniatures on one sheet. By Riza-i Abbasi

a. *The Dervish Abd al-Mutallib Selmnani (?), 1 Jumada I 1041 AH/ 25 November 1631 AD.*
7.3 x 16.4cm.
b. *A Shepherd. 25 Dhu-l-hijja 1043 AH/22 June 1634 AD.*
10.4 x 16.4cm.
c. *Love Scene. 1610s–1620s.*
7.4 x 10.4cm.
d. *Youth with a Hookah.*
1610s–1620s. 8.8 x 12cm.

The National Library of Russia, St Petersburg.
Inv. No. Dom 489, f. 73b.

212. Shah Abbas and Khan Alam. By Riza-i Abbasi. 17 Rajab 1042 AH/ 28 January 1633 AD
17.5 x 28.5cm. The National Library of Russia, St Petersburg.
Inv. No. Dom 489, f. 74a.

The art of the last great Iranian miniaturist, Riza-i Abbasi (see Cat. No.209), is fairly well represented in former Soviet collections: thirteen signed works of his are known, of which seven are reproduced in this book.

A well-known scholar of the Iranian miniature, I S Shchukin, has distinguished three periods in the artist's work. The majority of the miniatures reproduced in this book belong to the last (third) period in the art of Riza-i Abbasi. The large miniature *Shah Abbas and Khan Alam* is exceptional among his work; possibly it represents the genre of official ceremonial portraiture.
Bibliography:
Krachkovskaya 1927b, pp.42, 43; Mistetstvo 1930, No.480; Akimushkin and Ivanov 1968, pp.26–30, 39 (a reading of the signatures on the miniatures), Nos 65, 66.

213. Three samples of calligraphy. By Mir Imad. No later than 1615
Indian ink on paper. Size of sheet: 45 x 29.5cm; size of samples: 19.4 x 9.4cm (upper), 17.5 x 9cm (left), 17.5 x 9.2 cm (right).
Branch of the Institute of Oriental Studies of the Russian Academy of Sciences, St Petersburg (album E 14, sheet 95b).
Transferred 1921 from the Russian Museum, Petrograd.

The outstanding master of artistic calligraphy, Imad al-Mulk Muhammad ibn Husain (or Ibrahim) al-Husaini al-Saifi al-Qazwini (1551–1615), better known as Mir Imad, was a pupil of the famous calligraphers Malik Dailami (died 1562) and Muhammad-Husaini Tabrizi (died c.1578). He was the last reformer of the *nastaliq* script style and was famed for his art in writing samples of large and medium *nastaliq*. He worked for many years at the court of Shah Abbas I

(1587–1629). The album contains 188 samples of Mir Imad's artistic writing and 26 exercises.
Bibliography:
Akimushkin 1962; Murakka 1994, p.85.

214. Miniature: Girshasp Kills Afriqi in the Battle Against the Kirvan Padishah. By Afzal al-Husaini. 1055 AH/1645–46 AD
31 x 22.5cm. Manuscript: Shah-nama of Firdawsi. Calligrapher: Muhammad-Shafi' ibn Abd al-Jabbar, 1052-61 AH/1642-51 AD.
The National Library of Russia, St Petersburg.
Inv. No. Dom 333, f. 77.

An enormous copy of the Shahnama was prepared as a gift to Shah Abbas II: it was illuminated with 192 miniatures. A group of artists worked on the illustrations of this copy, although not all of them left their signatures. Afzal al-Husaini was one of them and signed 55 miniatures (some of the unsigned works may also be attributed to him). A muted grey-blue palette and a somewhat grotesque treatment of human figures are the characteristics of his style.

Bibliography:
Gyuzalyan and Dyakonov 1934, No.18 (description of the manuscript).

215. Miniature: Rustam Battles with the Monster. By Riza-i musawwir. 1640s
25 x 39cm. Manuscript: Shah-nama of Firdawsi. Calligrapher: Muhammad-Shafi' ibn Abd al-Jabbar, 1052-61 AH/1642-51 AD.
The National Library of Russia, St Petersburg.
Inv. No. Dom 333, f. 217a.

Riza-i musawwir was another of the artists who worked on the miniatures for the copy of the *Shah-nama* made for Abbas II (see Cat. No.214). Although this miniature bears no signature, all the characteristics of the artist's style are present here – the use of light colours and the treatment of the sky in the form of blue-white patches – and this allows one to attribute the work to him (there are miniatures with the artist's signature in another copy of the *Shah-nama* from the same library, PNS 381).
First publication.

216. BLADE OF A SABRE.
BY RAJAB-ALI ISFAHANI.
FIRST HALF OF 17TH CENTURY
Damask steel, forged and inlaid with gold. Length 99.6cm.
The Moscow Kremlin Armoury.
Inv. No. OR-1413. Presented to Tsar Alexei Mikhailovich by an Iranian merchant in 1664.

The sabre blade is of damask steel, slightly curved, with a two-edged tip. Downwards from the handle a wide channel has been hollowed out. Along the blunt edge on both sides there are cavities for pearls (the presence of pearls is attested by the Armoury Inventories before 1776). The heel of the blade is flat and decorated with gold inlay in three bands of different widths, forming an undulating design with a rhythmical interface of decoratively-shaped medallions. On the right side of the blade, at the heel, the mark of the craftsman is damascened in gold. The tang is slightly curved in towards the cutting edge of the blade; it is wide, flat and straight with two holes for mounting the hilt. There are two rectangular marks stamped on the tang, bearing the Arabic inscription "Made by Rajab-Ali Isfahani", plus the circular stamp of the Great Royal Treasury, with a double-headed eagle.

Bibliography:
Treasures of Applied Art 1979, p.22, No.13.

217. BRIDLE HEADPIECE.
EARLY 17TH CENTURY
Leather, gold and silver; chased, matt-tooled, filigreed, gilded and decorated with gems and glass. Height of forehead plaque 11.5cm; width 7cm.
The Moscow Kremlin Armoury.
Inv. No. K-1015. Brought by the ambassador Andi-beg from Shah Safi to Tsar Mikhail Fiodorovich in 1635.

The bridle headpiece consists of narrow leather straps with applied gold plaques, and a crosspiece – a forehead plaque linking the upper horizontal straps.

Bibliography:
Treasures of Applied Art 1979, p.24, No.25.

218. CUP.
16TH–17TH CENTURY
Gold, cast, turned and polished, decorated with rubies, emeralds, garnets, turquoises and glass. Diameter 12cm; height 3.5cm.
The Hermitage, St Petersburg.
Inv. No. VZ-722.

This small cup is richly decorated on the outside surface only, with 510 rubies, 114 emeralds, 6 garnets, and turquoise and glass mounted in low settings. On the inside of the foot two incomprehensible inscriptions are engraved in Arabic script: "forty two" (?) and a word possibly signifying the weight of the cup, written in *siyaqat* script. It is important to note the tooling of the ground between the stone settings: it is like fine granulation. This technique has parallels both among Iranian articles in the Armoury (Cat. Nos 217, 219) and on Iranian weapons, although their ground tends to be tooled with various punches (Cat. Nos 165, 248). This observation is of importance in identifying Iranian jewellery of the 15th–17th centuries, which are very little known and of which, apparently, very few survive. It is possible that a characteristic of Iranian gold jewellery with gems is that the stones are mounted in low settings, in contrast to the high settings with a rosette seen on Turkish articles and the setting of stones in deep recesses (flush with the object's surface) in Indian articles of the 16th–18th centuries.

Bibliography:
Oriental Jewellery 1984, No.51.

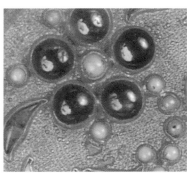

Stored in the Royal Treasury and known from ancient records, the horn has attracted the attention of scholars for a long time. It was first published in the middle of the 19th century and until recently was considered to have been made in Constantinople during the first half of the 17th century. I. Vishnevskaya has established the horn to be of Iranian manufacture of the 16th–17th century.
Bibliography:
Treasures of Applied Art 1979, p.32, No.55.

219. HORN.
FIRST HALF OF 17TH CENTURY
Buffalo horn in a gold mount, cast, chased, matt-tooled, enamelled and decorated with turquoises, rubies, tourmalines, spinel and glass. Length 41cm; diameter 8.4cm.
The Moscow Kremlin Armoury.

Inv. No. DK-264. Presented to Tsar Alexei Mikhailovich by the Dutch Embassy in 1665.

The mount is made of a fine sheet of gold chased in imitation of granulation. It consists of a terminal, one wide hoop at the rim and two narrow ones in the middle with supporting plaques fitted to them. The rims of the terminal and of the wide hoop are openwork tracery in the form of stylized lotus flowers. The mount is decorated with a great number of cabochon gems.

220. DAGGER AND SHEATH.
BY MUHAMMAD LARI.
BLADE AND HILT:
IRAN, 17TH CENTURY.
SHEATH:
TURKEY, 18TH CENTURY
Damask steel, gold, wood; forged and decorated with gemstones and enamel. Length 38.4cm.
The Moscow Kremlin Armoury.
Inv. No. OR-3877. Transferred 1810 from the Rüstkammer.

The two-edged blade of the dagger is of damask steel. The inscription "Muhammad Lari" is engraved on both sides of the heel.
The hilt is gold, richly ornamented with enamel and gemstones. The sheath is coated in gold leaf with a densely patterned vegetal ornament.
Bibliography:
Treasures of Applied Art 1979, p.24, No.24.

CAT N° 218

CAT N° 220

221. CANDLESTICK.
FIRST HALF OF 17TH CENTURY
*Bronze (brass), cast, forged and
engraved. Height 26.5cm.*
The Hermitage, St Petersburg.
*Inv. No. IR-2270. Acquired from the
Stroganov collection.*

Candlesticks of similar form
(nine other examples are known)
present art historians with several hitherto unresolved problems,
of which the main one is to
determine the date of manufacture of such objects.

All ten candlesticks have identical
sockets for the candles, in the
form of dragons' heads, and iden-

tical scaly ornament on the body.
The shape of the base on one of
the candlesticks dates back to
14th-century examples. The lower
part of this base has exactly the
same scaly ornament.

It could be suggested that this is a
15th-century candlestick preserved
intact (see Allan 1982b, p.39).
The bases of the remaining nine
candlesticks are distinguished by
their ornament (three of them
are without any decoration). The
shape of all the bases is virtually
identical and goes back to 15th-
century examples (see Cat. No,
163). The oldest of them (in the
Museum of Islamic Art, Cairo,

see Ivanov 1969a, No.2; SPA
1938-39, vol.VI, p.1377a; Grube
1974, fig.99) undoubtedly dates
from the last quarter of the 15th
century. It was made in the workshop of Shir- Ali ibn Muhammad
Dimashqi in Khurasan. G Wiet
has pointed out that the socket
of this candlestick is a later addition (see Wiet 1935, p.17).
Another similar candlestick is in
the Pars Museum in Shiraz.
Along the rim of the shoulders
is an openwork ornament of palmettes (absent from the other
bases). Melikian-Chirvani attributes it to the second half of
the 15th century (see Melikian-
Chirvani 1975, p.155, fig.6).
In the collection of F.R. Martin
there were once two such candlesticks (see Martin 1902, p.40).
The base of one of them was decorated with corrugated ornament only on the upper side
facet of the shoulders, while the
other, distinguished from similar
ones by its wide, low edge, was
richly decorated with engraved
vegetal ornament, which enables
one to date it no earlier than the
last quarter of the 16th century.
The candlestick reproduced here
is distinguished from others by a
lower rim to the base, in the
form of large palmettes.
The base is richly decorated with
figures of people and beasts, and
vegetal ornament, which makes it
possible to date it to the first half
of the 17th century. There is
another candlestick in the
Hermitage, two in the Museum
of Art and Culture in Samarkand
and one in the mausoleum of
khwaja Ahmad Yasawi in the
town of Turkestan, none of

which have any ornament on
their bases (the Hermitage one
has pierced applied plaques of
uncertain date). On all four
objects the socket and base are
made of the same metal (bronze
or brass) and they do not create
the impression of being articles
composed of variously dated
parts.
It is essential to point out that
there is one other type of candlestick with sockets in the form of
two dragons, but the heads are
treated differently from those of
the objects described above, and
the bases are of a different shape,
characteristic of a number of
17th-century candlesticks (see
Bulletin des Musées de France, 8th
year, No.4, Paris, 1936, p.63). This
type can be dated to the middle
of the 17th century.
Thus it is possible that in this
group one candlestick has survived intact, the base of another
is from the second half of the
15th century, while two other
bases can be assigned to the end
of the 16th-first half of the 17th
century. The dating of the
remaining bases is uncertain.
Candle sockets can be assigned to
the end of the Timurid era due to
the depiction of dragons, and
these are widely represented
among various types of objects
from the Khurasan of the second
half of the 15th-early 16th centuries (see Grube 1974, figs 38,
39, 80, 81, 103-08, 140, 145).
Whether the treatment of the
dragon heads on all the mentioned objects is close or not
remains difficult to decide.
At the same time it is hard to
imagine that the tradition of

making candle sockets in the form of two dragon heads should have been preserved virtually unaltered for about two hundred years. Yet it is possible to believe that such sockets were being produced in the 17th century as well. There is a strange object in the ethnographical section of the Janashia Museum of Georgia. It consists of a large brass torch of the first half of the 17th century (similar in its dimensions to the upper part of the lampstand-torch, Cat. No. 203) with a socket for candles attached to it, in the form of three intertwined dragon heads made of brass.

Therefore one would suppose that the Hermitage candlestick was also made in its entirety during the 17th century.

Bibliography:
SPA 1938–39, vol.VI, pl.1377b; Grube 1974, fig,100; E Grube, "Notes on the Decorative Arts of the Timurid Period, II", in: Islamic Arts, III, Genoa – New York, 1989, fig.7; Masterpieces 1990, No.108.

222. BOWL. BY MUHAMMAD-ZAMAN NAQQASH-I SHIRAZI. RAJAB 1052 AH/ SEPTEMBER-OCTOBER 1642 AD

Bronze (brass), cast and engraved.
Diameter 18.2 cm.
The Hermitage, St Petersburg.
Inv. No. IR-2264.

This bowl on a low foot-ring has sides which widen upwards to an extroverted rim and a small hemispherical protuberance in the centre of the base. This form of bowl emerged in the 16th century and

continued to exist, with few changes, until the beginning of the 20th century.

Bowls of this form are usually entirely covered with inscriptions from the Koran and were used either in folk medicine or for fortune-telling. The Hermitage bowl also has inscriptions from the Koran engraved inside it, and next to the protuberance there are Arabic verses in praise of Ali, but with the name of Muhammad added. On the outside surface there are quotations from various suras of the Koran (not even always entire verses). There is also an inscription with benedictions of the Shi'ite imams, and in another band the signs of the zodiac.

The protuberance bears verses from the Gulistan of Sa'di (*motaqareb* metre, *thuluth* script) and the craftsman's signature:

غرض نقشيست كز ماباز ماند *
كه هستى رانمى بينم بقائى
مگر صاحب دلى روزى برحمت *
كند در حق اين مسكين دعائى
كتبه العبد المذنب بالتقصير محمد زمان نقاش
شيرازى شهر رجب ١٠٥٢

"The aim of life is to leave behind a memory of oneself,
For I do not see eternity in being.
Perhaps occasionally some wise man will mercifully
Utter a prayer in memory of this poor man."

"This was written by a slave who has sinned through remission, Muhammad-Zaman naqqash-i Shirazi, the month of Rajab 1052."

The Hermitage collection includes a second bowl by the same craftsman, completed in 1037 AH/1627–28 AD. Here he

indicates his other professional title – *kendekar* (engraver). On the bowl reproduced here his title is *naqqash*, which is usually translated as "artist" (in the wider sense of the word), but the first meaning of this Arabic root is still "to engrave", so there is no particular discrepancy here.

It is possible that this craftsman was one of the Shiraz coppersmiths who, according to the traveller John Fryar, were the best in Iran during the 17th century. The craftsman's *nisba* "Shirazi" points to such a possibility. No other works by Shiraz craftsmen have yet been discovered.

First publication.

223. Casket. By Sadiq.
17th century
Copper, forged and engraved.
27 x 19,8cm.
Museum of Ethnology, St Petersburg.
Inv. No. 31-156. Acquired 1902.

This casket is apparently the sole surviving object in such a form. Its decoration is typical of the 17th century and the ground is tooled with diagonal hatching characteristic of Iranian copperware of that century.

A verse inscription (*ramal* metre, *nastaliq* script) is engraved on the casket. It is interesting in that it includes the craftsman's name, which is a very rare occurrence:

باددر عالم فانى باقى * عمل صادق استاد باقى

"In a transient world may the work remain of Sadiq – an eternal master !"

Another work of his – also a casket, but of a different shape – is now in a private collection in Geneva.
In the 19th century the side walls were engraved with figures of people, birds and beasts, and with a false date: 872 AH/1467–68 AD. First publication.

224. BOWL.
1113 AH/1701–02 AD
Copper, forged and engraved.
Height 15.5cm; diameter 31.5cm.
The Hermitage, St Petersburg.
Inv. No. IR-2158. Purchased 1980 from S Khanukayev.

Such bowls as this, on a fairly high foot, appear in the 17th century. Only the outside of the bowl is decorated. The inscription, in *nastaliq* script but with widely-spaced letters, is particularly striking. The background consists of scrolled stems with flowers and trefoils. The content of the inscription is a blessing upon the Shi'ite imams.

Similar inscriptions often appear on objects of applied art in Iran from the beginning of the 16th century, when the Shi'ite interpretation of Islam became an official religion. During the second half of the 17th century the curves and spacing of lettering became very wide. This exaggerated decorativeness became especially highly developed in the early 18th century.
First publication.

225. Flask. 17th century
Faience, with moulded decoration.
Height 18cm.
The Hermitage, St Petersburg.
Inv. No. VG-2354. Transferred 1925
from the museum attached to the former
Stieglitz School of Technical Design.

The flask is decorated with a relief design and covered with a light green glaze. On one of the sides there is a half-length portrait of the Madonna and Child, on the other a dragon against a background of a landscape. Relief vegetal ornament around the ribbing of the flask serves as a frame to these scenes. The flask is one of a small number of surviving examples of Safavid faience, which are notable for the originality of their technique (the paste is pressed into moulds), for their colour and their decoration. As a rule the wide sides of the flasks, mugs and bottles bear images on a variety of themes. The characteristic blend of Iranian, European and Chinese themes on ceramics of this type has already been noted in the literature, as has the close link of the images with those of the Isfahan school of miniatures. The European motif of the Madonna and Child could have been borrowed from European etchings which were widely circulated in Iran during the 17th century. But taking into account the fact that the Madonna's face reflects a canonical type from Isfahan miniatures, one can assume that this portrayal has as its basis some Persian miniature or other on a European theme. The same may be said of the Chinese motif on the other side of the flask: the Chinese

dragon is portrayed against a landscape characteristic of 17th-century Isfahan miniatures.
Bibliography:
Rapoport 1972, fig.2.

226. Spittoon.
Late 17th–early 18th century
Faience, painted in lustre; double firing. Height 13cm.
The Hermitage, St Petersburg.
Inv. No. VG-62. Transferred 1925 from the museum attached to the former Stieglitz School of Technical Design.

This light and very thin-walled vessel was made from a dense, white, porcelain-like paste, painted in lustre and covered with a transparent, colourless glaze.
Iranian craftsmen of the Safavid age revived the art of lustre painting, which had been highly developed in the 12th–14th centuries. This is the only type of Iranian Safavid ceramics virtually untouched by Chinese influences. However, the decoration on lustreware of this time (primarily small bowls, vases and high-necked bottles) does not repeat old traditional Iranian motifs either: they reflect the tastes of the Safavid period and stylistically owe much to designs on textiles and other products of Iranian applied art. More often than not plants are depicted, as on this spittoon, and sometimes birds and beasts portrayed, unlike an old lustreware, in silhouette and not "in reserve".
The majority of Safavid lustre faience articles are assigned to the second half of the 17th–first half

of the 18th centuries, on the basis of their shape and of the only dated example, with an indecipherably inscribed date which A. Lane has read as 1084 AH/ 1673-74 AD (Lane 1957, p.118, No.53).
It has not yet proved possible to determine the exact origin of this group of Iranian ceramics.
First publication.

227. Bottle. Late 16th–
first half of 17th century
Faience, with underglaze painting. Height 36.3cm.
The Hermitage, St Petersburg.
Inv. No. VG-290. Acquired from the State Museum Reserve.

This bottle is made of white faience, decorated with relief designs and painted with vivid blue cobalt point under a colourless glaze. The cobalt serves as a ground for motifs which stand out against it "in reserve" – a technique rarely encountered among examples of blue-and-white ceramics. Individual elements of the design executed in relief are outlined in black and the details are marked with black lines.
In contrast to the majority of cobalt wares with chiefly Chinese motifs, the themes here are purely Iranian. One side of the bottle presents a heron and a hunter shooting a gun at a fleeing animal, while the other shows a standing man in European dress with the slain animal thrown over his shoulder, and a woman with a bowl in her hand, kneeling in front of an unidentified object. Both scenes are united by a landscape with shrubs and trees with

birds perched on the branches. Four flying birds are also represented on the pear-shaped section at the tip of the neck.

These same decorations, with insignificant alterations, occur on three other bottles in the Hermitage collection, on a bottle in the Czartoryski collection in Cracow and on a bottle in the Victoria and Albert Museum in London. Although several of this group of bottles are plainly based on a single model, their painting varies in the level of artistic execution. Apparently the bottles were made at various times, which enables one to trace the evolution both of the themes themselves and of various details in terms of their simplification and degeneration. Lane (see Lane 1957, p.99) has ascribed the bottle in London to Mashhad, one of the largest centres for the production of cobalt ceramics in 16th- and 17th-century Iran. This localization can presumably be accepted for this particular bottle too, if we take into account the proximity of many of its features to those of ceramics attributed to Mashhad – a white paste, the use of black outlines, the manner of rendering plants with large leaves and flying birds "in reserve" on a cobalt ground and outlined in black.

Bibliography:
Rapoport 1975; Masterpieces 1990, No.100.

228. BOWL OF A HOOKAH. 17TH CENTURY

Faience, with slip decoration and underglaze painting. Height 27.2cm. The Hermitage, St Petersburg. Inv. No. VG-291. Transferred 1925 from the museum attached to the former Stieglitz School of Technical Design.

This hookah is decorated with painted designs in white and yellow slip on a blue ground, under a colourless, transparent glaze. At the side the vessel has an opening with a spout in the form of a flower, to which the tube for the mouthpiece was attached. The hookah's shape echoes that of Chinese porcelain wine vessels. However, the painting is based on a symmetrical composition, widespread in Iranian ceramics, and characteristic Iranian motifs serve as ornament - scalloped medallions filled with arabesque-*islimi*, clusters of long narrow leaves, carnation stalks and flowers.

Faience wares with polychrome painting on a white or coloured ground are tentatively ascribed to Kirman - one of the most important centres of ceramics production of Safavid times. In the Victoria and Albert Museum in London there is a vessel analogous in shape to that in the Hermitage and also painted in white and yellow slip on a blue ground, and this is dated 1049 AH/1658-59 AD (see Lane 1957, pl.88b).

Bibliography:
Masterpieces 1990, No.105.

229. BOTTLE. 17TH CENTURY

Faience, with slip decoration and underglaze painting. Height 26.4cm. The Hermitage, St Petersburg. Inv. No. VG-345. Transferred 1925 from the museum attached to the former Stieglitz School of Technical Design.

This type of polychrome painting is found on wares from Kirman.

Numerous shards have been discovered in Kirman itself and its surroundings, fragments of ceramic wares with painting in cobalt blue, red slip and sometimes green point. Dated examples of this type of ceramics are also known from the 1670s, allowing one to determine the period when it was produced (see Lane 1957, p.83).

Bibliography:
Kverfeldt 1947, p.107, pl.XXI.

230. PLATE. 17TH CENTURY

Faience, with slip decoration and underglaze painting. Diameter 33 cm. The Hermitage, St. Petersburg. Inv. No. VG-527. Purchased from S Magomedov (Kubachi).

The plate has been painted with wide, relief brushstrokes in red and yellow slip, and also with cobalt blue, green and brown point, all under a transparent, colourless glaze.

This plate belongs to the so-called Kubachi group (see Cat. No.161). In its range of colour this piece is reminiscent of Turkish faience; however, the decoration of human and animal figures, the flower and landscape motifs, all reflect features of the predominating style of 17th-century Iranian art.

As has already been pointed out, it is nowadays accepted that the so-called Kubachi ceramics were made at some centre or other in North-Western Iran. This type of ware is usually assigned to the late 16th–early 17th centuries.

Bibliography:
Great Art Treasures 1994, No.414.

CAT N° 227

CAT Nº 229

CAT N° 233

CAT N° 234

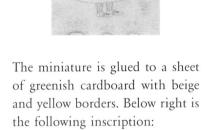

235. MINIATURE:
EUROPEAN LANDSCAPE.
BY ALI-QULI IBN MUHAMMAD.
1059 AH/1649 AD
9 x 12cm.
The Hermitage, St Petersburg.
Inv. No. VR-950.

The miniature depicts a provincial locality with a river crossed by a bridge in the foreground, a watermill and houses. At the bottom of the miniature is the artist's signature: "A painting by the most humble Ali-Quli son of Muhammad 1059."

European works were copied regularly in Iran from the 1670s on, but during the first half and middle of the century only isolated cases of Persian artists turning to European examples are known, one of them being this particular miniature.

It has been established by L Gyuzalyan that this miniature was copied from an engraving published by the Dutch engravers, Marco and Aegidius Sadeler. The engraving in turn was based on a canvas by the 17th-century landscape and animal pointer Roelandt Savery. The miniature is distinguished neither by artistry of execution nor by care and precision in copying the illustration.

The miniaturist has distorted the perspective of the buildings, renounced the play of light and shade and reinforced the harshness of line. Not only were the techniques of western painting new to the miniaturist, but also the motif itself. It is well known that "pure landscape" was never an independent genre in Persian painting, which is probably why the miniaturist supplemented the landscape

with figures absent in the original. Bibliography: Gyuzalyan 1972.

236. MINIATURE:
PORTRAIT OF IMAM-QULI KHAN.
BY MUHAMMAD MUSAWWIR. 1052
AH/BETWEEN 1 APRIL 1642 AND
21 MARCH 1643 AD
12.7 x 16.3cm.
Museum of Oriental Art, Moscow.
Inv. No. 1973-II. Acquired 1954
from the Board of Art Exhibitions
and Panoramas.

This portrait of the ruler of Bukhara, Imam-Quli Khan, is the only surviving picture of him. It was painted a year before his death: he died in Medina in 1053 AH/1643-44 AD. Imam-Quli set out on the *hajj* (pilgrimage to the holy places of Mecca and Medina) in November 1641 AD, having abdicated the throne. He travelled through Iran where he was ceremoniously received by Shah Abbas II. It was during his stay in Iran that this portrait was painted – a typical example of the Isfahan school of 17th-century miniature painting, as can be clearly seen in the treatment of the vegetation and clouds and the figure of the Khan himself.
Bibliography:
Ivanov 1968; Maslenitsyna 1975, No.120.

237. MINIATURE:
PORTRAIT OF AN INDIAN PRINCE.
BY BAHA AL-DIN GILANI.
RABI' II 1061 AH/BETWEEN 24
MARCH AND 21 APRIL 1651 AD
16.1 x 9.2cm.
The Hermitage, St Petersburg.
Inv. No. VR-740/XXVI.
Transferred in the 1930s from the
Academy of Arts of the USSR.

The miniature is glued to a sheet of greenish cardboard with beige and yellow borders. Below right is the following inscription:

هو در شهر ربیع الآخر سنه ١٠٦١ تحریر یافت در
شهر اصغهان .... بها الدین کیلانی

"He [i.e. God]. In the month of Rabi' II the year 1061 in the town of Isfahan painted by Baha al-Din Gilani".

The miniature shows all the basic characteristics of early 17th-century Mughal portraiture. The figure is portrayed full length and, as is usual in Mughal miniatures, the body is shown at a three-quarter angle while the face and legs are in profile.

The clothes are carefully painted, with all the peculiarities of fashion at the early 17th-century Mughal court: the white *jama* (outer garment) with the special shading of the armpit, often found on miniatures by Mughal artists in the first quarter of the 17th century; the brocade belt with its long narrow ends; the flat form of the turban. (In the second quarter of the 17th century details of clothing change.)

The colour treatment of the miniature is distinguished by its restraint: this drawing is rather lightly coloured in lilac, orange and gold – which is also characteristic of early 17th-century Mughal portraiture.

Hence this miniature portrait executed by a Persian painter of the mid-17th century is a copy of an early 17th-century Mughal painting. It should be noted that several specific characteristics of Indian dress were incomprehensible to the Persian painter, such as the

"construction" of the Indian turban and the fastening and ornamentation of the belt. The artist decided not to depict the striped cloth of the wide trousers beneath the transparent gown, limiting himself to the outline alone.
First publication.

238. MINIATURE:
SHAH AND COURTIERS.
BY ALI-QULI BEG JABBADAR.
SECOND HALF OF 17TH CENTURY
42.1 x 28.2cm.
Branch of the Institute of Oriental Studies of the Russian Academy of Sciences, St Petersburg. Album E 14, f. 98. Transferred 1921 from the Russian Museum, Petrograd.

The personality of the artist, Ali-Quli beg Jabbadar, remains something of a mystery. Nothing is known of his biography from contemporary sources (however, the same could be said of all the other artists who were his contemporaries). A short and very curious reference to him occurs in the poetry anthology *Atashkade* compiled in the third quarter of the 18th century by Lutf-Ali beg Isfahani.

The author of the anthology writes of the artist Muhammad-Ali beg, whose grandfather is "Ali-Quli beg Farangi, and in painting he is a second Mani". It follows from this text that Ali-Quli beg was a European (*farangi* means "European"), who had adopted Islam in Iran; this is Ali-Quli beg Jabbadar.

Whether he was a professional artist remains uncertain. The quality of his work shows that he was no novice at painting,

although some details do not indicate professional status. His nickname Jabbadar (literally "possessing armour") hints at a connection with armoury and it is not impossible that he could have been a European armourer. However, during the second half of the 17th century the supervision of works of art was part of the business of the *jabbakhana* (arsenal). Possibly this fact explains the artist's nickname.

His only accurately dated miniature, *Two Ladies and a Page* (in the same album as that which contains five signed works by Ali-Quli and another two which can with certainty be attributed to him), was painted at Qazwin in the month of Safar 1085 AH/May–June 1674 AD. All these miniatures have a common style.

Four of his miniatures portray Shah Suleiman (ruled 1666–94). This allows one to say that Ali-Quli was close to the Shah and was apparently an outstanding artist of the court workshop (among the works of his colleague and contemporary, Muhammad-Zaman, there are no portraits of Shah Suleiman, see Cat. No.239). The miniature *Shah and Courtiers* bears the signature:

هو غلام زاده قديم عليقلى جبادار

"He [i.e. Allah] ! Son of an ancient slave Ali-Quli Jabbadar".

Although the term ghulam-zade signifies "son of a slave born in the master's house", it hardly follows that one should understand it literally in this instance. It is most probably simply a humbling

formula. Above the two figures, to the left, are two Georgian inscriptions, but greatly distorted. Although the draughtsmanship of the miniature is Iranian, it shows evidence of Ali-Quli's close acquaintance with the techniques of European painting. But there are disruptions of perspective and of composition: the figure of a European to the left of the Shah is floating in mid-air.
Bibliography:
Ivanov 1962, pp.55–58, pl.99; De Bagdad à Ispahan 1994, p.255; Murakka 1994, p.29.

239. MINIATURE: VENUS AND CUPID. BY MUHAMMAD-ZAMAN. 1096 AH/1684-85 AD
17.9 x 24cm.
Branch of the Institute of Oriental Studies of the Russian Academy of Sciences, St Petersburg.
Album E 14, f. 89. Transferred 1921 from the Russian Museum, Petrograd.

The life and work of the artist Muhammad-Zaman, son of hajji Yusuf Qumi, have engaged the interest of scholars of the Persian miniature for a number of years. But although the first attempt to write his biography was undertaken in 1925, we still know next to nothing about him, the signatures on his miniatures being the only source of information.
Because the influence of European painting is very noticeable in his work and several miniatures are painted on Christian themes, for a long time it was considered that Muhammad-Zaman was sent to study painting in Rome, where he adopted the Christian faith,

returned to Iran, fled to India because of his devotion to Christianity, then returned once more to Iran and worked in Isfahan during the last quarter of the 17th century.
However, a careful study of all these facts has shown that most of them concern a different person – a certain Muhammad-Zaman "Farangikhwan" (*ie* "who reads European"), who did in fact adopt the Christian faith, but in Iran, and who went to India and lived there for some time.
The trouble is that the name Muhammad-Zaman is not unusual and at present no fewer than twenty people bearing this name are known in 17th-century Iran. However, among them there is no Muhammad-Zaman, son of hajji Yusuf Qumi.
The reliable information about Muhammad-Zaman can be reduced to the following few facts. His place and date of birth are unknown, he died before 1112 AH/1700-01 AD, most probably in Isfahan.
In 1086 AH/1675-76 AD he was working at the Shah's residence at Ashraf in the province of Mazandaran, and later in Isfahan, the capital of the Safavid state. At that time he was employed in the preparation of manuscripts at the court library workshop.
Miniatures with Christian subjects – Mary and Elizabeth, Abraham's Sacrifice, The Return from Egypt – were painted for the Shah and are copies of Flemish prints (the authors of the last two are known).
The earliest of his surviving miniatures are dated 1086 AH/

1675-76 AD and the latest 1100 AH/1688-89 AD.
The miniature *Venus and Cupid* has two inscriptions. The first includes the artist's signature: "Picture completed by the most worthless of slaves Muhammad-Zaman. The year 1087 [AH; 1676-77 AD]".
The second inscription is written in small *nastaliq*: "He [*ie* Allah] ! At the command of he who achieves his desires, the most noble, most sacred, supreme sovereign". This phrase in its entirety formed the standard appellation of the Shah.
The subject is borrowed from an engraving by R Sadeler (Hollstein 1980, XXI, p.248, No.174). A comparison of the miniature and the print shows that Muhammad-Zaman did not slavishly copy the subject, but only transferred to the miniature the figures of Venus and Cupid, meanwhile completely altering the background, and he left out the figure of a satyr, without which the posture of Cupid remains inexplicable. Meanwhile the painting technique remains purely Iranian.
Bibliography:
Ivanov 1962, p.44, 45, ill.83; Ivanov 1979b; Arts of Persia 1989, p.220, pl.38; De Bagdad à Ispahan 1994, p.253; Murakka 1994, p.69.

CAT N° 235

CAT Nº 238

CAT N° 239

240. QALAMDAN (PEN-CASE).
LATE 17TH CENTURY

Papier-mâché, painted and lacquered.
23.3 x 3.8 x 3.5cm.
The Hermitage, St Petersburg.
Inv. No. VR-125. Transferred 1925
from the museum attached to the former
Stieglitz School of Technical Design.

This oblong pen-case with rounded ends and a sliding internal section represents the commonest type of *qalamdan*. The portrait of a young European in armour is painted on it, framed by flower and foliate motifs in gold against a black ground.

This picture echoes a miniature previously in the collection of F. Martin and afterwards, from the early 1950s, in the Musée Guimet, Paris. Ivanov assigns the *qalamdan* to the late 17th century or the very beginning of the 18th century and considers the portrait represented on it to be a copy of a mid-17th century Dutch print.

He suggests that it is the young Louis XIV who is portrayed both on the *qalamdan* and in the miniature. He has also suggested that these works were reproductions from the same original and by a single artist - Ali-Quli beg Jabbadar, who worked in Iran during the second half of the 17th century (this name is written on the miniature in the Musée Guimet).

Ivanov considers that the inscription on the miniature is not authentic; nevertheless, he does not deny Jabbadar's authorship.

It should be added that the picture on the *qalamdan* was evident-ly not painted onto the case itself. In all probability a miniature on paper was used, trimmed around the edges and glued to a pen-case of standard dimensions.

Taking into account the great artistry of the miniature, one can assume that it did in fact bear the authentic signature of Jabbadar, which was lost when the picture was transferred onto the pen-case.

An argument in favour of the above conjecture is the fact that all of Jabbadar's known works, bearing signatures that are indisputable and in his own hand, are miniatures on paper. Besides this, examination of the painting on the *qalamdan* has shown that lacquer was poured over the portrait in the centre of the case when there were already large cracks in the paint layer and priming. The painting on the sides of the *qalamdan* is not finely cracked, which may be explained by the protective properties of the lacquer. Although the edges of the miniature portrait - which we have suggested was glued to the case - are deliberately masked with a thick layer of ornamen., Even so it is clearly visible that the black ground on which the painting is executed in gold is on a raised layer, above the portrait of the youth.

Bibliography:
Ivanov 1974; Busson 1978.

241. QALAMDAN (PEN-CASE).
BY MUHAMMAD-IBRAHIM IBN HAJJI YUSUF QUMI. ISFAHAN, RAJAB 1092 AH/BETWEEN 17 JULY AND 15 AUGUST 1681 AD

Papier-mâché, painted and lacquered.
24.5 x 4.5 x 3.6cm.

The Hermitage, St Petersburg.
Inv. No. VR-17. Transferred 1924 from
the museum attached to the former
Stieglitz School of Technical Design.

This *qalamdan* is one of the few surviving items of 17th-century lacquerware. Its decoration involves a combination of foliate ornament and calligraphic inscriptions.

The main role is played by the Arabic inscriptions in the five cartouches on the lid, their severity of line being dictated by their content: the central, largest, cartouche bears a prayer extremely popular among all Shi'ites, directed at the Imam Ali; in the four others there are verses in praise of Ali:

"Cry out to Ali, the performer of miracles,
You will find in him a support to bear griefs.
All cares and woes will vanish
Under your protection, o Ali, o Ali, o Ali!"
Ali ! The shield is the object of his affection.
He allots the Flame and the Garden [i.e. hell and heaven].
In truth he fulfils the will of the Chosen One [i.e. Muhammad],
He represents the line of men and the line of spirits."

Inscribed in yellow on a dark blue ground or in white on a bright green ground, these inscriptions not only convey a specific text but blend organically into the decoration on the case, forming part of a single ornamental composition together with the fine gold vegetal pattern filling the spaces between cartouches.

Four large cartouches on the sides bear Persian verses by Mir Abd al-Ghani Tafrishi:

"In that your brush performs miracles of writing,
It may be that the words might reveal a playful meaning.
Compared to any curve inscribed by you, the sky is only a slave with a ring in his ear,
For each line you extend the reward will be long days of existence."

In the four small medallions situated between the cartouches the following information is communicated: "Completed in the revered month of Rajab of the year 1092 in the capital city of Isfahan by the brush of this most humble slave protected by the heavenly angels of the Threshold ibn hajji Yusuf Muhammad-Ibrahim Qumi".

Muhammad-Ibrahim, who painted the *qalamdan*, was apparently the brother of one of the most famous Persian painters of the second half of the 17th century, Muhammad-Zaman (see Cat. No.239).

Bibliography:
Ivanov 1970b (the article includes the Arabic and Persian texts of the inscriptions); Adle 1980, pp.37–42, figs 19–23.

242. MINIATURE: A BIRD.
BY YUSUF-ZAMAN.
1108 AH/1696-97 AD

14.3 x 8.7cm.
The Hermitage, St Petersburg.
Inv. No. VR-707, f. 6 (glued into an
album of miniatures and samples of
calligraphy). Transferred 1924 from
the museum attached to the former
Stieglitz School of Technical Design.

Persian miniatures depicting flowers and birds appeared quite frequently in the mid-17th century. Usually they were included in

muraqqa' – special albums in which miniatures and samples of calligraphy were collected. This genre probably did not develop without the influence of the Mughal miniature, in which pictures of plants, birds and animals played a significant role from the very beginning of the 17th century. However, the earliest known Persian miniatures with depictions of flowers were copied from European prints.

The miniature reproduced here is executed in the European style, which had become established in Iranian painting during the second half of the 17th century. The figure of the bird is rendered three-dimensionally by means of chiaroscuro modelling. The miniature bears the artist's inscription:

نموده رقم يوسف زمان ۱۱۰۸

"Painted by Yusuf-Zaman. 1108".

First publication.

243. Box with hinged lid. By Muhammad-Ali ibn Muhammad-Zaman. 1112 AH/1700–01 AD

Papier-mâché, painted and lacquered. 26.9 x 6 x 4.8cm.
The Hermitage, St Petersburg.
Inv. No. VR-126. Transferred 1924 from the museum attached to the former Stieglitz School of Technical Design.

The landscape on the lid is painted in the European manner, using techniques of linear and aerial perspective. Behind the figures is a river, with trees and various buildings beyond i, and further still, light blue mountains.

On the side walls flowers are painted on a black ground. Chiaroscuro is rendered with exceptional delicacy, sometimes by means of fine hatching, sometimes through a very delicate pointillist technique.

The painter of this work, Muhammad-Ali, was the son of Muhammad-Zaman. Like his father

he painted miniatures on paper as well as on lacquerware. The box is one of the best and the earliest known of his works.

On the lid of a *qalamdan* dated 1119 AH/1708 AD (in the National Museum, Stockholm), Muhammad-Ali copied a miniature from a *qalamdan* apparently painted by his father, Muhammad-Zaman, in 1109 AH/1697–98 AD (see Wiet 1935, p.72, pi.57). A love scene is depicted against the background of a landscape which seems to be a continuation of the landscape on the Hermitage box. On yet another of Muhammad-Ali's *qalamdans*, dated 1133 AH/1720–21 AD, a pair of lovers appear against the background of mountain scenery.

There are other *qalamdans* too, painted in the course of the first two decades of the 18th century by various artists, depicting variations on one and the same theme upon their lids.

Adle, describing one of these *qalamdans*, links the theme of the

miniature to the ideas of Persian mystics and especially to Sufi poetry (see Adle 1980, pp.9–20, figs 1–7).

Muhammad-Ali's box is of interest in that it has enabled us to determine the approximate date of Muhammad-Zaman's death. On the lid is written: "The work of Muhammad-Ali's on the fate of Muhammad-Zaman. 1112".

The word "fate" in the artist's inscription, which does not appear in inscriptions on his subsequent works, shows that Muhammad-Zaman died no later than 1112 AH, and possibly in that very year, as was pointed out by Ivanov.

Bibliography: Ivanov 1960a.

CAT N° 245

CAT Nº 246

CAT Nº 256

256. MIRROR-CASE.
BY MUHAMMAD-BAQIR.
1177 AH/1763–64 AD
Papier-mâché, painted and lacquered,
17.5 x 12.2cm.
The Hermitage, St Petersburg.
Inv. No. VR-27. Transferred 1924 from
the museum attached to the former
Stieglitz School of Technical Design.

This mirror-case, decorated by Muhammad-Baqir, is among the best examples of Persian lacquer painting in the Hermitage. A branch of a blossoming fruit tree is depicted on the outside of the lid. Muhammad-Baqir tried to convey every natural feature by pictorial means: flowers are shown at all stages of development, from barely open buds to blossoms with half-scattered petals.

On the reverse of the case a branch of a hazlnut-tree is painted against the same background.
On the inside of the lid are the Madonna and St John, undoubtedly copied from the work of a European artist, and not apparently painted by Muhammad-Baqir, but by another, less skilful, painter.

Very little is known of Muhammad-Baqir, although, to judge by his work, he must have been one of the most important painters of the second half of the 18th century. In the mid-18th century he collaborated in designing an album of miniatures and examples of calligraphy. Apparently he worked in Shiraz at the court workshop of Karim-Khan Zand. This is attested by a miniature portrait of this ruler, with the inscription: "A drawing by the most humble slave of the court Muhammad-

Baqir". Miniatures on paper predominate among the known works of Muhammad-Baqir.
The inscription on the Hermitage mirror is written in gold and located on the outside of the lid at the top:

كمترين محمد باقر ١١٧٧

"the most humble Muhammad-Baqir. 1177".

First publication.

257. FLASK.
17TH–18TH CENTURY
Blown glass. Height 19cm.
The Hermitage, St Petersburg.
Inv. No. VG-2604. Transferred 1933
from the museum attached to the former
Stieglitz School of Technical Design.

Artistic glassware, which had been highly developed in pre-Mongol Iran, again became an important branch of applied arts from the 16th century onwards. According to the testimony of Europeans during the 17th–18th centuries, many towns in Iran had workshops for making artistic glassware, but the main centre was Shiraz. Here they made bowls, jugs and bottles for the famous Shiraz wine, and also rosewater sprinklers – vessels for scented water and attar of the Shiraz roses famed in verse. The forms of the glassware were laid down in the mid-16th century. Attention was concentrated on perfection of form, on a harmonious correspondence between its parts and also on colour (vessels were tinged in various colours by metal oxides).
First publication.

258. FLASK.
17TH–18TH CENTURY
Blown glass. Height 22cm.
The Hermitage, St Petersburg.
Inv. No. VG-2605. Transferred 1933
from the museum attached to the former
Stieglitz School of Technical Design.

This flask, distinguished by its particularly graceful form, may be reckoned among the highest achievements of Iranian artistic glassware. Its colour lends it particular beauty – darker in places where the fluxes and drips of molten glass have left traces and transparent in clear patches. First publication.

259. ROSEWATER SPRINKLER.
17TH–18TH CENTURY
Blown glass. Height 33cm.
The Hermitage, St Petersburg.
Inv. No. VG-2263. Transferred 1924
from the museum attached to the former
Stieglitz School of Technical Design.

It is hard to say exactly when this form of vessel emerged – the spherical body on a low foot-ring and the very long, curved (sometimes twisted) neck culminating in a bell-mouth flattened at the sides and with a pointed protuberance at the top. It was still very popular in the 17th century and gradually acquired ever more complicated features. In the fate 19th century rosewater sprinklers came into fashion and were much in demand in Europe.
First publication.

260. EWER.
17TH–18TH CENTURY
Blown glass. Height 26.3cm.
The Hermitage, St Petersburg.

Inv. No. VG-2267. Purchased 1926
from Pashayev (Kubachi).

This ewer has a tall body narrowing downwards, a high, narrow neck, a flattened, curved spout and curved handle. Its type of decoration was already generally current in the Seljuk age.
First publication.

261. MINIATURE:
GIRL AND YOUTH.
BY NAZAR-ALI.
LATE 18TH – EARLY 19TH CENTURY.
Watercolour. 19 x 13.5 cm.
Art Museum of Georgia, Tbilisi.
Inv. No. 354. Purchased 1920 from
Nalbandian.

The work of this artist is little known: less than ten of his miniatures have survived. To judge from the treatment of the landscape and figures, he was active during the second half of the 18th century and possibly at the very beginning of the 19th century.
First publication.

262. Youth with Hare.
Second half of 18th century
Oil on canvas, 142 x 74cm.
Museum of Oriental Art, Moscow.
Inv. No, 1560-II. Transferred 1930
from the museum in Ostafyevo.

To judge from the depiction of the landscape and the youth's headgear, the picture was painted during the second half of the 18th century and is a characteristic example of the painting of that period.
Bibliography:
Easel Painting 1973 (cover illustration); Maslenitsyna 1975, No.123.

263. Portrait of Fath-Ali Shah.
By Mihr-Ali.
1224 AH/1809–10 AD
Oil on canvas. 253 x 124cm.
The Hermitage, St Petersburg.
Inv. No. VR-1107. Transferred 1932
from the Gatchina Palace Museum.

It seems that in the late 18th-early 19th centuries during the reign of Fath-Ali Shah (1797–1834), Persian painting evolved a new style which was named "Qajar" after the ruling dynasty. Many factors influenced the formation of the Qajar style which was in essence eclectic though purely courtly in its spirit, but above all was the exorbitant claims of the Shah and nobility to have brought about in that age a "rebirth" of the grandeur of Achaemenid and Sassanian Iran.

In Qajar painting the leading genre was official portraiture, which in antiquity had been one of the foremost aspects of Iranian art and had a propagandist significance. The portraits of the Shah were intended both to decorate reception rooms of his palaces and to be presented to foreign rulers or ambassadors as gifts.

The portrait of Fath-Ali Shah was painted by the head of the court painters, Mihr-Ali, in 1224 AH. Despite the use of chiaroscuro and an oil painting technique adopted from the West in the age of the Safavids, paintings executed in the Qajar style should be assigned to the Iranian tradition, insofar as they reveal the clear predominance of Persian features and characteristics.

Above on the right in a medallion is written:

السلطان فتحعلی شاه قاجار

"al-sultan Fath-Ali Shah Qajar".

Beneath the medallion there are verses (metre *motaqareb*) in a rec-

tangular cartouche:

بکـام خـــودای پـاک بـرودکــــار ٭
زدی نقش ایـن نامـــور شـــهـریـار
چو ایـن آفـــرینـش بر آراسـتـى ٭
چنان اقــریدی کـه خـود خـواسـتى

"According to your desire, o You, most pure Creator,
You have portrayed this eminent Shah.
When You created this work,
You created it such as You desired."

In the lower left hand corner:

این پردة تصویر تمثال بیمثال شاهنشاه بیهمال
است کـه در خصـور باهر النور اقـدس مـلاحظه
شمایل مهر حمایل مبارک شده وبدون تغییر
رقمزد بکك خجسته...کمترین غلام مهر
علی آمده فى سنة ١٢٢٤

"This painting is a portrayal of the incomparable, the unequalled Shahanshah, who in the presence of a clear, sacred ray of light became the subject of observation... Accomplished by the brush of the most humble slave Mihr-Ali. 1224".

Bibliography:
Adamova 1971.

264. Woman with a Rose.
First quarter of 19th century
Oil on canvas, 184 x 94cm.
The Hermitage, St Petersburg.
Inv. No. VR-1113. Transferred 1932
from the Gatchina Palace Museum.

Among surviving Qajar oil paintings the great majority are pictures of young women, mainly intended as decorations for the reception rooms of the Shah's or the nobility's palaces. Evidence of this is shown specifically in the lancet top many of them have, including the *Woman with a Rose* from the Hermitage collection. In this painting, as in the majority of such works, the woman is portrayed against an open window.

Such a background is traditional (a greenish wall with an open frame, beyond which a blue sky is visible). Evidently the artists were striving to create the illusion of a window in the wall of the room decorated with paintings.

From its stylistic characteristics, the painting can be assigned to the early stage of the Qajar style. Here many elements of western art are noticeable: the oil-painting technique, the localized use of chiaroscuro modelling, the striving to convey the texture of cloths and the depiction of such features as drapery in the background. However, the predominant characteristics are those linked to the old tradition of Persian painting: local colour, a flat treatment of space and form, especially in depicting clothes where the carefully delineated patterns of the cloth play the role of an independent motif and create a general impression of richness and decorativeness.

The *Woman with a Rose* was previously kept in the Gatchina Palace Museum, together with the portraits of Fath-Ali Shah. It can be assumed that one of them was brought from Iran by the Russian ambassador Yermolov in 1817, according to the testimony of V Borozdna and M. Kotsebu. Possibly the *Woman with a Rose* was bought together with the portrait of Fath-Ali Shah and consequently was painted no later than 1817.
Bibliography:
Adamova 1970, fig.2.

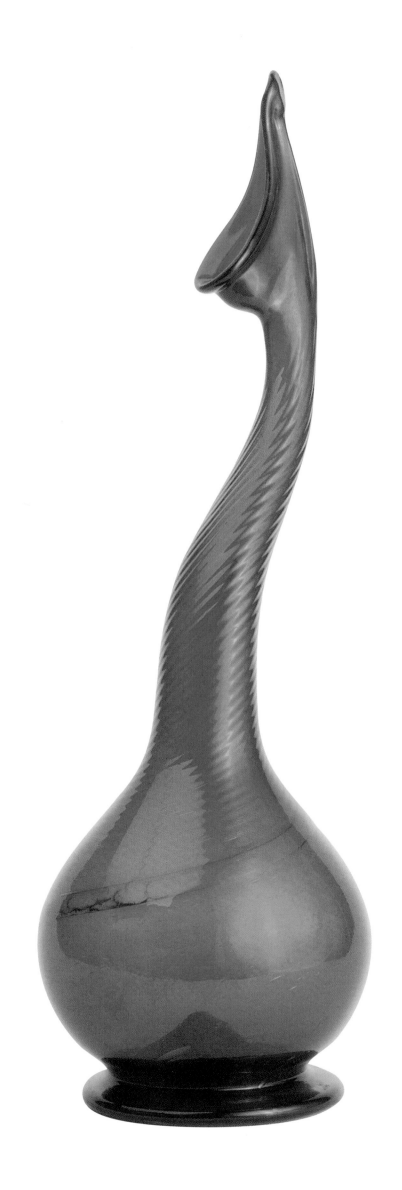

CAT N° 259

265. Portrait of Abbas-mirza. By Allahverdi Afshar. 1232 AH/1816–17 AD

Oil on canvas. 220 x 130cm. Museum of Oriental Art, Moscow. Inv. No, 1740-II. Purchased 1939 from Bakhrushin.

To date the artist Allahverdi Afshar is only known for this one work. He was probably active either at the court of Fath-Ali Shah or at the court of Abbas-mirza. His manner is characteristic of the Qajar court school of painting during the first third of the 19th century.
Bibliography:
Easel Painting 1973, No.7; Maslenitsyna 1975, No.124.

266. Dancing Woman with Castanets. By Ahmad. 1242 AH/1826 AD

Oil on canvas. 180 x 92.5cm. Museum of Oriental Art, Moscow.

Inv. No. 1413-II. Transferred 1933 from the museum in Yuryev-Polsky.

Two portraits of Fath-Ali Shah by this artist are known, and a portrait of Muhammad Shah, dated 1260 AH/1844 AD (see Robinson 1979a, pp.340-342). Hence this painter was active during the first half of the 19th century.
Bibliography:
Easel Painting 1973, No.8; Maslenitsyna 1975, No.125.

267. Portrait of Fath-Ali Shah Qajar. Late 1810s–early 1820s

Oil on canvas. 217 x 131cm. Museum of Oriental Art, Moscow. Inv. No. 1412-II. Acquired 1974 from G Gorbulevsky.

The portrait of Fath-Ali Shah was painted by the same artist who did the two other portraits of this Shah in the Hermitage (for one of

them, see Cat. No.263). Evidence of this is provided by identical medallions with the Shah's name and the same verses located on all three paintings. Judging by the portrayal of the Shah, the portrait was painted at the same period as one of the Hermitage pictures (Cat. No.263).
Bibliography:
Easel Painting 1973, No.10; Maslenitsyna 1975, No.127.

268. Miniature: Portrait of Muhammad Shah Qajar. By Abu-i-Hasan naqqash. 1260 AH/1844 AD

Watercolour. 13.5 x 19.2cm. Art Museum of Georgia, Tbilisi. Inv. No. 288. Transferred 1921 from the National Gallery of Georgia.

Abu-1-Hasan naqqash (1813–1867) was one of the leading artists during the reigns of Muhammad Shah Qajar (1834–1848) and Nasir al-Din Shah (1848–1896). He was well known as a portraitist.
He studied for several years in Italy and his art is characterized

by a total acceptance of the techniques of European painting. First publication.

269. Miniature: Portrait of a Dignitary Holding a Watch. Late 18th century

Watercolour. 7.8 x 6.6cm. Art Museum of Georgia, Tbilisi. Inv. No. 206. Acquired 1931 from the Transcaucasian Office for State Trade.

This small portrait of an unknown dignitary was executed in the style of late 18th-century miniatures and may be considered an example of miniature painting at the beginning of the rule of Fath-Ali Shah Qajar (1797–1834). First publication.

270. Sabre and scabbard. Early 19th century

Damask steel, forged, decorated with gold, gemstones and painted in enamels. Length of sabre: 92.7cm; length of scabbard: 85.7cm. The Hermitage, St Petersburg. Inv. No. OR-46. Transferred 1886 from the Tsarskoye Selo Arsenal (presented to Alexander II by Nasir al-Din Shah Qajar in 1880).

The sabre is a typical example of the work of court jewellers. Judging by the inscription on the blade, it

was made for Fath-Ali Shah Qajar (1797-1834). The hilt and obverse of the scabbard are studded with gems. There are 2,421 diamonds on the sabre, 143 brilliants, 503 emeralds, 20 rubies and 3 spinels. The reverse of the scabbard is covered with enamel. On the reverse of the hilt is the portrait, painted in enamels, of a youth in a high hat with an aigrette.

Bibliography:
Oriental Jewellery 1984, No.64.

271. Portrait of Hajfi Mirza Aghasi. By Abu-i-Hasan Ghaffari. 1261 AH/1845 AD

Tempera on paper. 33 x 26.2cm.
Museum of Oriental Art, Moscow.
Inv. No. 1554-II. Transferred 1924 from the History Museum, Moscow; formerly in the P. Shchukin collection.

The artist Abu-i-Hasan Ghaffari Kashani (1229-83 AH/1813-67 AD), given the name "Sani' al-Mulk" by the Shah, came from the town of Kashan, from a family of religious activists which produced a number of artists. He

was particularly active during the 1840s-1860s. During the late 1840s he studied in Italy and assimilated the techniques of European painting.

Bibliography:
Shchukin 1907, vol.XXXII; Maslenitsyna 1975, No.122.

272. Dagger and sheath. Late 18th-early 19th century

Steel, forged, inlaid with gold and painted in enamels. Length in sheath 59.2cm.
The Hermitage, St Petersburg.
Inv. No. OR-274. Transferred 1886 from the Tsarskoye Selo Arsenal.

The blade is decorated with gold foliage. The hilt is in the form of a bird's head. The slight relief of the enamelwork allows one to link this object with 18th-century ware and to date it to the end of the 18th or beginning of the 19th century.

Bibliography:
Oriental Jewellery 1984, No.61.

273. Bowl of a hookah. Early 19th century

Copper, forged, covered with gold leaf and painted in enamels. Height 20.2cm.
The Hermitage, St Petersburg.

Inv. No. VZ-296. Acquired 1927 from the State Museum Reserve.

The bowl of the hookah is in the form of a bottle, which is covered with gold leaf and decorated with floral ornament and eight scalloped medallions containing enamel portraits.

This object can be considered a typical example of the mid-19th century Qajar court style.

Bibliography:
Oriental Jewellery 1984, No.69.

274. Tray. 1800-1830

Gold, forged and painted in enamels. Diameter 45.5cm.
The Hermitage, St Petersburg.
Inv. No. VZ-751. Transferred 1934 from the Catherine Palace Museum in the town of Pushkin.

This massive gold tray with a scalloped edge is richly decorated with polychrome enamel. On the reverse, two short inscriptions are

engraved in Arabic script which have not yet been deciphered.

This is a typical example of the Qajar court style during the time of Fath-Ali Shah (1797-1834).

Bibliography:
Oriental Jewellery 1984, No.72.

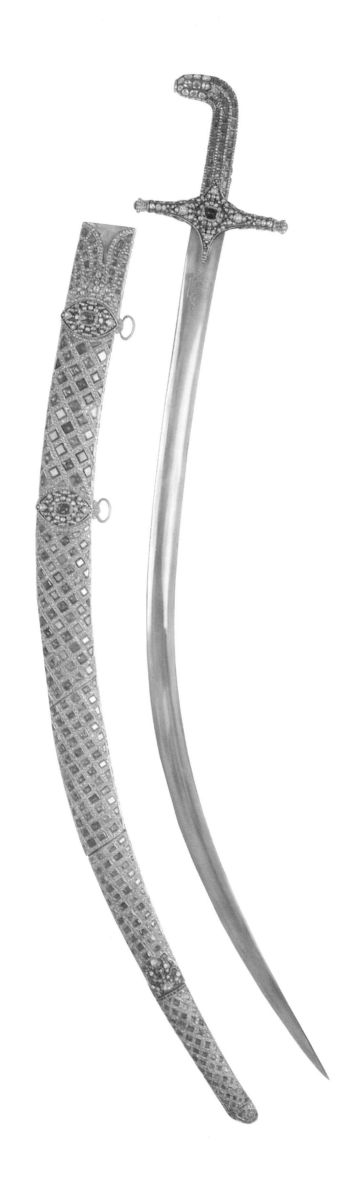

CAT N° 270

275. CURTAIN.
18TH–19TH CENTURY
Printed cotton. 170 x 100cm.
The Hermitage, St Petersburg.
Inv. No. VT-597. Transferred 1925
from the museum attached to the former
Stieglitz School of Technical Design.

Printed textiles were very popular in Iran. Usually they were decorated with illustrations, often of a gaudy nature reminiscent of popular prints. A similar type of curtain was common in India as well, but a number of the ornamental motifs have close parallels in Iranian decoration – in particular the figures of the peacocks, the foliage and the hill made of stones.
First publication.

276. MINIATURE: FLOWERS.
BY LUTF-ALI SHIRAZI.
30 JUMADA I 1278 AH /
3 DECEMBER 1861 AD
Watercolour. 17 x 10.2cm.
Art Museum of Georgia, Tbilisi.
Inv. No.363.

Lutf-Ali Shirazi (d.1872), nicknamed "Suratgar" (painter), was active during the first half of the 19th century. Pictures of flowers were a favourite theme in his work and this is a typical example.
First publication.

277. PEACOCK. BY HAJJI ABBAS.
LATE 19TH CENTURY
Steel, forged, inlaid with gold and engraved. Height 58cm.
The Hermitage, St Petersburg.
Inv. No. VS-858. Acquired 1924 from the I. Bagmanov collection.

This fairly large figure of a peacock was evidently a piece of decorative sculpture. There is the craftsman's inscription on the breast in *nastaliq* script:

عمل كمترين هادي عباس

"Made by the most humble hajji Abbas"

(about signed works of hajji Abbas, see Cat. No.253). The foliate ornament in gold enables one to date the manufacture of this figure to somewhere between the middle and end of the 19th century.
First publication.

278. LID.
BY MUHAMMAD HAKKAK.
1252 AH / 1836–37 AD
Copper, forged, tinned and engraved.
Height 14cm; diameter 19.8cm.
The Hermitage, St Petersburg.
Inv. No. VS-931. Acquired 1923 from the State Museum Reserve.

A number of lids with cupola-shaped projections in the centre have been preserved, although it is not clear for what sort of vessel they were intended. This object is

decorated in a slightly unusual manner: it is covered with engraved ornament executed on an untooled ground. This may be partly explained by the craftsman's professional title – "hakkak" (engraver) which was usually applied to a lapidary. The craftsman's inscription is situated on the projection in two medallions:

فرمان دوست محمد حكاك

"The friend of the king's decree – Muhammad hakkak".

Apart from this inscription there are also two verse quotations in *nastaliq* script on the projection. The first of them cannot be deciphered in full; the second is part of *ghazal* by Hafiz (metre *ramal*):

ساقيا برخيز و در ده جام را * خاك بر سر كن غم ايام را
ساعى مى در كفم نه تاز سر * برشم اين دلق ازرق فام را
كرچه بدنامست نزد عاقلان * ما نمىخواهيم نيك و نام را
باده درده چند اين زين باد غرور * خاك بر سر نقس نافر جام را ۱۲۵۲

"O wine servant, arise and bring a bowl,

Throw ashes on the head of days of sorrow!
Place the wine goblet in my hand so that I can
Tear off this azure dress!
Although the bad is known among wise men,
We wish for neither good nor glory for ourselves.
Bring wine! for how long [shall] this wind of arrogance [speak] !
Away with this dissolute desire! 1252."

Three other works by Muhammad hakkak are known - a copper bowl of 1243 AH/1827 AD in the Victoria and Albert Museum, London (see SPA 1938 – 39, vol.VI, pl.1387c), a copper bowl of 1259 AH/1843 AD in the Hermitage and an undated copper bowl in the collection of H. Rahimi (Iran) (see Zoka and Simsar, p.18, ill.17). From the dates on this craftsman's works it follows that he was active during the period from the 1820s to the 1840s.
First publication.

279. Ewer. By Baqir hakkak. Mid-19th century

Bronze (brass), cast and engraved.
Height 37cm.
The Hermitage, St Petersburg.
Inv. No. VS-556. Transferred 1925 from the museum attached to the former Stieglitz School of Technical Design.

This massive cast ewer has a curved handle, its ends decorated with a lion's and a dragon's heads, and is covered with ornament. The complex design of the decoration is formed by different types of medallion and cartouche within which are sited various real or fantastic scenes, the themes of which are not always comprehensible. The ground is matt-tooled which is very characteristic of 19th-century Iranian ware.

The craftsman's inscription is situated on the neck in two small medallions:

"made by the most humble Baqir hakkak".

As has already been noted (see Cat. No.278), the professional title "hakkak" (engraver) was usually applied to lapidaries of seals.
Bibliography:
Masterpieces 1990, No.119; Great Art Treasures 1994, No.412.

280. Bowl. Late 19th century

Bronze (brass), cast, turned and engraved. Diameter 20cm; height 6.3cm.
The Hermitage, St Petersburg.
Inv. No. VS-947. Purchased 1936.

On the outside, the bowl's decoration consists of five bands: the first contains an Arabic inscription (undeciphered); the third has various scenes in large deco-ratively-shaped cartouches with vegetal ornament between them. The theme of three scenes can be understood: two of them evoke episodes from Nizami's poems – *Khusrau Sees Shirin Bathing and Fitna with the Bullock* – while the third is probably *Joseph and the Women of Egypt*; two other scenes portray a banquet and a court reception.

In the centre of the bowl there is a round rosette with a double row of palmettes around the edge and a flower in the middle. The ground to the ornament and inscription is cross-hatched.

Part of the ground was evidently hollowed in the process of tooling, because all the ornamentation and letters of the inscription are in relief.

The treatment of the human figures is somewhat reminiscent of reliefs at Persepolis and Naqsh-i Rustam. This style emerged in the second half of the 19th century. First publication.

281. VASE.
LATE 19TH CENTURY
Bronze (brass), cast, turned, engraved and inlaid with silver.
Height: 13.5cm.
The Hermitage, St Petersburg.
Inv. No. VS-999. Purchased 1937.

The vase is a typical example of those objects whose motifs and decorative style evoke the Persepolis reliefs. The reversion to ancient Iranian imagery was one of the characteristic trends in Iranian art during the second half of the 19th century; the reasons for this revival are not yet entirely clear.

Around the neck and foot there are Arabic inscriptions which have not been deciphered. The vase is decorated with silver inlay; there were attempts during the 19th century to revive this defunct technique, but apparently it did not become widespread. First publication.

282. TRAY.
BY ABD AL-MUTALLIB ISFAHANI.
LATE 19TH CENTURY
Bronze (brass), forged and engraved.
57.5 x 38.5cm.
The Hermitage, St Petersburg.
Inv. No. IR-2165. Purchased 1981.

Rectangular trays with rounded corners are often found in late 19th-century metalwork. The rim of the tray is richly decorated with vegetal ornament. Three *ghazals* of Hafiz, excluding some baits, are engraved in 24 cartouches separated by four-lobed medallions. These verses clash with the pictures in the centre of the tray (one would rather have expected verses from the *Shahnama*): there the Sasanid shahanshahs are represented in 30 medallions, and also Umar ibn al-Khattab, under whom the conquest of Iran by the Arabs began. In the third medallion from the left on the lower row is the craftsman's inscription:

عمل عبد المطلب اصفهانى

"Made by Abd al-Mutallib Isfahani".

Another tray by this craftsman is in the History Museum, Moscow. The portraits of the Sasanid shahanshahs on this tray are of interest (the name of the shah is written in each medallion). Undoubtedly the craftsman had before him some European publication on the history of the Sassanids, in which Sassanian coins were reproduced. In particular, this publication reproduced a rare type of coin of Ardashir I (in a *kulah* with a star on it), but did not reproduce rare coins of the later Sasanid shahanshahs. Obviously using the chronological list appended to this publication, Abd al-Mutallib Isfahani engraved their portraits, depicting such crowns as his own imagination dictated. Insofar as Sassanian coins show only the bust of the shahanshah, the craftsman "dressed them up" in the fashion of his own times, while for the portraits of the two queens – Puran (in the inscription – "Purandukht") and Azarmedukht – he simply presented the portraits of two late 19th-century noblewomen. (Genuine Sassanian coins of Puran are extraordinarily rare; coins of Azarmedukht have only recently been discovered.)

Since the book which the artist was using reproduced a rare type of coin of Ardashir I, there is the possibility of identifying the publication and determining the exact date of the tray's manufacture. First publication.

283. MINIATURE: PORTRAIT OF A NOBLEWOMAN. BY MUHAMMAD-HASAN AFSHAR. 1291 AH/1874 AD

Watercolour. 12.9 x 18.4cm.
Art Museum of Georgia, Tbilisi.
Inv. No. 144. Transferred 1934 from the National Gallery of Georgia.

The work of the artist Muhammad-Hasan Afshar has not been studied, although more than ten of his miniatures are known. He came from a family of artists which produced several interesting masters (see Cat. No. 284). *The Portrait of a Noblewoman* is one of his latest works.
Bibliography:
Grigoliya 1971, pp.124, 125.

284. PORTRAIT OF MIRZA ALI-KHAN. BY BEGLAR-KHAN NAQ-QASHBASHI AFSHAR. 1284 AH / 1867–68 AD

Watercolour. 28.5 x 20.5cm.
Art Museum of Georgia, Tbilisi.
Inv. No. 136. Transferred 1934 from the National Gallery of Georgia.

The artist Beglar-khan of the Afshar family evidently held an eminent position at the court of Nasir al-Din Shah Qajar (1848–1896) since

his title is *naqqashbashi* (chief artist). From the signatures on his works it follows that he was the son of Muhammad-Hasan Afshar (Cat. No.283) and that his works were produced in the 1850s-1860s.
Bibliography:
Grigoliya 1971, pp.126–131.

285. TABLE. BY ABU-I-QASIM AL-HUSAINI AL-ISFAHANI. 1301 AH/1883–84 AD

Wood, painted and lacquered. Height 77cm; diameter of top 52.5cm.
The Hermitage, St Petersburg.
Inv. No. VR-1281. Purchased 1977 from M V Itin.

In four cartouches on the top of the table there are quatrains attributed to Omar Khayyam (from the reading by L Gyuzalyan):

من هیچ ندانم کـه مـرا آنکه سـرشت *
بود اهل بهشت خـوب یا دوزخ راستراشت
خـالی ولبی وبـربطی أو لب کـشت *
این هرسـه مـرا نـقد وترا نسیـه بهشت

"I know not whether he who made me was a denizen of blessed paradise or cursed hell.
But one thing [I know] full well: I have a birthmark [on a beauty's cheek], [her] lips and a lute in [my] hands, and you [my maker] have only paradise, and that is a pledge."

In a wide band around the edge of the table, in small cartouches, there is an excerpt in hemistichs from a *ghazal* of Hafiz (from the reading by L Gyuzalyan):

بلبلی برگ گلی خـوش رنگ در منقار داشت *
وندر ان برگ نواخـوش نالهـای زار داشت
گفتمش درعین وصل این ناله وفریاد چیست *
گفت مارا شهوه (؟) معشوق درایـن کار داشت
بار اگر نشست بامـا نیست جای گفتگو *
پادشـاه کـامـران بود گدایان عار داشت
خیـز تابر کلک این نقاش جان افشان کنیم *
کاین همه نقش عجب در گردش پرگار داشت

"A nightingale held a beautiful rose petal in its beak and poured harmonious and grievous moans into this petal.

I asked him: whence these complaints and pleas for salvation, since you are at one [with the rose]? He said: the passion of a lover has brought me to this.

If the beloved had not sat down with us, there would be nothing of which to speak. You were a queen who did not condescend to the beggarly rabble. Arise and let us lay our souls before the brush of this artist who has drawn all these amazing designs with the aid of compasses' turning."

In the central circle, above the heads of the birds, is the craftsman's inscription:

عمل ابو القاسم الحسين الاصفهانى ١٣٠١

"Made by Abu-1-Qasim al-Husaini al-Isfahani, 1301".

In the Hermitage there is a box with pictures of flowers and birds and numerous inscriptions, dated 1319 AH/1901–02 AD, and also a picture frame decorated with architectural and landscape motifs and verses from Hafiz's *ghazal*, dated the same year. Both bear the signature of Abu-I- Qasim. In Tbilisi there are two decorative panels in the Art Museum of Georgia. They are executed on cardboard and covered with lacquer. These works are also signed by Abu-I-Qasim al-Isfahani and dated 1313 AH/1895–96 AD and 1319 AH/ 1901–02 AD. Lacquerware by this artist usually features large flowers and leaves, composed either into "bouquets" or groups. Their characteristic feature is a vigorous chiaroscuro stressing mass and volume, and vivid, contrasting colour combinations.
First publication.

286. TABLE.
19TH CENTURY
Wood and faience, painted and fired.
Height 61.5cm; diameter 57.5cm.
The Hermitage, St Petersburg.
Inv. No. VG-2651. Acquired 1927 from the State Museum Reserve.

A circular tile is fixed to the table-top: it is painted in cobalt, manganese, olive and turquoise paints under a transparent, colourless glaze. It depicts the heroes of Firdawsi's poem *Shah-nama*. In the centre King Kay-Khusrau sits on a throne, holding a sceptre; on either side of him are Zal, Rustam, Godarz and Giv (their names are written in cartouches). Dancing boys are portrayed below; above is an architectural background. Black outlines are drawn round the figures, traces of gilding are visible on the surface of the file.
The tile belongs to the Qajar period. The choice of subject reflects the efforts of the Qajar shahs to revive the artistic traditions and themes of former times. According to the testimony of Europeans who visited Iran in the 19th century, the walls of the Qajar shahs' palaces were decorated with similar court reception scenes showing the ancient kings of Iran.
The buildings in the upper part of the composition are painted in spatial recession. At the same time the figures are placed on an even cobalt ground with the space between them evenly filled with flowers and vessels.
First publication.

287. Cover. 19th century

Wool, silk; appliqué, embroidery, 186 x 115cm.

The Hermitage, St Petersburg.

Inv. No. VT-496. Acquired 1925 from the museum attached to the former Stieglitz School of Technical Design.

The composition of the pattern reveals a similarity to the bindings of manuscripts. Embroidered articles of a similar kind were widely used in everyday life – as prayer rugs, saddle-cloths, curtains and table-cloths. The town of Rasht is considered to have been their centre of production. First publication.

288. CARPET.
1311 AH/1893–94 AD
Pile-woven wool, 125 x 198cm.
The Hermitage, St Petersburg.
Inv. No. VT-1643. Purchased 1970.

In the centre is the Achæmenid king, Artaxerxes I, seated on a throne beneath a canopy; behind, a servant holds a fan, whilst above is the symbol of the supreme god, Ahura Mazda. Below, the king's throne is supported by subjects arranged in three tiers. On the border in a rectangular frame is the Persian inscription: "The order of the commander-in-chief of the sovereign Abd al-Husaini Mirza" and the date "1311". At the bottom there is an inscription in French: Personnages anciens à Persepolis. Several carpets are known which show analogous scenes and have two inscriptions with dates. Evidently the carpets were made from a single drawing, reproducing scenes from the reliefs decorating the south gate to the Hundred Column Hall in the palace at Persepolis.
First publication.

289. BOWL. BY MUHAMMAD-ALI. 1233 AH/1817–18 AD

Faience, with underglaze painting.
Height 8cm; diameter 19cm.
The Hermitage, St Petersburg.
Inv. No. VG-145. Purchased 1925
from R. Magomedov (Kubachi).

The internal and external surfaces of the bowl are totally filled with ornament, executed in cobalt beneath a transparent, colourless glaze. The dark shade of cobalt has flowed under the glaze, forming indistinct outlines and giving the white ground a tinge of light blue. A worsening in the quality of cobalt, which loses its softness of tone and flows under the glaze, can already be observed in late 17th-century wares and becomes more pronounced in 18th- and 19th-century ceramics.
The Hermitage bowl is of interest as a rare example of one bearing the craftsman's name, the date and the owner's name. Written in blue paint on the outside of the base is:

عمل محمد علی ١٢٣٣ صاحبه زین العابدین

"Made by Muhammad-Ali. 1233. Owner Zain al-Abidin".

There is a plate by this craftsman, also painted in cobalt and decorated with flower motifs, in the Victoria and Albert Museum, London. The craftsman also put his name and the date (1232 AH/ 1816–17 AD) on this one, as well as the name of the owner (Ahmad). First publication.

290. PLATE.

19TH CENTURY

Faience, with underglaze painting.
Diameter 21.4cm.
The Hermitage, St Petersburg.
Inv. No. VG-2199. Purchased 1938
from A. Shavanova (Kubachi).

The plate is painted in dark blue, brown (two shades) and black. There are a number of similarly painted articles in the Hermitage collection. They are covered with a thick layer of transparent glaze of a greenish tinge.
More often than not, these are small bowls and plates and their entire surface is filled with gaudy illustrations resembling popular prints. Round the rim of the plate there is a narrow band of floral and foliate patterns and inscriptions.

The picture on the plate represents an elephant driver (an Indian mahout); above there is a young warrior with a sword in his hand and a shield behind his back; to the left there is a griffin (?).
The subject was possibly borrowed from folk tales; however, it is more likely that we are faced here with imagery that has undergone changes over the years and is presented in a distorted form on the plate: the prince wearing the crown who should be mounted on the elephant turns up hanging in mid-air or flying like a genie through the clouds, while the mahout has taken his place on the elephant.
Images of a young prince riding an elephant, with a driver on the elephant's neck, framed by Arabic or Persian blessings, are often found on 12th- and 13th-century faience.

The inscriptions are located in four cartouches in a band round the rim of the plate. Three cartouches repeat one and the same benedictory formula:

ابصادبکرامت شکرانه سلامت

"O, lord of mercy, [accept] a grateful desire for health".

In the fourth cartouche:

روزی ده نقدسی درویشی

"You, most holy provider of the dervish order".

First publication.

LIST OF ABBREVIATIONS

Abayev 1958
* V I Abayev, *A Historical and Etymological Dictionary of the Ossetian Language*, M L, 1958.

Adamova 1970
* A T Adamova, *"Two Paintings from the Early Qajar Period"*, in: *Central Asia and Iran*, L, 1970, pp.170–77.

Adamova 1971
* A T Adamova, "Two Portraits of Fath-Ali Shah from the Hermitage Collection, and the Qajar Official Style", *SGE*, L, 1971, XXXIII, pp.85–88.

Adle 1980
C Adle, *Écriture de l'Union. Reflets du temps des troubles. Œuvre picturale (1083-1124/1673-1712) de Hâjjî Mohammad*, Paris, 1980.

Akimushkin 1962
* O F Akimushkin, "Mir Imad", in: *Album of Indian and Persian Miniatures of the 16th-18th Centuries*, M, 1962, pp.60–72.

Akimushkin and Ivanov 1968
* O F Akimushkin and A A *Ivanov, Persian Miniatures of the 14th-17th Centuries*, M, 1968

Akimushkin and Ivanov 1979
O F Akimushkin and A A Ivanov, "The Art of Illumination", in: *The Arts of the Book in Central Asia: 14th-16th Centuries*, UNESCO, 1979, pp.35–57.

Allan 1976
* J Allan, "Review: G Fehérvári. Islamic Metalwork of the Eighth to the Fifteenth Century in the Keir Collection", *Oriental Art*, vol.XXXII, No.3, 1976, pp.299–302.

Allan 1982a
* J W Allan, "Abbas, Hajji", in: *Encyclopaedia Iranica*, vol.I, fasc.1, London, Boston, 1982, pp.76, 77.

Allan 1982b
* J Allan, "Copper, Brass and Steel", in: *Tulips, Arabesques and Turbans. Decorative Arts from the Ottoman Empire*, London, 1982, pp.33–43.

Allan 1982c
J W Allan, *Islamic Metalwork. The Nuhad es-Said Collection*, London, 1982.

Apakidze et al. 1958
* A Apakidze, G Gobedzhishvili, A Kalandadze and G Lomtatidze, "Archaeological Relics of Armaziskhe-vi. From Excavations of 1937-1946", in: *Itogi arkheologicheskikh issledovany*, vol.I (*Mtskheta*), Tbilisi, 1958.

Arakelian 1976
* B Arakelian, *An Outline of the History of the Art of Ancient Armenia (6th Century BC-3rd Century AD)*, Yerevan, 1976.

Artamonov 1962
* M I Artamonov, "On the Question of the Origin of Scythian Art", in: *Omaglu lui George Oprescu*, Budapest, 1962.

Artamonov 1973
* M I Artamonov, *The Treasure of the Saki*, M, 1973. Art of Central Asia 1980. *The Art of Central Asia During the Age of Avicenna*, Dushanbe, 1980.

Arts de l'Islam 1971
Arts de l'Islam des origines à 1700 dans les collections publiques françaises, Paris, 1971.

Arts of Islam 1976
The Arts of Islam. Exhibition Catalogue. Hayward Gallery, 8 April-4 July 1976, London, 1976.

Arts of Islam 1981
The Arts of Islam. Masterpieces from the Metropolitan Museum of Art, New York. Exhibition Catalogue. Museum für Islamische Kunst, 20 June-23 August 1981, Berlin, 1981.

Arts of Persia 1989
The Arts of Persia. Ed. by R W Ferrier, New Haven-London, 1989.

Ashrafi 1966
* M M Ashrafi, *Miniatures of the 16th Century in Manuscripts of Jami's Works in the Collections of the USSR*, M, 1966.

Atagarryyev and Khodzhageldyyev 1972
* E Atagarryyev and A Khodzhageldy-yev, "The Art of Resonant Metal", in: *Monuments of Turkmenistan*, Ashkhabad, 1972, No.2 (14), pp.27–32.

Bader 1949
* O Bader, "The Bartym Bowl", *KSI-IMK*, M, 1949, XXIX, p.85.

Bader and Smirnov 1954
* O Bader and A Smirnov, *"Zakamskoye Silver" of the First Centuries AD*, M, 1954.

Bahrami 1937
M Bahrami, *Recherches sur les carreaux de revêtement lustrés dans la céramique persane du XIIIᵉ au XVᵉ siècle (étoiles et croix)*, Paris, 1937.

Bahrami 1949
M Bahrami, *Gurgan Faiences*, Cairo, 1949.

Balashova 1940
* G N Balashova, *"A Bronze Mirror with a Hunting Scene"*, TOVGE, vol.III, L, 1940.

Balashova 1972
* G N Balashova, "A Clay Jug of the 12th-13th Century with Epic Scenes", in: *Central Asia and Iran*, L, 1972, pp.91–106.

Bartold 1969-77
* V V Bartold, *Collected Works*, 9 vols, M, 1969–77.

Belenitsky, Bentovich, Bolshakov 1974
* A M Belenitsky, I B Bentovich and O G Bolshakov, *The Medieval City in Central Asia*, L, 1974.

Bemshtam 1937
* A Bernshtam, "The Hun Burial Site of Noin-ula and Its Historical and Archaeological Significance", *Izvestiya AN SSSR*, L, 1937.

Bertels 1960
* E Bertels, *A History of Persian-Tajik Literature*, M, 1960.

Bertels 1962
* E Bertels, *Selected Works: Nizami and Fuzuli*, M, 1962.

Bolshakov 1969
* O G Bolshakov, "Islam and Figurative Art", *TGE*, vol.X, L, 1969, pp.142–56.

Borisov and Lukonin 1963
* A Y Borisov and V G Lukonin, *Sasanian Gems*, L, 1963.

Boyce 1957
"The Parthian *Gōsan* and Iranian Minstrel Tradition", *Journal of the Royal Asiatic Society*, London, 1957, I, II, pp.10–45.

Bretanitsky 1964
* L S Bretanitsky, "On the Problem of Style in Connection with the Periodification of Architecture of the Countries of the Near East", *Peoples of Asia and Africa*, M, 1964, No.4.

Bretanitsky 1966
* L S Bretanitsky, *The Architecture of Azerbaijan in the 12th-15th Centuries and its Place in the Architecture of the Near East*, M, 1966.

Bretanizki 1988
L Bretanizki, B Weimarn, B Brentjes, *Die Kunst Azerbaidshans vom 4. bis zum 18. Jahrhundert*, Leipzig, 1988.

Busson 1978
A Busson, "Note sur une miniature moghole d'influence européenne", *Arts Asiatiques*, vol.XXXIV, Paris, 1978, pp.133–38.

Carswell 1972
J Carswell, "Eastern and Western Influence on the Art of the Seventeenth Century in Iran", in: *The Memorial Volume of the 5th international Congress of Iranian Art and Archaeology*, Tehran, 1972, pp.277–82.

Collections 1902
* *The Collections of the Caucasian Museum: Archaeology*, vol.V, Tiflis, 1902.

Cullican 1965
W Cullican, *The Medes and Persians*, New York, 1965.

Cuyler Young 1965
T Cuyler Young, "A Comparative

Ceramic Chronology for Western Iran. 1500-500 BC", *Iran*, vol.III, London, 1965.

DANDAMAYEV AND LUKONIN 1980
* M A Dandamayev and V G Lukonin, *The Culture and Economy of Ancient Iran*, M, 1980.

DAVIDS-SAMLING 1975
C L Davids-Samling, Islamisk Kunst, Copenhagen, 1975.

DE BAGDAD À ISPAHAN 1994
De Bagdad à Ispahan. Manuscrits islamiques de la Filiale de Saint-Pétersbourg de l'Institut d'Etudes Orientales, Académie des Sciences de Russie, LuganoMilan, 1994.

DODKHUDOYEVA 1982
* L N Dodkhudoyeva, "The Literary Wasf and Its Equivalents in Painting", in: *Written Records and the Problems of the History of Culture of Oriental Peoples. 16th Annual Scientific Session of the Leningrad Branch of the USSR Academy of Sciences Institute of Oriental Studies*, II, M, 1982.

DYAKONOV 1936
* M M Dyakonov, *A Bronze Aquamanile of 1206 as a Work of Art and Historical Source. Summary of Dissertation*, L, 1936.

DYAKONOV 1938
* M M Dyakonov, "The Shirvan Aquamanile of 1206", in: *Monuments of the Age of Rustaveli*, M-L, 1938, pp.247-54.

DYAKONOV 1939
* M M Dyakonov, "A Bronze Aquamanile of 1206", in: *The Third international Congress on the Art and Archaeology of Iran*. Reports, M-L, 1939, pp.45-51.

DYAKONOV 1940
* M M Dyakonov, "The 1431 Manuscript of Nizami's *Khamsa* and Its Significance for the History of Miniature Painting in the East", TOVGE, vol.III, L, 1940, pp.275-86.

DYAKONOV 1947A
* M.M. Dyakonov, "On an Early

Arabic Inscription", *EV*, M-L, 1947, 1, pp.5-8.

DYAKONOV 1947B
* M M Dyakonov, "Bronze Sculpture During the First Centuries of the Hijra", *TOVGE*, vol.IV, L, 1947, pp.155-78.

DYAKONOV 1951
* M M Dyakonov, "An Arabic Inscription on a Bronze Eagle from the Collection of the State Hermitage", *EV*, M-L, 1951, IV, pp.24-27.

DYAKONOV 1956
* M Dyakonov, *A History of Media*, M, 1956.

DYAKONOV 1961
* M Dyakonov, "An Interpretation of Iranian Languages Using Heterographic Scripts", in: *I Fridrikh, The Deciphering of Forgotten Scripts and Languages*, M, 1961.

DYSON 1969
R Dyson, "Digging in Iran. Hasanlu, 1958", *Expedition*, vol.XI, 1969.

DYSON 1973
R Dyson, "The Archaeological Evidence of the Second Millennium BC on the Persian Plateau", in: *Cambridge Ancient History*, vol.II, Cambridge, 1973, pl.I.

EASEL PAINTING 1973
* *Easel Painting in Iran in the 18th-19th Centuries. Catalogue*, M, 1973.

ERGINSOY 1978
U Erginsoy, *Islam maden sanatinin gelismesi*, Istanbul, 1978.

ETTINGHAUSEN 1957
R Ettinghausen, "The Wade Cup in the Cleveland Museum of Art, Its Origin and Decorations", *Ars Orientalis*, vol.II, Ann Arbor, 1957, pp.327-66.

ETTINGHAUSEN 1964
"7000 Years of Iranian Art. Exhibition" Circulated by the Smithsonian Institute. 1964-1965, Washington, 1964.

ETTINGHAUSEN 1969
R Ettinghausen, "Some Comments on Medieval Iranian Art (A Propos the Publication of the Cambridge History of Iran)", *Artibus Asiae*, vol.XXXI, No.4, Ascona, 1969, pp.276-300.

FEHÉRVÁRI (S.A.)
G Fehérvári, "Some Problems of Seljuq Art", in: *The Art of Iran and Anatolia from the 11th to the 13th Century AD. Colloquies on Art and Archaeology in Asia, No.4*, London (s.a.), pp.1-12.

FEHÉRVÁRI 1973
G Fehérvári, *Islamic Pottery*, Glasgow, 1973.

FEHÉRVÁRI 1976
G Fehérvári, *Islamic Metalwork of the Eighth to the Fifteenth Centuries in the Keir Collection*, London, 1976.

FEHÉRVÁRI AND SAFADI 1981
G. Fehérvári and Y.H. Safadi, *1400 Years of Islamic Art. A Descriptive Catalogue*, London, 1981.

FRYE 1972
* R.N. Frye, *The Heritage of Iran*, M., 1972.

GHIRSHMAN 1962
R Ghirshman, *Iran, Partes et Sassanides*, Paris, 1962.

GHIRSHMAN 1962A
R Ghirshman, *Perse proto-iraniennes, Mèdes achéménides*, Paris, 1962.

GHIRSHMAN 1979
R Ghirshman, *Tombe princière de Ziwiyé et le début de l'art animalier scythe*, Paris, 1979.

GIUZALIAN 1968
L T Giuzalian, "The Bronze Qalamdan (Pencase) 542/1148 from the Hermitage Collection (1936-1965)", *Ars Orientalis*, vol.VII, Ann Arbor, 1968, pp.95-119.

GONCHAROVA 1964
* A A Goncharova, "Ancient State Regalia", in: *The Armoury*, M, 1964, pp.257-90.

GRABAR 1968A
O Grabar, "The Visual Arts:

1050-1350", in: *The Cambridge History of Iran*, vol.V, Cambridge, 1968, pp.626-58.

GRABAR 1968B
O Grabar, "Les Arts mineurs de l'Orient musulman à partir du milieu du XIIᵉ siècle", *Cahiers de civilisation médiévale*, vol.XI, No.2, 1968, pp.181-190.

GRABAR AND BLAIR 1980
O Grabar and S Blair, *Epic images and Contemporary History. The illustrations of the Great Mongol Shahnama*, Chicago-London, 1980.

GRANTOVSKY 1970
* E A Grantovsky, *An Early History of the Tribes of the Near East*, M, 1970.

GREAT ART TREASURES 1994
Great Art Treasures of the Hermitage Museum, St Petersburg, New York, London, 1994, vols I, II.

GRIGOLIYA 1971
* A M Grigoliya, "The Art of the Miniaturists of the Afshar Line from Documents in the Georgian SSR Museum of Art", in: *The Art and Archaeology of Iran. All-Union Conference (1969). Reports*, M, 1971, pp.121-33.

GRUBE 1966
E J Grube, *The World of Islam*, London, 1966.

GRUBE 1970
E J Grube, "Islamic Art - a Proposed New Classification", in: *Islamic Art Across the World. An Exhibition Prepared by Theodore Bowie in Partial Celebration of the 150th Anniversary of Indiana University*, Indiana, 1970, pp.7-16.

GRUBE 1974
E J Grube, "Notes on the Decorative Arts of the Timurid Period", *Gururajamanjarika. Studi in onore di Giuseppe Tucci*, Naples, 1974, pp.23379.

GUEST 1943
G D Guest, "Notes on the Miniatures of the Thirteenth Century", *Ars Islamica*, vol.X, 1943.

Gyuzalyan 1938
* L T Gyuzalyan, "A Bronze Ewer of 1182 AH", in: *Monuments of the Age of Rustaveli*, L, 1938, pp.227-36.

G[yuzalyan] 1949
* L G[yuzalyan], "A Bronze Incense Burner in the Shape of an Eagle", in: *Sokrovishcha Ermitazha*, M-L, 1949, pp.129, 130.

Gyuzalyan 1953
* L T Gyuzalyan, "Two Extracts from Nizami on Tiles of the 13th-14th Centuries", EV, M-L, 1953, VII, pp.17-25.

Gyuzalyan 1956
* L T Gyuzalyan, "Inscription on a Lustre Tile of 624/1227 AD in the Kiev Museum", *EV*, M-L, 1956, XI, pp.33-43.

Gyuzalyan 1963
* L T Gyuzalyan, "Three Injuid Bronze Vessels. On the Question of Locating the South-Western Group of Iranian Medieval Artistic Bronzes", in: *Papers of the 25th international Congress of Orientalists*. Moscow, 9th-16th August, 1960, vol.II, M, 1963, pp.174-78.

Gyuzalyan 1972
* L T Gyuzalyan, "Oriental Miniatures Depicting a Western Landscape", in: *Central Asia and Iran*, L, 1972, pp.163-69.

Gyuzalyan 1978
* L T Gyuzalyan, "The Second Herat Bucket (the Fould Bucket)", *TGE*, vol.XIX, L, 1978, pp.52-83.

Gyuzalyan and Dyakonov 1934
* L T Gyuzalyan, M M Dyakonov, *Manuscripts of the Shah-nama in Leningrad Collections*, L, 1934.

Hakemi 1973
A Hakemi, "Excavations in Kaluraz, Gilan", *Bulletin of the Asia Institute*, Shiraz, 1973.

Hambly 1964
G Hambly, "An Introduction to the Economic Organisation of Early

Qajar Iran", *Iran*, vol.II, London, 1964, pp.69-81.

Harper and Meyers 1981
P Harper and P Meyers, *Silver Vessels of the Sasanian Period*, vol.I (Royal Imagery), New York, 1981.

Hill and Grabar 1964
D Hill and O Grabar, *Islamic Architecture and Its Decoration*, Chicago, 1964.

Hollstein 1980
Hollstein's Dutch and Flemish Etchings, Engravings and Woodcuts, ca 1450-1700, vols XXI, XXII, Amsterdam, 1980.

IDM 1982
* *Istoriya drevnego mira [History of the Ancient World]*, M, 1982.

Iemsalimskaya 1972
* A A Iemsalimskaya, "A New Discovery of the So-Called 'Sassanian' Silk with Senmurvs", *SGE*, L, 1972, XXXIV, pp.II-15.

Islam 1985
Islam. Art and Culture, Stockholm, 1985.

Ivanov 1960a
* A A Ivanov, "A Small Box with the Name of Muhammad-Ali, Son of Muhammad-Zaman", *SGE*, L, 1960, XVIII, pp.52, 53.

Ivanov 1960b
* A A Ivanov, "A Copper Bowl of 8 ii AH (1408-09 AD) with Verses of Hafiz", *SGE*, L, 1960, XIX, pp.41-44.

Ivanov 1960c
* A A Ivanov, "On the Original Purpose of the So-Called Iranian 'Candlesticks' of the 16th-17th Centuries", in: *investigations into the Cultural History of the Peoples of the East*, M-L, 1960, pp.337-45.

Ivanov 1961
* A A Ivanov, "On the Principles of Dating l5th- to 18th-Century Iranian Copper and Bronze Wares", *TGE*, vol.V, L, 1961, pp.243-50.

Ivanov 1962
* A A Ivanov, "Persian Miniatures",

in: *Album of Persian and Indian Miniatures of the 16th-18th Centuries*, M, 1962, pp.44-59.

Ivanov 1964
* A A Ivanov, "Khurasan Bronze and Copper Wares of the Second Half of the lst-Early 16th Centuries", in: *Summary of Reports to the Jubilee Academic Session (State Hermitage)*. October, 1964, L, 1964, pp.56, 57.

Ivanov 1966
* A A Ivanov, "The Base of a Candlestick of 880 AH (1475-76 AD) with Verses by the Poet Salihi", *SGE*, L, 1966, XXVII, pp.67-70.

Ivanov 1968
* A A Ivanov, "On the Portrait of Imam-Quli Khan", in: *The Near and Middle East: History, Culture, Study of Sources*, M, 1968, pp.61-66.

Ivanov 1969a
* A A Ivanov, "A Group of Khurasan Copper and Bronze Wares of the Second Half of the lst Century. Works of the Master Shir-Ali ibn Muhammad Dimashqi", *TGE*, vol.X, L, 1969, pp.157-67.

Ivanov 1969b
* A A Ivanov, "Artistic Bronzes of the Near and Middle East (7th-20th Centuries)", *SGE*, L, 1969, XXX, pp.31-36.

Ivanov 1970a
* A A Ivanov, "On the Production of Bronze Objects in Mavera al-Nahr in pre-Mongol Times", *Kratkiye soobshcheniya instituta arkheologii AN SSSR*, M, 1970, No.122, pp.101-105.

Ivanov 1970b
* A A Ivanov, "A Persian Qalamdan of 1092 AlI/1681 AD", *Palestinsky sbornik*, L, 1970, No.21 (84), pp.229-32.

Ivanov 1971a
* A A Ivanov, *Copper and Bronze (Brass) Objects in Iran during the Second Half of the 14th-First Half of the 18th Centuries (indications of Date and the Problem of Localization)*.

Author's Abstract of Dissertation, L, 1971.

Ivanov 1971b
* A A Ivanov, "The Seal of Gouhar-Shad", *Strany i narody Vostoka*, M, 1971, No.10, pp.199-201.

Ivanov 1971c
* A A Ivanov, "Three Objects with Verses by Jami", *EV*, M-L, 1971, XX, pp.97-103.

Ivanov 1973
* A A Ivanov, "On the Periodization of Iranian Art of the 14th-18th Centuries", in: *Summaries of Reports to the Second All Union Conference on the Art and Archaeology of Iran*, M, 1973, pp.4-6.

Ivanov 1974
* A A Ivanov, "A Qalamdan with the Portrait of a Youth in Armour", *SGE*, L, 1974, XXXIX, pp.56-59.

Ivanov 1976
* A A Ivanov, "The Periodization of the Production of Copper and Bronze (Brass) Wares in Iran During the 14th-18th Centuries", in: *Bartoldian Studies*. 1976. Third Year, M, 1976, pp.45-47.

Ivanov 1977
* A A Ivanov, "A History of the Study of the Mavera al-Nahr (Central Asian) School of Miniatures (Article I)", in: *Central Asia in Antiquity and the Middle Ages (History and Culture)*, M, 1977, pp.144-59.

Ivanov 1979a
A A Ivanov, "A Group of Iranian Daggers of the Period from the Fifteenth Century to the Beginning of the Seventeenth with Persian Inscriptions", in: *Islamic Arms and Armour* (ed. R Elgood), London, 1979, pp.64-77.

Ivanov 1979b
A A Ivanov, "The Life of Muhammad-Zaman: a Reconsideration", *Iran*, vol.XVII, London, 1979, pp.65-70.

Ivanov 1980a
* A A Ivanov, "A Faience Plate of the

l5th Century from Mashhad", *SGE*, L, 1980, XLV, pp.64–66.

IVANOV 1980B
* A A Ivanov, "With Reference to an Articleby G A Pugachenkova", *lskusstvo*, M, 1980, No.11, pp.67–70.

IVANOV 1982
* A A Ivanov, "An Iranian Silver Talisman of the 16th Century", *SGE*, L, 1982, XLVII, pp.73, 74.

IVANOV 1985
* A A Ivanov, "A Bronze Bowl from Khunzakh", in: *Problems of Oriental Culture*, L, 1985.

IVANOV AND ORAZOV 1984
* A A Ivanov and O Orazov, "A Hoard of Bronze Objects from the Site of Old Serakhs", *EV*, L, 1984, XXII, pp.52–56.

JEROUSSALIMSKAJA 1978
A Jeroussalimskaja, "Le Cafetan aux simourghs du tombeau de Mocht-chevaja Balka", *Studia Iranica*, vol.VII, fasc.2, Leiden, 1978, pp.183–211.

KALTER 1982
J Kalter, "Der islamische Orient", in: Ausstellungskatalog "Ferne Völker frühe Zeiten". *Kunsnverke aus dem Linden-Museum Stuttgart. Staatliches Museum für Völkerkunde*, vol.2, Recklinghausen, 1982.

KESATI 1940
* R Kesati, "The Bronze Figure of an Eagle", *SGE*, L, 1940, 1, pp.12, 13.

KETSKHOVELI 1972
M Ketskhoveli, "A Fragment of Silk Textile from Upper Svaneti", in: *Dzeglis Megobari*, 29, Tbilisi, 1972, pp.41–45 (in Georgian, with summary in Russian).

KHALILOV 1976
* D Khalilov, "A Silver Dish with Gilding from Ancient Shemakha", *Vestnik drevney istorii*, M, 1976, No.3, pp.146–49.

KHODZHAGELDYYEV 1974
* A Khodzhageldyyev, "Cauldrons by Ancient Masters", in: *Monuments of Turkmenistan*, Ashkhabad, 1974, No.2(18), pp.23, 24.

KHODZHAGELDYYEV 1975
* A Khodzhageldyyev, "Bronze Cauldrons from Southern Turkmenistan", in: *Monuments of Turkmenistan*, Ashkhabad, 1975, No.2(20), pp.21–23.

KHODZHAGELDYYEV 1976
* A Khodzhageldyyev, "On the Question of the Place of Manufacture of Bronze Cauldrons of the Open Type (the Work of Abu Bakr ibn Ahmad Marwazi)", in: *Summary of Reports to the 1st Scientific Conference of Young Scholars of the Turkmen SSR Academy of Sciences*, Ashkhabad, 1976, pp.10, 11.

KHODZHAGELDYYEV 1979
* A Khodzhageldyyev, "Bronze Cauldrons of Southern Turkmenistan of the 12th-13th Centuries", in: *Karakumskiye drevnosti*, Ashkhabad, 1979, No.8, pp.106–112.

KIBALCHICH 1910
* T Kibalchich, *South Russian Gems*, Berlin, 1910.

KINZHALOV 1959
* R Kinzhalov, "A Silver Plaque with a Depiction of a Parthian King", *Sovetskaya arkheologiya*, M, 1959, No.2, pp.197-204.

KOMAROFF 1980
L Komaroff, "Timurid to Safavid Iran: Continuity and Change", *Marsyas*, vol.XX, New York, 1980, pp.11–16.

KOMAROFF 1992
L Komaroff, *The Golden Disk of Heaven. Metalwork of Timurid Iran*, Costa Mesa and New York, 1992.

KONDRATYEVA 1961
* F A Kondratyeva, "Green Glaze Ceramics from Paikend", *TGE*, vol.V, L, 1961, pp.216–27.

KÖNIG 1934
F M König, "Älteste Geschichte der Meder und Perser", *Der Alte Orient*, vol.XXXIII, Leipzig, 1934.

KRACHKOVSKAYA 1927A
* V A Krachkovskaya, "The Tiled Lustre Mihrab in the Hermitage", *Iran*, vol.I, L, 1927, pp.73–86.

KRACHKOVSKAYA 1927B
* V A Krachkovskaya, "Islamic Art in the Khanenko Collection", in: *Zapiski kollegii vostokovedov*, vol.II, L, 1927, pp.1–50.

KRACHKOVSKY 1930
* I Y Krachkovsky, "Abu Nuwaz on a Sassanian Bowl with Illustrations", *Doklady AN SSSR*, L, 1930, No.10.

KÜHNEL 1931
E Kühnel, "Dated Persian Lustred Pottery", *Eastern Art*, vol.III, 1931, pp.221–36.

KVERFELDT 1940
* E K Kverfeldt, "Realistic Features in Illustrations on Fabrics and Carpets from Safavid Times", *TOVGE*, vol.III, L, 1940, pp.263–74.

KVERFELDT 1947
* E K Kverfeldt, *Ceramics of the Near East*, L, 1947.

LANE 1957
A Lane, *Later Islamic Pottery. Persia, Syria, Egypt, Turkey*, London, 1957.

LITVINSKY 1978
* B T Litvinsky, *Burial Grounds of Western FerghanaIV. Tools and Utensils from the Burial Grounds of Western Ferghana*, M, 1978.

LIVSHITS 1979
* V Livshits, "Rulers of Punch (Sogdian and Turkic)", *Peoples of Asia and Africa*, 1979, No.4, p.57, note 6.

LIVSHITS AND LUKONIN 1964
* V A Livshits and V G Lukonin, "Middle Persian and Sogdian Inscriptions on Silver Vessels", *Vestnik drevnei istorii*, 1964, No.3.

LUKENS-SWIETOCHOWSKI 1979
M Lukens-Swietochowski, "The School of Herat from 1450 to 1506", in: *The Arts of the Book in Central Asia. 14th-16th Centuries*, UNESCO, 1979, pp.179–214.

LUKONIN 1961
* V Lukonin, *Iran in the Age of the First Sassanids*, L, 1961.

LUKONIN 1967
* V Lukonin, "Kushan-Sassanian Coins", *EV*, XVIII, M-L, 1967, pp.16–33.

LUKONIN 1971
* V G Lukonin, *Treasures of Art from Ancient Iran, the Caucasus and Centrai Asia*, L, 1971.

LUKONIN 1977A
* V G Lukonin, "Archaeological Relics from Iran of the 2nd-1st Millennium BC and New Exhibits in the Oriental Department", *SGE*, XLII, 1977.

LUKONIN 1977B
* V G Lukonin, *The Art of Ancient Iran*, M, 1977.

LUKONIN 1980
* V G Lukonin, *Iran in the 3rd Century. New Material and an Attempt at Historical Reconstruction*, M, 1980.

LUKONIN 1983
V Lukonin, "Parthian and Sassanian Administration, Trade and Taxes", in: *The Cambridge History of Iran*, vol.III, Oxford, 1983, pl.2.

MACHABELI 1976
* K Machabeli, *Late Antique Metalwork of Georgia*, Tbilisi, 1976.

MAHBOUBIAN 1970
Treasures of Persian Art after Islam. The Mahboubian Collection, New York, 1970.

MAISTROV 1968
* Scientific Devices. Compiled and edited by L Maistrov, M, 1968.

MARSCHAK 1986
B Marschak, *Silberschätze des Orients. Metallkunst des 3.-13. Jahrhunderts und ihre Kontinuität*, Leipzig, 1986.

Marshak 1971
* B I Marshak, *Sogdian Silver. Essays on Oriental Metalwork*, M, 1971.

Marshak 1972
* B I Marshak, "A Bronze Ewer from Samarqand", in: *Central Asia and Iran*, L, 1972, pp.61–90.

Marshak 1976
* B I Marshak, "Silver Vessels of the 10th–11th Centuries, Their Significance for the Periodization of the Art of Iran and Central Asia", in: *The Art and Archaeology of Iran. Second All-Union Conference. 19-23 November, 1973. Reports*, M, 1976, pp.148–73.

Marshak 1978
* B I Marshak, "Early Islamic Bronze Plates (the Syro–Egyptian Traditions in the Art of the Caliphate", *TGE*, vol.XIX, L, 1978, pp.26–52.

Marshak and Krikis 1969
* B Marshak and Y Krikis, "The Chilek Bowls", *TGE*, vol.X, L, 1969, pp.62–66.

Martin 1902
F R Martin, *Ältere Kupferarbeiten aus dem Orient*, Stockholm, 1902.

Martin 1912
F R Martin, *The Miniature Painting and Painters of Persia, India and Turkey from the 8th to the 18th Century*, vols I, II, London, 1912.

Maslenitsyna 1975
S Maslenitsyna, *Persian Art in the Collection of the Museum of Oriental Art*, L, 1975.

Maslenitsyna 1976
* S P Maslenitsyna, "The Beginning of a New Period of Medieval Ceramics in Iran (14th Century)", in: *The Art and Archaeology of Iran. Second All-Union Conference. 19-23 November, 1973. Reports*, M, 1976, pp.174–81.

Masterpieces 1990
Masterpieces of Islamic Art in the Hermitage Museum, Kuwait, 1990.

Mayer 1956
L A Mayer, *Islamic Astrolabists and Their Works*, Geneva, 1956.

Mayer 1959
L A Mayer, *Islamic Metalworkers and Their Works*, Geneva, 1959.

Meinecke 1971
M Meinecke, "Zur Entwicklung des islamischen Architekturdekors im Mittelalter", *Der Islam*, vol.XLVII, Berlin, 1971, pp.200–35.

Meisterwerke 1912
Die Ausstellung von Meisterwerken muhammedanischer Kunst in München, 1910, Munich, 1912.

Melikhov 1952
* A Melikhov, "A Silver Plate from Krasnaya Polyana", *KSIIMK*, vol.X, M, 1952.

Melikian-Chirvani (s.a.)
A S Melikian-Chirvani, "The Westward Progress of Khorassanian Culture under the Seljuks", in: *The Art of Iran and Anatolia from the 11th to the 13th Century AD. Colloquies on Art and Archaeology in Asia, No.4*, London (s.a.), pp.110–25.

Melikian-Chirvani 1969
A S Melikian-Chirvani, "L'Ecole du Fars au XIVᵉ siècle", *Journal Asiatique*, vol.CCLVII, Nos 1, 2, Paris, 1969, pp.19–36.

Melikian-Chirvani 1970
A S Melikian-Chirvani, "Le roman de Varqe et Golsâh", *Arts Asiatiques*, vol.XXII, Paris, 1970.

Melikian-Chirvani 1972a
A S Melikian-Chirvani, *Le Bronze iranien*, Paris, 1972.

Melikian-Chirvani 1972b
A S Melikian-Chirvani, "Les Calligraphes et l'art du bronze", *Iran*, Paris, 1972, pp.138–49.

Melikian-Chirvani 1974
A S Melikian-Chirvani, "The White Bronzes of Early Islamic Iran", *Metropolitan Museum Journal*, vol.IX, New York, 1974, pp.123–51.

Melikian-Chirvani 1975
A S Melikian-Chirvani, "Recherches sur l'école du bronze ottoman au XVIe siècle", *Turcica*, Paris-Strasbourg, 1975, pp.146–67.

Melikian-Chirvani 1976a
A S Melikian-Chirvani, "Four Pieces of Islamic Metalwork. Some Notes on Previously Unknown School", *Art and Archaeology Research Papers*, London, 1976, No.10, pp.24–30.

Melikian-Chirvani 1976b
A S Melikian-Chirvani, "Iranian Metalwork and the Written Word", *Apollo*, vol.CIII, No.170, London, 1976, pp.286–91.

Melikian-Chirvani 1976c
A S Melikian-Chirvani, "Les Bronzes du Khorâssân 4. Bronzes inédits du Khorâssân oriental", Studia Iranica, vol.V, fasc.2, Paris, 1976, pp.203–12.

Melikian-Chirvani 1976d
A S Melikian-Chirvani, *Islamic Metalwork from Iranian Lands (8th-18th Centuries). Exhibition Catalogue. Victoria and Albert Museum, April–May 1976*, London, 1976.

Melikian-Chirvani 1977a
A S Melikian-Chirvani, "Les Thèmes ésotériques et les thèmes mystiques dans l'art du bronze iranien", in: *Mélanges offerts à Henry Corbin*, Tehran, 1977, pp.367–406.

Melikian-Chirvani 1977b
J Sourdel-Thomine and B Spuler, "Die Kunst des Islam", in: *Propyläen Kunstgeschichte*, vol.IV, Berlin, 1977, p.187.

Melikian-Chirvani 1979
A S Melikian-Chirvani, "The Tabarzins of Lotf'ali", in: *Islamic Arms and Armour* (ed. R Elgood), London, 1979, pp.117–35, 240–41.

Melikian-Chirvani 1982
A S Melikian-Chirvani, *Victoria and Albert Museum Catalogue: Islamic Metalwork from the Iranian World, 8th-18th Centuries*, London, 1982.

Mellink 1966
M J Mellink, "The Hasanlu Bowl in

Anatolian Perspective", *Iranica Antiqua*, vol.VI, 1966.

Mishukov 1954
* F Y Mishukov, "Gold Damascening and Inlay on Antique Weapons", in: *State Armoury of the Moscow Kremlin*, M, 1954.

Mistetstvo 1930
Mistetstvo kraïn islyamu. Catalogue. Compiled by M Vyazmitina, Kiev, 1930 (in Ukrainian).

Moghaddam 1972
H Moghaddam, "Prospection archéologique au Dailaman", in: *The Memorial Volume of the 5th International Congress of Iranian Art and Archaeology*, vol.I, Tehran, 1972.

Murakka 1994
O F Akimushkin, *Il Murakka di San Pietroburgo*, Lugano-Milan, 1994.

Nasr 1975
S H Nasr, "Sufism", in: *The Cambridge History of Iran*, Cambridge, vol.IV, 1975, pp.442–64.

Negahban 1964
E Negahban, *A Preliminary Report of Marlik Excavation*, Tehran, 1964.

Negahban 1972
E Negahban, "Pottery Figurines of Marlik", in: *The Memorial Volume of the 5th international Congress of Iranian Art and Archaeology*, vol.I, Tehran, 1972.

Negahban 1977
E Negahban, "The Seals of Marlik-Tepe", *Journal of the Near Eastern Studies*, vol.XXXVI, No.2, New York, 1977.

Nizami Aruzi Samarqandi 1963
* Nizami Aruzi Samarqandi, *Collected Rarities or Four Conversations*, M, 1963.

Nylander 1970
C Nylander, *Ionians in Pasargadae. Studies in Old Persian Architecture*, Uppsala, 1970.

Orbeli 1938
* I A Orbeli, "A Bronze Incense

Burner of the 12th Century in the Form of a Snow Leopard", in: *Mouments of the age of Rustaveli*, L, 1938, pp.293–300.

ORBELI AND TREVER 1935
* I A Orbeli and K V Trever, *Sassanian Metal*, L, 1935.

ORIENTAL JEWELLERY 1984
* A A Ivanov, V G Lukonin and L S Smesova, *Oriental Jewellery. Catalogue*, M, 1984.

ORIENTAL MINIATURES 1980
* Oriental Miniatures in the Collection of the Abu-al-Rayhan Biruni Institutel Studies of the Uzbek SSR Academy of Sciences, Tashkent, 1980. Wasifi

PETROV 1949
* G M Petrov, "A Brief Sketch of the Development of Russo-Iranian Economic and Political Relations in the 18th Century", *Sovetskoye vostokovedeniye*, vol.VI, M-L, 1949, pp.327–35.

PETMSHEVSKY 1966
* I P Petmshevsky, *Islam in Iran During the 7th-15th Centuries*, L, 1966.

PIRVERDIAN 1969
* N A Pirverdian, "On the Time of Manufacture of One Persian Fabric", *SGE*, L, 1969, XXX, pp.39–42.

PIRVERDIAN 1975
* N A Pirverdian, "On the Dating of Iranian Brocaded Fabrics with Figural Compositions", *SGE*, L, 1975, XL, pp.53–56.

POPE 1969
A U Pope, *Persian Architecture*, Shiraz, 1969.

PORADA 1965
E Porada, *The Art of Ancient Iran*, New York, 1965.

PORADA 1971
E Porada, "Problems of Iranian Iconography", in: *The Memorial Volume of the 5th International Congress of Iranian Art and Archaeology*, vol.I, Tehran, 1971.

PROPYLÄEN KUNSTGESCHICHTE 1977
J Sourdel-Thomine and B Spuler, "Die Kunst des Islam", *Propyläen Kunstgeschichte*, vol.IV, Berlin, 1977.

PUGACHENKOVA 1953
* G A Pugachenkova, "On the Dating and Origin of the Khamsa manuscript of Amir Khusrau Dihlawi in the Collection of the Oriental Institute of the Uzbek SSR Academy of Sciences", *Trudy AN Tadzhikskoy SSR. Institut Istorii, Arkheologii i Etnografii*, vol. XVII, Stalinabad, 1953, pp.187–96.

PUGACHENKOVA 1967
* G Pugachenkova, *The Art of Turkmenistan*, M, 1967.

PUGACHENKOVA 1979
* G A Pugachenkova, "Towards a Discussion of the Central Asian School of Miniature Painting in the 15th Century", *Iskusstvo*, M, 1979, No.2, pp.5053.

PUGACHENKOVA 1980
* G A Pugachenkova, "Miniature Painting. in Central Asia in the 14th-15th Centuries", in: *Adaby Meros, Tashkent*, 1980, No.4 (16), pp.60–89.

PUGACHENKOVA AND REMPEL 1982
* G A Pugachenkova and L I Rempel, *An Outline of the Art of Central Asia*, M, 1982.

RAPOPORT 1972
* I V Rapoport, "Monochrome Ceramics of Iran in the 16th-17th Centuries, with Relief Depictions", in: *Central Asia and Iran*, L, 1972, pp.149–56.

RAPOPORT 1975
* I V Rapoport, "On One Group of Iranian Faience Bottles", *SGE*, L, 1975, XL, pp.50–53.

RAYEVSKAYA 1971
* T Rayevskaya, "Towards the Question of the Method of Dating Some Monuments of Sassanian Glyptics", in: *Art and Archaeology of Iran. All-Union Conference (1969). Reports*, M, 1971, pp.263–68.

RAYEVSKY 1984
* D S Rayevsky, "Towards a Characterization of the Basic Tendencies in the History of Scythian Art", in: *Problems of Oriental Culture*, L, 1984.

REITLINGER 1961
G Reitlinger, "Recension on A Lane. Later Islamic Pottery: Persia, Syria, Egypt, Turkey", *Ars Orientalis*, vol.IV, 1961, pp.400–09.

RICE 1955
D S Rice, *The Wade Cup in the Cleveland Museum of Art*, Paris, 1955.

ROBINSON 1958
B W Robinson, *A Descriptive Catalogue of Persian Paintings in the Bodleian Library*, Oxford, 1958.

ROBINSON 1967
B W Robinson, *Persian Miniature Painting from Collections in the British Isles. Exhibition Catalogue*, London, 1967.

ROBINSON 1979A
B W Robinson, "Persian Painting in the Qajar Period", in: *Highlights of Persian Art, Boulder*, Colorado, 1979, pp.331–61.

ROBINSON 1979B
B W Robinson, "The Turkman School to 1503", in: *The Arts of the Book in Central Asia: 14th-16th Centuries*, UNESCO, 1979, pp.215–47.

ROBINSON 1980
B W Robinson, *Persian Paintings in the John Rylands Library. A Descriptive Catalogue*, London, 1980.

ROBINSON 1982
B W Robinson, "A Survey of Persian Painting (1350-1896)", in: *Art et société dans le monde iranien*, Paris, 1982, pp.13–89.

ROGERS 1973
J M Rogers, "The 11th Century – a Turning Point in the Architecture of Mashriq?", in: *Islamic Civilisation: 950-1150*, Oxford, 1973, pp.211–49.

SCERRATO 1969
U Scerrato, "Ogetti metallici di età

islamica in Afghanistan", *Annali*, vol.XIV, 2, Naples, 1969, pp.673–714.

SCHLUMBERGER 1970
D Schlumberger, *L'Orient hellénisé*, Paris, 1970.

SHANDROVSKAYA 1960
* V S Shandrovskaya, *The Culture and Art of the Near and Middle East: 4th Millennium BC-18th Century AD and Byzantium of the 4th-15th Centuries*, L, 1960.

SHEFER 1982
* Shefer, *The Golden Peaches of Samarqand*, M, 1982.

SHIKHSAIDOV 1969
* A R Shikhsaidov, *Inscriptions Speak*, Makhachkala, 1969.

SHIKHSAIDOV 1984
* A R Shikhsaidov, *Epigraphic Monuments of Daghestan in the 10th-17th Centuries as a Historical Source*, M, 1984.

SHILEIKO 1925
* V Shileiko, "The Seal of the King Artaxerxes", *Zhizn muzeya*, M, 1925, pp.17–19.

SMIRNOV 1909
* Y I Smirnov, *Oriental Silver*, St Petersburg, 1909.

SMIRNOV 1934
* Y I Smirnov, *The Akhalgori Hoard*, Tiflis, 1934.

SMIRNOV 1957
* A Smirnov, "New Finds of Oriental Silver in the Urals Region", *Trudy Gosudarstvennogo Istoricheskogo Muzeya. Pamyatniki kultury*, M, 1957, XXV.

SOROKIN 1972
* S S Sorokin, "A Twisting Beast from Ziwiye", *SGE*, L, 1972, XXXIV, pp.75–78.

SOURDEL-THOMINE 1973
J Sourdel-Thomine, "Renouvellement et tradition dans l'architecture Saljuquide", in: *Islamic Civilisation: 950-1150*, Oxford, 1973, pp.251–63.

SPA 1938–39
A Survey of Persian Art (ed. A.Il. Pope), London-New York, 1938-39, vols I-VI.

Splendeur 1993
Splendeur des Sassanides. L'Empire perse entre Rome et la Chine (224-642), 12 February-25 April 1993, Brussels, 1993.

Stchoukine 1907
* P I Stchoukine, *Persian Pieces in the Stchoukine Collection*, M, 1907.

Stchoukine 1954
I Stchoukine, *Les Peintures des manuscrits timurides*, Paris, 1954.

Stchoukine 1964
I Stchoukine, *Les Peintures des manuscrits de Shah Abbas Iᵉ à la fin des Safavis*, Paris, 1964.

Stronach 1973
D Stronach, "Median and Achaemenid Parallels in Architecture", *Bulletin of the Asia Institute of Pahlavi University*, Shiraz, 1973.

Sztuka 1935
Sztuka perska (ira'nska) i jej wplywy, Warsaw, 1935.

Tafazzoli 1974
A Tafazzoli, "A List of Trades and Crafts in Sassanian Period", *Archaeologische Mitteilungen aus Iran*, N F, vol.VII, Berlin, 1974.

Talbot Rice and Gray
D Talbot Rice, *The Illustrations of the "World History of Rashid al-Din"* (ed. B Gray), Edinburgh, 1976.

Tavadia 1952
J S Tavadia, "Tajik", *Zeitschrift der Deutschen Morgenländischen Gesellschaft*, vol.CII, 1952.

Thiesenhausen 1884
* V Thiesenhausen, *Collected Materials Relating to the History of the Golden Horde. Vol.I. Extracts from Arabic Works*, St Petersburg, 1884.

Thompson 1974
D Thompson, "A Fragmentary Stucco Plaque in the Royal Ontario Museum", in: *Near Eastern Numismatics, Iconography, Epigraphy and History. Studies in the Honour of George Miles*, Beirut, 1974.

Timur 1989
T W Lentz and G D Lowry, Timur and the Princely Vision. *Persian Art and Culture in the Fifleenth Century*, Los Angeles, 1989.

Transactions 1949
* *Transactions of the South-Turkmen Archaeological Expedition*, vol.I, Moscow-Ashkhabad, 1949.

Treasures 1994
Treasures from the Hermitage, St Petersburg. *The European Fine Art Fair, MECC*, Maastricht, the Netherlands, 12–20 March 1994.

Treasures of Applied Art 1979
* *Treasures of Applied Art of Iran and Turkey of the 16th-17th Centuries*, M, 1979.

Trever 1932
C Trever, *Excavations in Northern Mongolia (1924-1925)*, L, 1932.

Trever 1937
* K Trever, *New Sassanian Plates in the Hermitage*, L, 1937.

Trever 1940
* K Trever, *Monuments of Graeco-Bactrian Art*, M-L, 1940.

Trever 1959
* K Trever, *Outline of the History and Culture of Caucasian Albania*, M-L, 1959.

Trever 1960
* K V Trever, "A New 'Sassanian' Saucer in the Hermitage (From the History of the Culture of the Peoples of Central Asia)", in: *Research into the History of Culture of the Peoples of the East*, M-L, 1960, pp.256-79.

Trever and Lukonin 1987
* K V Trever and V G Lukonin, *Sassanian Silverware from the Collection of the Hermitage*, M, 1987.

Tushingham 1972
A D Tushingham, "Persian Enamels", in: *The Memorial Volume of the 5th international Congress of Iranian Art and Archaeology*, vol.II, Tehran, 1972, pp.211–22.

Vanden Berghe 1982
L Vanden Berghe, Luristan, *Een verdenen Bronskunst uit West-Iran*, Brussels, 1982.

Veselovsky 1910a
* N I Veselovsky, *The Herat Bronze Bucket of 559 AH (1163 AD) from the Collection of Count A.A. Bobrinsky*, St Petersburg, 1910.

Veselovsky 1910b
* N I Veselovsky, "A Signet-Ring of Miran-Shah Mirza, Son of Tamerlane", in: *The Kaufman Coliection of Articles, published in Memory of the 25th Anniversary of the Death of the Subjugator and Administrator of the Turkestan Region*, General-Adjudant K P von Kaufman I. M, 1910, pp.229–34.

Vorozheikina 1984
Z N Vorozheikina, "Literary Service at the Medieval Iranian Courts (from Documents of the Isfahan Literary School)", in: *Ocherki istorii kultury srednevekovogo lrana. Pismennost i literatura*, M, 1984, pp.140–91.

Watson 1975
O Watson, "Persian Lustre Ware from the 14th to the 19th Century", in: *Le Monde iranien et l'Islam*, vol.III, Paris, 1975, pp.63–80.

Weitzman 1964
K Weitzman, "Mount Sinai's Holy Treasures", *National Geographical Magazine*, vol.CXXV, No.1, 1964, p.122.

Wiet 1935
G Wiet, *Exposition d'art persan*, Cairo, 1935.

Wilber 1955
D Wilber, *The Architecture of Islamic Iran*. The Il-Khanid Period, Princeton, 1955.

Wilkinson (s.a.)
C K Wilkinson, Nishapur. *Pottery of the Early Islamic Period*, The Metropolitan Museum of Art, New York.

Wilkinson 1975
C K Wilkinson, *Ivories from Ziwiye*, Bern, 1975.

Yakubovsky 1938
* A Y Yakubovsky, "A Vase with Illustrations of Musicians and a Game of Polo", in: *Monuments of the Age of Rustaveli*, L, 1938, pp.201–08.

---

* Works marked with an asterisk are in Russian.

EV – *Epigrafika Vostoka.*

KSIIMK – *Kratkiye soobshcheniya instituta istorii JnateriaInoy kultury AN SSSR.*

SGE – *Soobshcheniya Gosudarstvennogo Ennitazha.*

TGE – *Trudy Gosudarstvenno go Ennitazha.*

TOVGE – *Trudy otdela Vostoka Gosudarstvennogo Ennitazha.*

L – *Leningrad.*

M – *Moscow.*